Essentials of Money and Capital Markets

Fixed Income Markets and Institutions

Fourth Edition

Miles B. Livingston

University of Florida

cognella | ACADEMIC PUBLISHING

Bassim Hamadeh, CEO and Publisher
Jennifer McCarthy, Field Acquisitions Editor
Amy Smith, Project Editor
Abbey Hastings, Associate Production Editor
Jess Estrella, Senior Graphic Designer
Sara Schennum, Licensing Associate
Natalie Piccotti, Senior Marketing Manager
Kassie Graves, Vice President of Editorial
Jamie Giganti, Director of Academic Publishing

Dedicated to My Wife Nubia

Contents

Introduction

T HE MAGNITUDES OF debt obligations in the United States and many other countries are very large and play vital roles in economic systems. Changes in the debt markets have major impacts on individuals, corporations and governments. The goal of this chapter is to provide an overview of several important patterns and trends in the debt markets.

DEBT LEVELS IN THE UNITED STATES

We will first look at changes in debt levels of five varieties of debt in the United States. Debt levels can be measured in terms of absolute value, but a more revealing measure is the amount of debt relative to the level of output in the economy, specifically debt divided by gross domestic product (GDP). Figure 0.1 shows the levels of five major types of debt in the United States as a percentage of Gross Domestic Product (GDP). The period covered is from 1945 until the present.

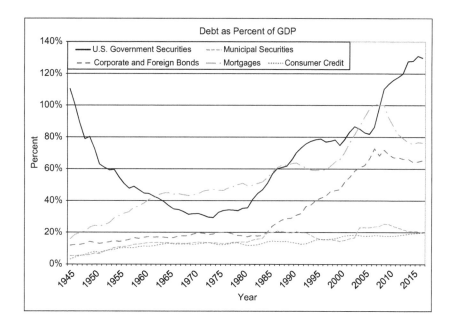

FIGURE 0.1 Varieties of United States Debt as % of GDP.

Source: U.S. Treasury and Federal Reserve.

Federal Government Debt

When the government spends more money than it receives in tax revenues, the shortfall is financed with borrowing and is added to the national debt. The level of government borrowing is influenced by a number of factors including the business cycle, government expenditures, government taxes, and wars.

In 1945 at the end of World War II, US government debt as a percentage of gross domestic product was very large as a result of large borrowing by the government to finance expenditures during the war. Although debt as a percentage of GDP has declined at times, the absolute level of debt has virtually always increased.

From 1945 until 1980, the relative growth of GDP (a measure of output in the economy) increased faster than the increase in the amount of federal government debt. Although the absolute level of US government debt continued to increase, debt as a percentage of GDP declined steadily until approximately 1980 because GDP grew faster. Since 1980, the US government debt has increased steadily as percentage of GDP. The increases in debt since 1980 have been largely a result of lower tax rates and increased spending by the federal government that have increased the size of the annual deficits and added to the national debt.

Mortgage Debt

Mortgage debt as a percentage of GDP in the United States has increased steadily since 1945. Beginning in the late 1990s, there was a very dramatic increase in mortgage debt that ended in 2007. This growth in mortgage debt helped to fuel the large run-up in housing prices in the United States during 2000–2007, followed by a sharp decline in housing prices and construction activity. The drop-off in construction activity contributed to a recession in the entire economy of the US. During the boom period of 2000–2007, many homes were purchased at increasingly higher prices and financed with mortgages. The result was a classic bubble in which prices of homes increased to unrealistic levels. Many homes were purchased based upon the "bigger fool theory," the idea that an asset is worth whatever the next buyer (fool) is willing to pay for it. When the bubble burst, housing prices declined sharply. Many homeowners were left with mortgage debt that exceeded the market value of the home. A new word became popular in describing these homes: "underwater." The result was a large number of defaults on mortgages and resulting losses for lenders.

Corporate Debt

Corporate debt began increasing markedly in the 1990s. This expansion continued until the financial crisis of 2007–2009. The large increase in corporate borrowing contributed to the strong economy in the early 2000s. After the financial crisis, many corporations have continued to borrow large amounts of money as a result of very low interest rates.

Municipal Government Debt and Consumer Debt

The other two components of debt in the United States, consumer non-mortgage debt and municipal (state and local) government debt, have remained at a relatively stable percentage of gross domestic product, although the absolute value of the debt increased as the economy grew.

THE VARIABILITY OF INTEREST RATES

Figure 0.2 shows the history of interest rates in the United States since 1945 as represented by the rates on 10-year US Treasury securities and 90-day US Treasury bills. During the 1970s, the United States began to experience higher levels of price increases (inflation). To stop the inflation, the US Federal Reserve, under the leadership of Paul Volcker, followed a very restrictive monetary policy, driving interest rates to extremely high levels, and causing a recession. The resulting recession stopped the inflation.

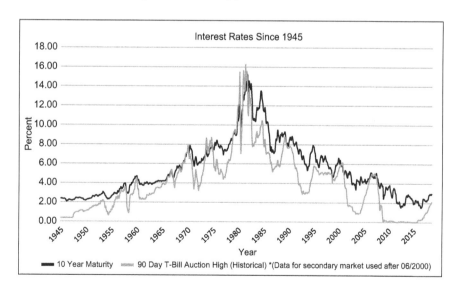

FIGURE 0.2 Variability of Interest Rates.

Source: U.S. Treasury and Federal Reserve.

When recessions occur, interest rates typically drop. During the recession of the early 1980s, interest rates dropped significantly. Since 1980 there has been a long-term decline in interest rates in the United States, with considerable variability about this long-term trend. One of the factors contributing to the expansion of mortgage and business debt has been the steady decline in interest rates since 1980.

Figure 0.2 shows that short-term interest rates have been far more variable than long-term interest rates in the US. The variability of interest rates for different maturities has important implications for both borrowers and for lenders. Borrowers and lenders have a choice of short-term or long-term loans. If a borrower believes that future interest rates are going to be higher than current interest rates, the best type of loan is a long-term loan to lock-in the current low interest rates. A borrower forecasting lower future rates of interest will find it desirable to borrow short-term now and roll the short-term loan into a longer-term loan if interest rates become lower in the future. These strategies are shown in Table 0.1.

Table 0.1. Strategies of Borrowers

Borrower's Forecast	Best Strategy	What Can go Wrong
High Current Interest Rates	Borrow short-term and roll over loan.	Interest rates may rise and new loan is at higher interest rates.
Low Current Interest Rates	Borrow long-term, locking-in the interest rate.	Interest rates may fall and the chance to borrow at lower rates is lost.

The best strategies for lenders are shown in Table 0.2. These are the opposite of the best strategies for borrowers. Suppose the lender thinks current interest rates are low and will rise in the future. The best strategy is to lend short-term and roll-over the loan at future higher interest rates. If the forecast is wrong and interest rates fall, the loan must be rolled-over at lower interest rates.

Table 0.2. Strategies of Lenders

Lender's Forecast	Best Strategy	What Can go Wrong
High Current Interest Rates	Lend long-term and lock-in high interest rate.	Interest rates may rise and opportunity to lend at higher interest rate is lost.
Low Current Interest Rates	Lend short-term, expecting to rollover at higher future interest rates.	Interest rates may fall and the loan must be rolled over at a lower interest rate.

EFFICIENT SECURITY MARKETS AND BUBBLES

In an efficient security market, all public information is very rapidly reflected in security prices. The opposite of an efficient market is a situation where prices do not immediately reflect public information. One possibility is for prices to be slow to adjust. Another possibility is for prices to overreact in the short run and eventually adjust to their new value. Figure 0.3 illustrates the ideas of under-reaction and overreaction.

Suppose there is a company that makes shoelaces and its stock price is relatively stable over time. Suddenly the company discovers a new form of shoelace that enables users of this new shoelace to run faster. When the company announces this new information to the public, the price of the company's stock should jump instantaneously to reflect the added value from this new product in an informationally efficient security market. If the information is public, sellers of the stock should be willing to sell at the new higher price and buyers willing to buy at this higher price.

The driving force behind market efficiency is competition. If the value of the new information is not immediately reflected in the stock price, buyers will enter the market and drive the price to its new value. If the market overreacts, holders of the company's stock will sell the stock and buy back when the price equals the new fair value.

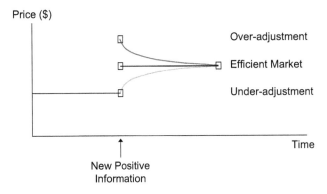

Public information is rapidly reflected in security prices.
Driving force: Competition for profits.

FIGURE 0.3 Efficient Markets.

If security markets are efficient, all public information about interest rates should be rapidly reflected in market interest rates. Consequently, future interest rate changes are not easily predicted. Because of the difficulty in predicting future interest rates in an efficient market, a reasonable strategy for borrowers and lenders is to have a variety of debt maturities in order to avoid major mistakes from incorrect predictions of future interest rates.

The efficient market hypothesis focuses primarily on the short run impact of new information. Many academic studies have shown that security markets adjust very rapidly to information that becomes public and will obviously affect prices.

However, over longer periods of time, there are boom and bust cycles in asset markets as discussed extensively in Malkiel's book *A Random Walk Down Wall Street*. One of the classic examples of an asset bubble is the tulip mania that engulfed Holland several hundred years ago. Tulips are valued for their beauty, something that is very subjective and for which there is no indisputable measure. The Dutch were able to develop hybrid tulips with unique characteristics. A buying frenzy for the "most beautiful" tulips ensued that drove prices to exorbitant levels. Eventually the price bubble burst and the prices of tulips dropped precipitously. Many Dutch people who had devoted their energies to developing ever more beautiful varieties suffered losses as tulip prices collapsed.

The housing boom of 2000–2007 is another example of an asset bubble. Although some individuals may have realized that housing prices had reached unreasonable levels, there was no way for a small number of individuals to take action to bring housing prices to a more reasonable level. Their only practical option would be to sell their properties. If there are a sufficient number of very enthusiastic buyers, the impact of the realists will not stop the bubble.

While asset markets are efficient in the short run, markets are not efficient over long horizons. Asset bubbles have appeared many times in the past and will probably appear again in the future.

DERIVATIVE SECURITIES

A derivative security is a security that is based upon another security or asset. In recent years, many derivative securities based upon debt instruments have been created. Mortgage-backed securities are one example in which many mortgages are packaged into a pool and claims on the pool sold as securities. Another example is credit default swaps (CDS), which guarantee the payments on mortgage-backed securities or on bonds in the event of default. Credit default swaps are a form of insurance. Other examples of derivative securities include call and put options and futures contracts. Derivative securities allow the partitioning of the risks and rewards from individual securities to be sold to other market participants.

Derivatives allow market participants to reduce their risk and reduce potential rewards, while other market participants increase their risk and increase their potential rewards. Firms finding a particular risk to be undesirable are able to transfer that risk to someone else, who may find that risk appealing. While derivatives allow individuals or firms to transfer risk, the risk does not disappear from the entire financial system.

A large number of derivative securities are traded over-the-counter instead of on organized exchanges. Over-the-counter trading involves a network of dealers. Over-the-counter markets do not have a formal, publicly available record of all trades. Thus, over-the-counter markets lacked transparency compared to organized exchanges.

If one party to an over-the-counter derivative security defaults, another party will suffer a loss. Because over-the-counter dealers are interconnected, default by one dealer or several dealers can set off an avalanche effect in which many dealers fail. This possibility has been called *systemic risk*. Many critics believe that the growth of over-the-counter derivatives has increased the risk of widespread failures of security dealers and financial institutions, which will in turn adversely affect the economy.

FINANCIAL CRISIS OF 2007–2009

The United States experienced a financial crisis in 2007–2009. During the years 2000–2006 housing prices in the United States rose dramatically. In some areas prices tripled over this time interval, a sign of a price bubble. By 2007 housing prices began to decline and borrowers began to default on their mortgages. Many mortgages had been *securitized*, or put into portfolios of mortgages (mortgage-backed securities) that were sold to investors. The default by individual borrowers led to defaults on mortgage-backed securities.

In 2008, two financial firms, Bear Stearns and Lehman Brothers, failed because of holdings of mortgage-backed securities and extreme reliance on very short-term financing. The environment of falling housing prices, default on mortgage-backed securities, and failing securities firms created great fear in the security markets. In an atmosphere of fear of defaults, it became extremely difficult to borrow money, resulting in reduced construction and business activity. The consequence was a large increase in unemployment.

As discussed more fully below, the US government took several actions in response to this crisis. First, large amounts of money were injected into the financial system by the Federal Reserve. Second, the Congress passed a spending bill to stimulate the economy. Third, the Dodd-Frank Act was passed to reduce the chance of a reoccurrence of a similar crisis.

The details of various parts of this crisis will be discussed in later sections of this book. However, it is strongly suggested that all readers of this book watch two videos from the public broadcasting system:. "The Warning" (one hour) and "Money Power and Wall Street" (four hours). These videos highlight the important controversy about free markets versus regulation.

SUMMARY

Since 1980, total United States debt as a percentage of gross domestic product has increased substantially, especially federal government debt, mortgage debt, and corporate debt. Historically, interest rates on short-term debt instruments have greater variability than the interest rates on long-term debt instruments.

There has been a large expansion in over-the-counter derivatives securities such as mortgage-backed debt and credit default swaps in recent years. These derivatives allow individuals to transfer risk to other individuals, but create the possibility of systemic risk in which failure of one security dealer may bring down other security dealers and have an adverse impact upon the level of economic activity.

REFERENCES

Malkiel, Burton Gordon. 1973. *A Random Walk Down Wall Street: The Time-tested Strategy for Successful Investing*. New York: W.W. Norton. ISBN 0-393-05500-0.

Frontline. "The Warning." Season 28, Episode 2. Public Broadcasting System. Aired October 20, 2009. Available at https://www.pbs.org/video/frontline-the-warning/.

Frontline. "Money, Power and Wall Street." Season 30, Episode 11. Public Broadcasting System. Aired April 24, 2012. Available at https://www.pbs.org/wgbh/frontline/film/money-power-wall-street/.

CHAPTER 1

Determinants of Interest Rates

While many varieties of debt instruments exist, all debt instruments are affected by macroeconomic factors determining the underlying interest rate. This chapter discusses these macroeconomic factors affecting interest rates. The first part of the chapter presents the loanable funds model to show the impact of business, consumer, and government borrowing, saving, and the money supply on the level of interest rates. The second part of the chapter deals with models of the impact of inflation on interest rates. The third part discusses the main features of the Federal Reserve, the US central bank.

LOANABLE FUNDS APPROACH

The loanable funds approach provides a simple and intuitive analysis of the major macroeconomic factors that determine the level of interest rates. The model shows that the short-term interest rate is determined by borrowing by businesses, consumers, and government; personal and business savings; and the supply of money. Later chapters will deal with other factors that determine the level of interest rates, such as the maturity of debt instruments and default risk.

According to the loanable funds approach, the interest rate is determined by the supply of and the demand for loanable funds. This approach is shown schematically in Figure 1.1. The demand curve shows the relationship between the demand for funds and the interest rate. This curve is drawn with a downward slope, indicating that borrowers will borrow more at lower interest rates. The supply curve shows the relationship between the supply of funds and the interest rate. The supply curve has an upward slope; at higher interest rates lenders will supply more funds to the market. The interest rate and the amount of funds changing hands are determined by the point where the two curves cross.

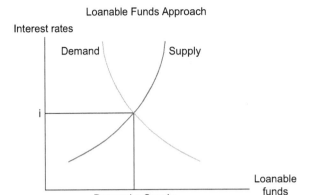

FIGURE 1.1 The Loanable Funds Approach.

The Demand for Funds

The total demand for funds has several components: business borrowing for investment in plant and equipment, consumer borrowing for consumption, and governmental borrowing. The demand curve shows the aggregate of these three components. We have drawn the total demand curve as downward-sloping, but some controversy exists about the demand curves for the components.

Business borrowing for investment in plant and equipment is affected by the level of the interest rate. Businesses estimate the rates of return on their investments and then list the investments from the highest to the lowest rate of return. The demand curve for business investment is essentially a list of investments from those with the highest rates of return to those with the lowest rates of return. See Figure 1.2. The return on investments is then compared to the cost of financing these investments. In the Loanable Funds framework, the cost of financing is assumed to be the interest rate. Investments with returns higher than the interest rate are profitable and are undertaken. Investments with returns less than the interest rate are rejected. As the interest rate falls (rises), some investments become profitable (unprofitable). Thus, with low interest rates, there is greater business investment in plant and equipment. With high interest rates, business investment is curtailed. This pattern translates into a downward-sloping demand curve.

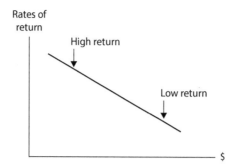

Rates of
return

High return

Low return

$

FIGURE 1.2 Demand Curve for Business Investment.

Consumer borrowing for "big ticket" items is interest-rate sensitive. High interest rates cause reductions in consumer purchases of homes and automobiles, but purchases of relatively low-priced items are not likely to be affected by interest rates. Thus, the demand curve for expensive consumer goods is downward-sloping. For other consumer goods, the slope is unclear. For the aggregate of all consumer goods, the demand curve is probably downward-sloping, meaning at lower interest rates consumers will borrow more.

Government borrowing is also included in the demand for funds. Federal government borrowing is not substantially affected by interest rates. Thus, federal government borrowing can be added as a constant to business and consumer borrowing. State and local governments borrow substantial amounts for capital expenditures. Some state and local government expenditures may be affected by the interest rate. When interest rates are quite low, state and local governments are more willing to borrow. Thus, the demand for state and local government borrowing is interest-rate sensitive.

The Supply of Funds

The total amount of funds supplied to the market includes savings from individual consumers, business savings, and increases in the money supply. The supply curve has been drawn with an upward slope; higher interest rates lead to a larger supply of funds, but economists debate the slopes of the components of the supply curve. By saving and lending these funds, consumers are giving up current consumption. They expect a higher interest rate to compensate them for the price of foregone consumption. The consumer might be willing to give up $1 today in exchange for receiving $1.05 one time period later allowing the consumer to consume more in the future.

Consumers save from current income for future consumption. The amount of individual saving depends upon preferences, current income, wealth, and interest rates. The direction of the effect of interest rates on savings is debatable. On the one hand, higher interest rates may attract funds from people who are willing to give up current consumption for a more attractive rate of return and resulting higher consumption in the future; this is called the *substitution effect* and implies an upward-sloping supply curve. On the other hand, some savers have a target goal for total future income derived from savings. These individuals are able to reduce the amount saved and maintain the same future income level as interest rates rise. This is called the *income effect* and implies a downward-sloping supply curve. The net impact of these two effects upon total savings is not clear on purely deductive grounds. We have drawn an upward-sloping supply curve, assuming that the substitution effect is dominant.

The impact of the interest rate on business savings is not entirely clear either. Business savings represent retained earnings and depreciation. Depreciation is a function of physical wear and tear on equipment and is probably not substantially affected by interest rates. The impact of the interest rate on retained earnings is ambiguous. Retained earnings equal earnings minus dividends. Thus, the impact of the interest rate on retained earnings can be decomposed into the impact of the interest rate on earnings and on dividends. Each of these impacts has an unclear direction. For example, the earnings of some firms, such as banks, may be very sensitive to interest rates, whereas other firms' earnings may be totally unaffected by interest rates. Most likely, interest rates are a minor determinant of retained earnings.

The supply of money is determined by the central bank. Increases in the supply of money shift the supply of funds curve to the right, and decreases in the money supply shift it to the left. This will be discussed in more detail below.

In summary, the level of interest rates is affected by business borrowing, consumer borrowing, government borrowing, business savings, and consumer savings.

GOVERNMENT POLICIES AND INTEREST RATES

The actions of the government can significantly affect the level of interest rates. The following discussion focuses upon two government policies: increases in the money supply and increases in government borrowing.

Changes in the Money Supply

The money supply in the economy is largely determined by the central bank as it carries out monetary policy. If the government increases the supply of money, the supply curve of funds will shift to the right, tending to lower interest rates. Reducing the supply of money will shift the supply curve to the left and tend to increase interest rates. Figure 1.3 shows how an increase in the money supply reduces interest rates, other things equal.

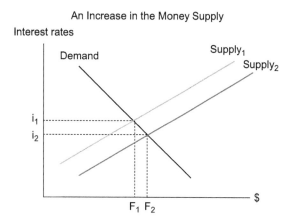

FIGURE 1.3 Impact of an Increase in the Money Supply.

The initial decline in interest rates tends to stimulate business investment. An increase in business investment increases output in the economy. John Keynes argued that an increase in business investment had a multiplicative effect on output in the economy because the initial business investment becomes wages of employees, who in turn spend these wages and create additional output, which becomes wages of more employees, etc. Therefore, an increase in business investment of $100 can increase output and income by much more than $100. Since total income must equal total output for the economy as a whole, a policy of increasing business investment will therefore increase total income and total employment.

Possibly, large increases in the money supply may generate expectations of inflation. These inflationary expectations may raise interest rates, as described later in the chapter. Thus, the net impact of increases in the money supply upon interest rates is somewhat ambiguous.

In recent years, central banks have driven interest rates to very low levels. If interest rates are very low, further cuts in the interest rate will have minimal impact upon economic activity. This possibility has been called the liquidity trap. Japan is often described as an example of the liquidity trap. In the early 1990s, the Japanese central bank reduced interest rates. The Japanese economy remained weak nevertheless.

The impact of an increase in the money supply on interest rates and business investment depends upon the slope of the demand curve. In a weak economy, businesses will face limited demand for their products and have limited incentives to invest. Then lowering interest rates will have a minimal impact upon business investment. Figure 1.4 shows an example where the demand for funds is very steep (implying very few business investment opportunities). In this case a shift in the supply curve does not make many investment opportunities profitable, and central bank reductions in the interest rate have little impact upon business and consumer borrowing.

Lower interest rates have some adverse effects. With lower interest rates, bond investors earn lower rates of return. Some bond investors may shift their holdings from risk-free bond investments to risky equity investments driving up the returns on equity investments. The result is a wealth transfer from bond investors. In addition, some financial institutions such as insurance companies that typically invest heavily in bonds earn relatively low rates of return. The consequence may be shifting to riskier investments, charging higher premiums on their insurance, or even declining to issue some types of insurance such as long-term care policies, which require investment by the insurance company over a very long horizon.

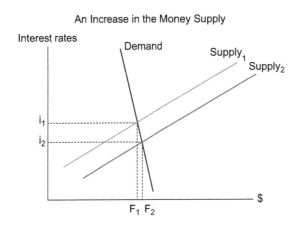

FIGURE 1.4 Steep Demand Curve for Funds.

In some cases, central banks have contracted the money supply to increase interest rates and curtail the level of economic activity. One dramatic example occurred in the United States beginning in 1979. During the late 1970s, the inflation rate in the United States increased significantly. In order to stop inflation, the Federal Reserve contracted the money supply and dramatically increased interest rates causing a recession and ending the inflation.

Increases in Government Borrowing

In the loanable funds framework, an increase in the government deficit (financed by additional borrowing) raises the total demand for funds, resulting in a shift to the right of the demand curve for funds. As shown in Figure 1.5, the shift in the demand curve causes a rise in the interest rate. Consequently, increased government borrowing tends to make consumer and business borrowing more expensive, thus reducing some consumer expenditures and business capital expenditures in the private economy. Some nongovernment borrowers are crowded out by the government borrowing. This effect is strong when the economy is at full capacity utilization, but is a weak effect when the economy is operating below full capacity utilization.

If the government borrows money and then spends it, the spending has an impact upon production. For the economy as a whole, total spending equals total income. A government policy that increases total spending also increases total income, and can reduce the level of unemployment in the entire economy.

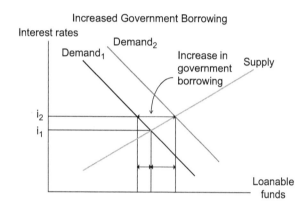

FIGURE 1.5 Increased Government Borrowing.

The amount of government borrowing is affected by the level of tax revenues. An economy in recession has lower income and lower taxes. Consequently, a constant level of government spending during a recession will tend to force the government to borrow as tax revenues decline. This increased government borrowing (caused by declining tax revenues during the recession) tends to offset the impact of the recession on production, income, and employment, a countercyclical policy. Additional government borrowing and spending during recessions offsets declines in output and income in the private sector. The Loanable Funds approach does not explicitly consider taxes, although they are an important component of government fiscal policy.

Increasing Government Borrowing Combined with Increasing Money Supply

Since the financial crisis of 2007–2009, the United States has followed a policy of high levels of federal government borrowing combined with an increasing money supply. The policy of increasing the money supply dramatically has been called *quantitative easing*. The combined impact of these two government policies is a decline in interest rates as shown in Figure 1.6.

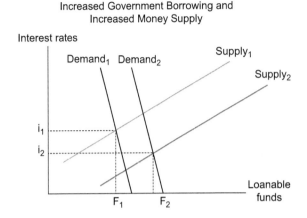

FIGURE 1.6 Increased Government Borrowing and Increased Money Supply.

INFLATION AND INTEREST RATES

The term *inflation* means a process with a continual increase in the general price level. As prices go up, individuals try to protect their purchasing power and take actions which may inadvertently perpetuate the inflation. For example, employees may try to protect themselves from inflation by having their wages tied to the cost of living. As prices rise, wages are forced up, which raises production costs, which raises selling prices, and so on, in a never-ending cycle. Throughout history, inflation has been a frequent occurrence. Generally, inflation has a significant impact upon economic activity, including interest rates.

Inflation is undesirable for two reasons. First, during inflationary periods, people try to stay ahead of inflation or even benefit in real terms. Strategies include trying to increase wages and prices and purchasing real assets. If some people are smarter or luckier than others, inflation may result in a redistribution of wealth, meaning that some people may be poorer and some people wealthier in real terms as a result of inflation. Second, people's efforts may be directed at keeping ahead of inflation and deflected from productive economic activity. The real wealth and economic growth may suffer. In effect, inflation may reduce real economic growth, curtailing total wealth. Thus, inflation can reduce the total economic pie and alter its distribution.

Precisely measuring the rate of inflation is a difficult task. The consumer inflation rate depends upon the price changes of individual consumer goods and the amounts consumed by actual consumers. Since consumer choices change as relative prices change, the basket of goods purchased by the average consumer changes over time. Finding the correct basket of goods is a major problem in measuring the inflation rate. Thus, considerable disagreement exists about the true inflation rate. Government statistics provide several price indexes: a consumer price index, a producer price index, and a GDP deflator. The rate of change in these indexes should each measure the inflation rate. But these rates of change can differ. This discussion overlooks these pragmatic problems in measuring the inflation rate and assumes a hypothetical inflation rate.

THE FISHER MODEL

Intelligent investors try to forecast important factors affecting their investment returns. Because inflation affects return, investors form expectations of the future inflation rate, based upon all available current information. These anticipations of the future inflation rate are reflected immediately in security prices and interest rates.

The most clear-cut relationship between inflation and interest rates occurs in the model of Irving Fisher when the inflation-free interest rate and the future inflation rate are known with certainty, when the actions of borrowers are ignored, and when there is only a single time period. As explained shortly, lenders add an inflation premium to the interest rate to compensate for declining purchasing power.

The inflation-free (real) rate of interest is defined as the rate that would prevail in an inflation-free world. Denote the inflation-free interest rate by r. Let the completely certain inflation rate be denoted by p. Let the observed, nominal (that is, money terms) interest rate be i. In order to compensate lenders exactly for the declining purchasing power of money, the following condition must hold:

$$i = r + p + rp \qquad \textbf{1.1}$$

The following example illustrates this expression. The inflation-free interest rate is 2% and the inflation rate is 5%. Then the nominal rate, i, must equal the inflation-free rate, r (0.02), plus the inflation rate, p (0.05), plus the product of the two, rp (0.02)(0.05):

$$i = 0.02 + 0.05 + (0.02)(0.05) = 0.0710 \qquad \textbf{1.2}$$

Adding the inflation rate, p, compensates the lender for the declining value of the principal (5%). Adding the term rp compensates the lender for the declining value of the inflation-free interest. This last term is frequently omitted, since the product of two rates has small absolute value. Thus, the nominal rate is frequently approximated by the first two terms.

Uncertainty

If the inflation rate is uncertain, the impact of inflation upon interest rates is not as clear-cut. In a widely held view, the anticipated inflation rate is added to the real interest rate. In addition, a risk premium should be added, so that:

$$i = r + E(p) + h \qquad \textbf{1.3}$$

Where $E(p)$ is the expected inflation rate and h is a risk premium. This premium compensates the lender for the possibility of a higher actual inflation rate than expected rate. To illustrate, if the inflation-free interest rate is 2%, the expected inflation rate is 5%, and the risk premium is 3%, the nominal interest rate is:

$$i = 0.02 + 0.05 + 0.03 = 0.08 \qquad \textbf{1.4}$$

Empirical Tests

Empirically testing the relationship between inflation and interest rates is difficult because the inflation-free interest rate and the anticipated inflation rate are not directly observable. Several ways of estimating the inflation-free interest rate as well as anticipations have been suggested, but these methods carry with them considerable chance of errors.

Some researchers have tried to see whether the nominal interest rate changes in unison with the observed inflation rate. Figure 1.7 illustrates the method of fitting a line to the relationship between the observed interest rate (vertical axis) and the recently observed inflation rate (horizontal axis). The slope of the fitted line represents the sensitivity of interest rates to recent inflation. The estimated slope is typically less than 1.0. For example, if the estimated slope is 0.50, approximately 50% of the recent inflation rate gets reflected in interest rates.

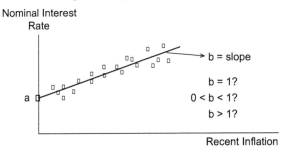

FIGURE 1.7 Nominal Interest Rate Versus Recent Inflation.

THE QUANTITY THEORY OF MONEY

The economist Milton Friedman was a strong advocate of the quantity theory of money. This theory says that changes in the money supply can have an impact upon the inflation rate.

$$P \times Q = M \times V \qquad \textbf{1.5}$$

Where:

P = price level.

Q = quantity of goods.

M = money supply.

V = velocity of money; # times money turns over in a year.

Consider the following numerical example:

$$6 \times 50 = 100 \times 3$$

This example indicates that the total output in money terms is $300, which is equal to $6 per unit of output times 50 units of output. The total output is also equal to the money supply of $100 times a velocity of 3, or $300.

If the economy is at full capacity, a percentage increase in the money supply will result in the same percentage increase in the price level. The following numerical example with an initial money supply of $100 and an increase in the money supply to $150 illustrates that a 50% increase in the money supply at full capacity will bring about a 50% increase in the price level.

$$P \times Q = M \times V \qquad \textbf{1.6}$$

$$6 \times 50 = 100 \times 3$$

$$9 \times 50 = 150 \times 3$$

If an increase in the money supply causes inflation or increasing inflationary expectations, interest rates will rise as described in the Fisher effect.

If the economy has excess capacity, then an increase in the money supply will increase physical output, but not change the price level. In the example, the 50% change in the money supply from $100 to $150 causes a 50% increase in production from 50 units to 75 units.

$$P \times Q = M \times V \qquad \textbf{1.7}$$

$$6 \times 50 = 100 \times 3$$

$$6 \times 75 = 150 \times 3$$

In the Friedman analysis, if there is full capacity an increase in the money supply might conceivably increase the velocity of money leading to hyperinflation, the situation in which the inflation rate increases at an increasing rate over time.

The Quantity Theory versus Loanable Funds

In the Quantity Theory of Money, changes in the money supply directly impact spending by both consumers and businesses. In the Loanable Funds Framework (a variant of the Keynesian model), an increase in the money supply changes interest rates, which changes business investment, which in turn affects production and income in the economy. In practice, both of these effects may work. The change in the money supply may directly affect spending as well as changing interest rates and affect business investment decisions.

A change in the money supply has multiple impacts. In the Quantity Theory of Money, a large increase in the money supply can create expectations of rising future prices, especially if the economy is at full capacity or expected to be at full capacity soon. In the Loanable Funds analysis, an increase in the money supply reduces interest rates. In practice, both of these effects may be operative.

THE UNITED STATES FEDERAL RESERVE SYSTEM

The Federal Reserve System is the central bank of the United States. The major functions of the Federal Reserve are to:

1. Set and administer monetary policy. This involves controlling the money supply and interest rates to foster economic growth, stable price levels, and high employment.
2. Act as a lender of last resort to banks through the discount window.
3. Assist in the payments and collections systems. The Federal Reserve System plays a major role in the check clearing process and the electronic wire transfer of funds.
4. Regulate commercial banks. The Federal Reserve System, the Comptroller of the Currency (part of the US Treasury), the Federal Deposit Insurance Corporation (FDIC), and state bank authorities have regulatory authority over commercial banks.

Federal Reserve Organization

The Federal Reserve System consists of two major parts: the Board of Governors and the twelve Federal Reserve District banks and branches. The Federal Reserve Board is composed of seven members appointed by the President for fourteen-year terms with the consent of the United States Senate. The terms are staggered so that a new governor must be appointed every two years. Often governors do not serve out their entire terms, and then a new governor is appointed for the remainder of the fourteen-year term.

One of the governors is appointed by the president as Chairman of the Board of Governors for a four-year term. In practice, the chairman has considerable power in setting the course of monetary policy. The chairman is the leader of the Federal Reserve System. He serves as the spokesperson for the Federal Reserve and makes regular presentations to both houses of the US Congress, as well as presentations at a wide variety of meetings and conferences. The chairman also has the power to act on behalf of the Federal Reserve in emergency situations requiring immediate action.

The Federal Reserve System is composed of twelve districts, each of which has a Federal Reserve district bank (and branches). These Federal Reserve banks are privately owned by the commercial banks that are Federal Reserve members in that district. Each district Federal Reserve Bank has nine directors, six of which are selected by commercial banks that are members of that district and three selected by the Board of Governors. Three of the directors selected by the commercial banks in the district are required to be non-bankers. The President of the Federal Reserve District Bank is chosen by the three directors selected by the Board of Governors and the three nonbanking directors. The president of the district bank participates in the Federal Open Market Committee.

The Federal Open Market Committee

The Federal Open Market Committee (FOMC) sets monetary policy. The FOMC has eight regular meetings a year attended by the seven governors and the Presidents of the twelve Federal Reserve districts. The Federal Open Market Committee discusses the economic and monetary situation and develops a directive for monetary policy. The directive is approved by the members of the FOMC with a special set of voting rules. The voting members of the FOMC are the seven governors, the president of the Federal Reserve district bank of New York, and four presidents of the other Federal Reserve district banks on a rotating basis. Thus there are twelve voting members. Seven of these twelve voting members are governors who comprise a majority of the committee and whose outlook focuses upon the economy as a whole, as opposed to a specific region of the country. Having all twelve presidents of the Federal Reserve districts present allows them to present information about particular regions of the United States. But the FOMC directive is focused upon the country as a whole.

Since the 2007–2009 financial crisis, the FOMC directive has announced a target rate for the federal funds rate and for the inflation rate. Short-term interest rates are closely related to the federal funds rate. Thus, this part of the directive is setting a target for short-term interest rates. The financial crisis created a fear of deflation. Consequently, the Federal Reserve has set a target to keep the inflation rate close to a target rate of approximately 2%.

The federal funds rate is the rate of interest at which banks borrow and lend deposits at the Federal Reserve Bank. These are interbank loans, loans between different banks. The United States has a fractional reserve system, which means that specified percentages of deposits have to be kept on deposit at the Federal Reserve. Banks with excess reserves can lend these reserves to banks that need reserves. The rate of interest on these loans is called the federal funds rate.

In earlier years, the FOMC directive also set targets for the growth rate of the money supply. Because the money supply is hard to measure, the Federal Reserve has focused recently on the federal funds rate.

The directive of the Federal Open Market Committee is released to the public shortly after the end of the meeting. In earlier years, this directive was kept secret for six weeks. During the weeks of delay, market participants were constantly watching the actions of the Federal Reserve, and the contents of the directive were effectively well known.

Independence of the Federal Reserve

The Federal Reserve is technically independent for two reasons. First, the Federal Reserve earns more money from its operations than it needs to cover its operating expenses and, consequently, does not have to ask Congress for funds. The earnings of the Federal Reserve are largely interest earned on securities held in order to carry out monetary policy. The amount of interest earned by the Federal Reserve is large.

Second, the Federal Reserve System is not directly subject to control by the executive and legislative branches of the government because the members of the Board of Governors are appointed for fourteen-year terms and because the twelve Federal Reserve Banks are privately owned. That is, the Federal Reserve has the power to set monetary policy independent of the wishes of the President and both houses of Congress. However, since the Federal Reserve was established by an act of Congress and since Federal Reserve powers can be changed by further congressional action, the Federal Reserve is subject in the long run to pressure from Congress. Thus, the Federal Reserve's actions cannot be too far out of line with Congressional preferences.

Independence of the Federal Reserve has pros and cons. On the one hand, independence from the rest of the government has the advantage that the Federal Reserve can look at policy from a long-run perspective. The Federal Reserve can follow a policy that should be good for the whole economy in the long run, as opposed to a shortsighted policy motivated by political expediency. On the other hand, too much independence may be undesirable if the policies of the Federal Reserve are in direct conflict with the rest of government economic policy. There is evidence that countries with relatively independent central banks have relatively low inflation rates in the long run, one of the primary targets of the central bank.

Goals of Monetary Policy

The goals of monetary policy are to promote economic growth, full employment, and low inflation. These three policy goals can be competing, forcing the Federal Reserve to make difficult policy choices.

Economic growth refers to increases in the wealth of the overall economy. On a per capita basis, wealth can be increased if the average worker produces more or if productivity increases. Productivity can be improved by increasing the amount of equipment available to workers and/or by making better use of that equipment.

Full employment refers to a situation in which all people who want to work are able to find work. In practice, full employment does not mean 100% employment and 0% unemployment. Because of so-called frictions, most economists feel that some people are always between jobs. Some unemployment is quite normal even though the economy is strong.

Historically, central banks have made *low inflation* a major target because inflation may reduce economic growth and create inequities since people on fixed incomes, holding money, or holding investments in dollar-denominated securities such as bonds lose from unanticipated inflation.

Monetary Policy Tools

The primary task of the Federal Reserve is to establish and administer monetary policy guidelines for the interest rates. Technically, there are three traditional tools of monetary policy available:

1. Open market operations
2. Changing reserve requirements
3. The Federal Reserve discount window

Open Market Operations

Open market operations have generally involved the purchase and sale by the Federal Reserve of U.S. Treasury securities in the open market. When the Federal Reserve purchases securities, the prices of these securities tend to increase and the interest rates tend to fall. If the Federal Reserve buys bonds in the open market from an individual, the seller's commercial bank account is increased by the sale price, increasing the money supply. If the Federal Reserve sells bonds to an individual, the security's price declines and the interest rate rises. The buyer's bank account is reduced and the money supply goes down. Because the Federal Reserve is able to electronically increase bank balances with a few strokes of the computer keyboard, it has virtually unlimited power to create money.

Purchases of securities by the Federal Reserve increase the balances of banks on deposit at the Federal Reserve. Deposits in excess of required reserves can be withdrawn by the bank and used to make loans. In this way, open market purchases of securities tend to increase the ability of banks to make bank loans.

In carrying out monetary policy, the Federal Reserve maintains a large portfolio of US Treasury and other securities, upon which it earns interest. Part of this interest is used by the Federal Reserve to pay its operating expenses, and the rest is returned to the Treasury.

Traditionally the Federal Reserve has primarily restricted open market purchases to US Treasury bills. Since the 2007–2009 financial crisis, the Federal Reserve has expanded the types of securities purchased to include longer-term Treasury securities and mortgage-backed securities in a process called *quantitative easing*. These purchases of securities have injected large amounts of funds into the banking system.

Open market operations are the most frequently used tools of the Federal Reserve for several reasons. Open market operations can be used effectively to make small adjustments in policy. Open market purchases and sales can be implemented very rapidly. They may also be reversed rapidly if necessary. Thus the Federal Reserve can rapidly inject reserves into the banking system and then rapidly withdraw them. In contrast, changing reserve requirements or changing the discount rate tends to result in large and inflexible changes in policy.

Reserve Requirements

Commercial banks are required to keep a proportion of their deposits as reserves. Required reserves may be kept as vault cash (coins and currency) and deposits with the Federal Reserve. The Federal Reserve has the power to change reserve requirements on bank deposits within legislatively set bounds.

Superficially, reserves are required for safety to meet emergency cash needs. Since reserves continue to be required as long as deposits exist, required reserves can never be withdrawn if bank deposit levels are unchanged. Therefore, safety is not the primary motive for reserve requirements. Required commercial bank reserves on deposit at the Federal Reserve allow the Federal Reserve to control the money supply and related monetary conditions by changing reserve requirements. For example, reducing reserve requirements gives banks excess reserves that are available for additional bank loans. In the past, the Federal Reserve has occasionally used the power to change reserve requirements to alter monetary conditions. In recent years, however, the Federal Reserve has focused upon open market operations.

Discount Window

The Federal Reserve makes loans directly to banks through the discount window. The discount window allows the Federal Reserve to be a lender of last resort to banks in need.

Three types of loans are available from the Federal Reserve. First, banks that are temporarily short of reserves to meet reserve requirements have access to loans from the Federal Reserve. The Federal Reserve is not required to make these loans. For example, if a bank tries to borrow too often, the Federal Reserve can refuse to make further loans.

Second, the Federal Reserve makes seasonal loans to some banks. For example, banks serving agricultural communities may have a marked seasonal demand for funds which the Federal Reserve may help to meet through seasonal loans.

Third, the Federal Reserve makes loans to banks in serious financial trouble. These loans are intended to give the troubled bank some time to work out its problems. Before establishment of the Federal Reserve, bank failures sometimes precipitated runs on healthy banks and a generalized banking panic. A bank run occurs when depositors become concerned about the safety of their funds. Consequently, they "run" to the bank to withdraw their funds. Because most of a bank's assets are working assets, very little cash is available to pay depositors. Large withdrawal requests may force a bank to close its doors. The closing of one bank may provoke depositors in other banks to become nervous about the safety of their deposits, causing runs on these banks and more closings in an avalanche effect. Large-scale closings can easily precipitate a recession or depression in the overall economy. Federal Reserve loans to troubled institutions are one tool for trying to prevent such dire events.

Quantitative Easing

The financial crisis of 2007–2009 caused the Federal Reserve to begin a program called *quantitative easing*, involving the purchase of securities other than short-term Treasury securities. The Federal Reserve expanded its purchases to longer-term treasury securities, mortgage-backed securities, and government agency securities. This policy was motivated by two objectives: first, to lower long-term interest rates as well as short-term interest rates in order to stimulate business loans for all maturities; second, to provide injections of funds into financial institutions by purchasing mortgage backed securities from them. The amount of securities purchased and held by the Federal Reserve have been enormous as evidenced by Figure 1.8.

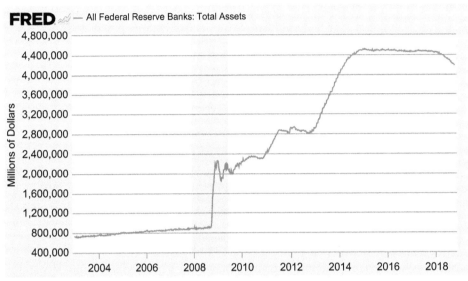

Shaded areas indicate U.S. recessions. Source: Board of Governors of the Federal Reserve System (US)

FIGURE 1.8 Changes in Federal Reserve Balance Sheet, Federal Reserve Bank of St. Louis.

Before the quantitative easing program, the Federal Reserve held a portfolio of shorter-term treasury securities of approximately three quarters of $1 trillion dollars. Quantitative easing increased the holdings of the Federal Reserve to over $4 trillion, providing an enormous inflow of funds into the financial system and the economy and driving down interest rates across the board. This program softened the impact of the recession.

Other Fed Actions to Stabilize Markets

The Federal Reserve has the power and obligation to stabilize financial markets in crises. The following are two examples of this type of Fed action.

On October 19, 1987, the stock market crashed, with prices declining more than 20% in one day. This crash resulted in massive losses for security dealers. On the following morning, many banks with outstanding loans to these dealers were hesitant to provide any more credit to them. If the dealers were denied credit, they would have been unable to operate as dealers and undoubtedly security prices would have taken a further dramatic plunge. To calm the situation, the Federal Reserve informed the banks that loans to dealers would be guaranteed by the Federal Reserve. The resulting injection of funds to dealers allowed them to continue to operate and gave the security markets some time to calm down.

In another example, a major money center bank had both its main computer systems and backup systems fail. This meant that very large payments could not be settled at the end of the day. Payments by the institution with failed computers were necessary for many other banks to settle their accounts for the day. Because of the effect of falling dominoes, default by one bank could bring the entire payments system to a close. To prevent this from occurring, the Federal Reserve immediately stepped in and made payments of the likely obligations of the bank with a guarantee that the Federal Reserve would pick up the tab if unresolved discrepancies occurred later. By acting quickly, the Federal Reserve was able to keep the payments systems moving smoothly.

Funds Transfer and Check Clearing

The Federal Reserve plays an important role in the wire (electronic) transfer of funds over the Federal Reserve Wire. Banks can rapidly transfer funds over the Federal Reserve Wire for a fee. This allows transactions to be completed on the same day.

The Federal Reserve plays an important role in the clearing and collection of checks. When a check is deposited in a bank, the check is immediately scanned. Then this electronic image is sent through the Federal Reserve System for collection. Within two days, funds are transferred from the bank on which the check is written to the receiving bank.

Credit Regulation

The Federal Reserve has the power to regulate borrowing for the purchase of securities, a so-called margin purchase. For example, in recent years the Federal Reserve has required the buyer of common stock to put down at least 50% of the original purchase price. For other types of securities and transactions, the margin requirement has been different.

Use of borrowed funds to buy securities is a form of financial leverage. The percentage changes in a levered (or margined) position are greater than the percentage changes in the underlying security. Overlooking dividends and interest, the percentage change in the equity of the levered position is equal to the percentage change in the underlying price divided by the percentage put down as collateral. That is,

$$\% \text{ change} = [\% \text{ change underlying}] / [\% \text{ collateral}] \qquad \textbf{1.8}$$

1 / [% collateral] is the leverage factor. This leverage factor increases as the percentage put down as collateral decreases. If 10% is put down, the leverage factor is 10.0. If 50% is put down as collateral, the leverage factor is 2.0.

The Federal Reserve has been given power over security margin purchases because of concern that excessive use of security credit might contribute to boom and bust cycles in security prices and in the overall economy. An example of a boom–bust cycle is the period of the late 1920s and early 1930s. In the 1920s, security margin was not regulated. The typical margin for common stocks was 10%. An investor putting down equity of $10 could borrow $90 and buy a stock worth $100. If the stock went up 10% to $110, the investor's equity would increase 100% to $20. Another $90 could be borrowed and more stock purchased. If many investors borrowed more as their profit increased, a snowballing effect would result. Rising prices would tend to bring about further rises until eventually prices would reach absurd levels and prices would collapse.

The very low margin requirements of the 1920s apparently contributed to the sharp rises in security prices during the late 1920s and the subsequent precipitous decline from 1929 to 1932. Some authorities claim that the stock market boom-bust cycle contributed to a similar boom-bust in the economy. The effect of the stock market is two-fold. First, changes in stock prices can affect consumption spending, with higher stock prices causing greater spending. The reason appears to be that higher stock prices increase consumers' perceived wealth. The wealth is perceived rather than actual. Market values do not represent actual wealth because, if all holders of stock tried to "cash in" their holdings, market values would rapidly sink. With higher perceived wealth, consumers tend to spend more. Second, a firm's cost of capital is affected by the level of stock prices, with the resulting impact upon firms' investment spending. Fear of a repetition of the events of the boom and bust cycle of the 1920s and early 1930s and concern about the impact of security credit upon the entire economy has motivated Federal Reserve control of security credit.

SUMMARY

In the Loanable Funds framework, the interest rate is determined by the demand for investment funds by businesses, by consumers, and by government, and by the supply of savings from individuals and businesses and the supply of money.

Because investors include anticipations of the future in current security prices, anticipated inflation rates have an impact upon the current interest rate. In the case of complete certainty about future inflation, the inflation rate is added to the real interest rate to arrive at the observed nominal interest rate. If the future is uncertain, the nominal interest rate equals the real interest rate plus the anticipated inflation rate plus some risk premium.

The Federal Reserve is the Central Bank of the United States. Its primary functions are to set and administer monetary policy, be a lender of last resort, expedite payments and collections, and regulate commercial banks. The goal of monetary policy is to promote economic growth, stability, full employment, and low inflation. These goals can be competing, creating difficult policy choices for the Federal Reserve.

Federal Reserve monetary policy has usually focused upon open market operations involving the purchase and sale of short maturity US Treasuries. Since the financial crisis of 2007–2009, the Federal Reserve has engaged in quantitative easing, in which the Federal Reserve has purchased mortgage-backed securities in the open market and longer maturity US Treasury bonds and notes. As a result of these additional purchases, the size of assets in the Federal Reserve balance sheet has increased dramatically. The purchases of additional securities in the quantitative easing program has injected large amounts of money into the financial system and pushed interest rates to very low levels in order to stimulate the level of economic activity.

QUESTIONS AND PROBLEMS

1. Explain the conflicting policy goals of the Federal Reserve.
2. Describe the determinants of the demand for funds and the supply of funds in the loanable funds framework.
3. Assume that the inflation-free rate of interest is 3% and that the inflation rate is 10% with complete certainty and no taxes. Determine the nominal interest rate.
4. In a world of certainty with no taxes, the nominal interest rate is 10% and the inflation-free interest rate is 5%. What is the inflation rate?
5. Assume no taxes. Suppose the inflation-free interest rate is 5%. The market forecasts a deflation rate of 15%. What is the nominal interest rate?

CHAPTER 2

Bond Issuers

This chapter discusses the major issuers of bonds in the United States. U.S. Treasury bonds, municipal bonds, and corporate bonds are discussed.

THE US TREASURY

The US Treasury has the responsibility of paying US federal government expenditures, collecting taxes, and borrowing to meet any deficit between expenditures and taxes. This borrowing is accomplished by selling debt securities of various types.

Figure 2.1 shows the first page of the September 2018 *Monthly Statement of the Public Debt* available from the US Treasury website. As shown in Figure 2.1, the national debt of the United States was approximately $21.5 trillion in February 2018. Over $6 trillion was in the form of nonmarketable debt, which is composed primarily of the Social Security Trust Fund and government employees' retirement funds. The total marketable debt was over $15 trillion. The marketable debt is composed of Treasury bills, Treasury notes, Treasury bonds, inflation-protected securities, and floating rate notes.

The lower part of the table shows the statutory limit on the debt. This debt limit was originally imposed during the First World War. This limit has been raised over time as the debt has grown.

MONTHLY STATEMENT OF THE PUBLIC DEBT
OF THE UNITED STATES

SEPTEMBER 30, 2018

(Details may not add to totals)

TABLE I -- SUMMARY OF TREASURY SECURITIES OUTSTANDING, SEPTEMBER 30, 2018

(Millions of dollars)

	Amount Outstanding		Totals
	Debt Held By the Public	Intragovernmental Holdings	
Marketable:			
Bills..	2,239,473	463	2,239,936
Notes..	9,150,301	4,079	9,154,380
Bonds...	2,114,982	12,840	2,127,823
Treasury Inflation-Protected Securities........	1,376,180	246	1,376,426
Floating Rate Notes [20]	369,142	0	369,142
Federal Financing Bank [1]	0	10,339	10,339
Total Marketable [a]..........................	**15,250,078**	**27,967** [2]	**15,278,045**
Nonmarketable:			
Domestic Series....................................	29,995	0	29,995
Foreign Series......................................	264	0	264
State and Local Government Series............	71,753	0	71,753
United States Savings Securities...............	156,809	0	156,809
Government Account Series.....................	250,680	5,726,936	5,977,617
Other..	1,575	0	1,575
Total Nonmarketable [b].....................	**511,077**	**5,726,936**	**6,238,013**
Total Public Debt Outstanding	**15,761,155**	**5,754,904**	**21,516,058**

TABLE II -- STATUTORY DEBT LIMIT, SEPTEMBER 30, 2018

(Millions of dollars)

	Amount Outstanding		Totals
Title	Debt Held By the Public [17, 19]	Intragovernmental Holdings	
Debt Subject to Limit: [17, 19]			
Total Public Debt Outstanding............................	15,761,155	5,754,904	21,516,058
Less Debt Not Subject to Limit:			
Other Debt	480	0	480
Unamortized Discount [3].........................	20,222	10,169	30,390
Federal Financing Bank [1]	0	10,339	10,339
Plus Other Debt Subject to Limit:			
Guaranteed Debt of Government Agencies [4]	*	0	*
Total Public Debt Subject to Limit	**15,740,453**	**5,734,396**	**21,474,848**
Statutory Debt Limit [5].......................................			0

COMPILED AND PUBLISHED BY
THE BUREAU OF THE FISCAL SERVICE

www.TreasuryDirect.gov

FIGURE 2.1 Public Debt of the United States September 2018.

Source: https://www.treasurydirect.gov/govt/reports/pd/mspd/mspd.htm.

Subsequent pages of the *Monthly Statement* provide details about the components of the debt. With regard to the marketable debt, there are over 300 issues of notes and bonds. The size of each issue is large; issue sizes of $20 billion and up are standard. The size of these individual issues means that they are extremely liquid compared to corporate bonds with average issue sizes of $200 million–$300 million. Thus, the US Treasury note and bond issues are approximately one hundred times bigger on average than the typical corporate bond issue.

Treasury securities are held by the Federal Reserve, by foreigners, by commercial banks, by nonbank financial institutions, and by individuals. When the United States runs deficits in its balance of trade (imports are greater than exports), foreigners accumulate dollar holdings including holdings of US Treasury securities. Foreigners often hold Treasury securities because they are essentially default-free and denominated in dollars, a relatively safe currency. The United States has frequently run trade deficits with China and Japan, and these countries are large holders of US Treasury securities. Many governments hold US Treasury securities as foreign exchange reserves.

Commercial banks hold Treasury securities as secondary reserves, that is, assets that can readily be turned into cash as the need arises. Nonbank financial institutions such as pension funds, insurance companies, and finance companies are large holders of debt obligations. These obligations have allowed nonbank financial institutions to control their risk by matching the institutions' fixed obligations to pensioners or policyholders with fixed income investments in bonds.

Individual investors hold Treasury securities because they are default-free, free of state income tax, and highly marketable. However, individuals hold a relatively small proportion of Treasury debt directly in their portfolios.

Types of Marketable Treasury Securities

The Treasury sells primarily four major types of marketable debt: (1) bills, (2) notes, (3) bonds, and (4) inflation-protected securities.

Treasury bills have maturities up to one year. They are issued on a discount basis, meaning no coupon payments. The buyer pays the purchase price and receives the par value at maturity. The difference is interest. See Figure 2.2.

FIGURE 2.2 Cash Flows for Treasury Bills.

Treasury notes and bonds are originally issued with maturities exceeding one year. United States Treasury notes and bonds pay semiannual coupon interest to the owners. See Figure 2.3. Notes have original maturities of up to ten years. Bonds have original maturities of between ten and thirty years, although thirty years has been the most common original maturity. The most recently issued thirty-year Treasury bond is often called the long bond.

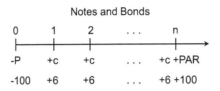

FIGURE 2.3 Cash Flows for US Treasury Notes and Bonds.

In many other countries, long-term coupon-bearing bonds have annual coupons instead of semiannual coupons.

The United States Treasury allows notes and bonds to be stripped by designated Treasury security dealers. The dealers are allowed to take a coupon-bearing security and to sell the individual coupons and principal separately. See Figure 2.4.

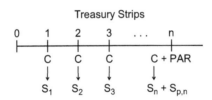

FIGURE 2.4 Example of Stripping of US Treasury Securities.

These securities are designated as STRIPS, which stands for Separate Trading of Registered Interest and Principal Securities. In the remainder of this book, STRIPS will frequently be called strips. Strips are actively traded. Bond dealers are permitted to strip designated securities and to reconstitute a bond by packaging strips back together to make the original bond. The *Monthly Statement of the Public Debt of the United States* provides details about the amount of individual bonds and notes held as STRIPS. US Treasury bonds and notes pay coupons every six months (semiannually), meaning that stripping of a ten-year Treasury results in twenty coupon strips and one principal strip.

The most recently issued Treasury securities are generally called on-the-run. Generally, there is a more active market in the most recently issued securities, increasing their liquidity, raising their prices, and lowering their yields compared to older securities that already exist.

Treasury inflation-protected securities specify an initial interest rate as a percentage of the par value. The par value is tied to an index of inflation, namely the consumer price index. If the consumer price index increases during a particular period of time, the par value increases proportionally and so does the coupon. For example, suppose that the stated coupon rate is 2% and the original par value is $100. If the consumer price index in the first time period increases by 1%, the par value increases to $100 (1.01) and the coupon becomes $100 (1.01) (0.02). If the consumer price index in the second time period increases by 3%, the par value becomes $100 (1.01) (1.03) and the coupon paid becomes $100 (1.01) (1.03) (0.02).

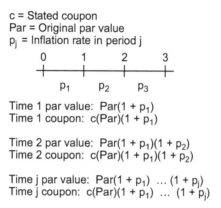

FIGURE 2.5 Treasury Inflation-Protected Securities (TIPS).

In the United States, the coupon paid on TIPS is subject to regular income tax, meaning that the inflationary increase in the coupon is taxed. In addition, the increase in the par value is subject to income tax. This tax treatment in the United States makes TIPS appealing to those in a low or zero tax brackets. Other countries often have a more favorable tax treatment of inflation-protected securities. In Britain the increase in the value of the principal resulting from inflation is not taxed although the inflationary increase in coupons is subject to British income taxes.

Suppose that non-indexed-linked bonds have the anticipated inflation rate incorporated into the yield to maturity (consistent with the Fisher hypothesis). Subsequent actual inflation can differ from anticipated inflation. If actual inflation is higher (lower) than anticipated inflation already incorporated into bond yields, investors in non-indexed-linked lose (gain) in real terms. By the same token, borrowers gain (lose) in real terms when actual inflation exceeds (falls below) the inflation premium incorporated into bond yields. If anticipations of inflation increase (decrease), interest rates on existing bonds tend to increase (decrease), and bond prices fall (rise). Thus changes in inflationary expectations will affect the market prices of existing bonds.

In contrast, index-linked bonds protect investors from all increases in the consumer price index whether they are anticipated or not. Therefore, index-linked bonds appeal to investors who do not want to bear the risks or rewards if actual inflation differs from anticipated inflation. Issuers of index-linked bonds are required to make higher payments if there is actual inflation. If inflation results in proportionally higher tax revenues, governments should have funds available to make the additional payments. With some rare exceptions, corporations do not issue index-linked bonds tied to a consumer price index because the inflation rate for corporations may differ from the inflation rate included in the consumer price index.

Treasury Debt Management Issues

Issue Pattern

Every year the Treasury needs to sell large amounts of debt. A current-year deficit requires sales of Treasury securities. The remaining sales result from the refinancing of maturing issues. Because of the enormous sums to be raised, the Treasury spreads its issues out over the course of the year. There are typically weekly auctions of various types of Treasury debt. In addition, the Treasury regularizes its pattern for issuing securities so that the market is not surprised by a particular issue. The Treasury feels that a regular pattern results in lower yields on average. To illustrate, the Treasury might announce the following issue pattern: thirteen-week and twenty-six-week bills every week, two-year notes every month, ten-year notes and thirty-year bonds every quarter, etc. Besides regularly scheduled auctions, there are additional auctions depending upon the cash needs of the Treasury.

Debt Maturity

The maturity of its debt is an important issue for the Treasury for two reasons. First, since short-term interest rates usually are lower than long-term interest rates, issuing short-term debt results in lower interest costs on average. Figure 2.6 shows an upward sloping yield curve that has been typical in recent years. Since the long-term interest rate is usually higher than the short-term interest rate, short-term securities have an immediate cost saving compared to long-term securities.

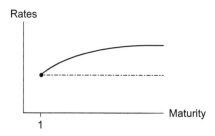

FIGURE 2.6 Upward-Sloping Yield Curve.

Second, short-term debt has to be refinanced more frequently than long-term debt. Since short-term interest rates fluctuate considerably, the rollover of short-maturity debt may take place at very high interest rates. A policy of issuing exclusively short maturities has lower total interest cost on average—but greater variability of total interest cost—than issuing long maturities.

Since a considerable part of the United States current deficit is interest on outstanding debt, the question of debt maturity affects the level and variability of deficits themselves. If the US Treasury followed a policy of issuing only short-term debt, the average interest cost of the debt would be relatively low compared to issuing exclusively long-term debt. However, the interest cost of the debt would be closely tied to the level of interest rates. When rates were high, the interest cost of the debt would be very high. The political consequences might be considerable if the interest on the debt increased at the same time that the other components of the federal deficit were high. A policy of issuing long-term debt exclusively makes the interest cost higher, but more stable. The US Treasury and most other countries follow a policy of issuing debt instruments with a variety of maturities. This mixed maturity policy makes the total interest on the debt relatively stable although somewhat dependent upon changes in interest rates.

The United States Treasury website provides details about the interest on the debt. In recent years, the annual interest on the national debt has been close to $500 billion. If interest rates were to rise or the total debt size increase, the total interest cost would increase considerably.

Procedures for Issuing Treasury Securities

Because of the enormous amounts of money involved, the procedures for issuing Treasury securities are quite important. The Treasury sells securities through sealed bid auctions. In sealed bid auctions, bidders are not aware of the bids of other bidders. Because of the enormous amounts of money that must be raised to cover deficits and to refinance existing securities reaching final maturity, the US Treasury conducts many auctions during the year.

Several days ahead of the auction, the Treasury announces the type of securities and the amount of par value of securities in a particular auction. Bids are submitted in terms of yield to maturity. The Treasury accepts bids starting with the lowest yield to maturity until the desired size of the issue is reached. With coupon-bearing bond issues, the coupon is not set until after the auction as explained below.

Bids may be competitive or noncompetitive as described below.

Noncompetitive Bids

Noncompetitive bids must not exceed $5 million par value. The noncompetitive bidder does not specify a yield, but merely specifies the par value of the securities desired. Noncompetitive bidders agree to accept the average yield of the accepted competitive bids. All noncompetitive bids are accepted by the Treasury.

Competitive Bids

All bids for $5 million or more of par value are competitive. These bidders are Treasury bond dealers or other financial institutions. The bidder specifies the yield. The Treasury accepts the competitive bids with the lowest interest rates (highest prices) and rejects the others. For an auction with coupon bearing bonds, the coupon rate is set at the 1/8 immediately below the highest winning yield. For example, if the highest winning yield is 4.90%, the coupon is set equal to 4.875%, or 4 7/8. Figure 2.7 illustrates a yield auction.

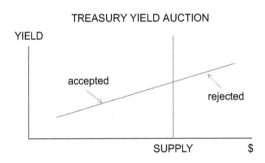

FIGURE 2.7 A Treasury Yield Auction.

Currently, the United States Treasury uses a procedure called uniform auctions in which all accepted bids are at the yield of the highest accepted winning competitive bidder. To illustrate the acceptance procedure, suppose the Treasury announces a sale of $43 billion par value of two-year Treasury notes. Three billion dollars of noncompetitive bids are received. The $3 billion of noncompetitive bids are accepted, and the $40 billion of competitive bids with the lowest yields (highest prices) are accepted. Since the highest winning competitive bid is 4.52%, the coupon on the auction would be set at 4.5%.

Table 2.1. Example of a Treasury Yield Auction

	Yield	Par Amount	Cumulative Par Amount
Accept	4.46%	$15 billion	$15 billion
Accept	4.49%	$15 billion	$30 billion
Accept	4.52%	$10 billion	$40 billion
Reject	4.56%	$10 billion	
Reject	4.60%	$10 billion	

In the past, the Treasury used a procedure called discriminatory auctions. In discriminatory auctions, all accepted competitive bidders receive the specific yield that they bid. In a discriminatory auction, the noncompetitive bidders pay the average of these accepted competitive bid yields.

Uniform versus Discriminatory Auctions

Since winning bidders in discriminatory auctions earn the interest rate that they bid, these bidders are more likely to place their purchase offers at high yields to avoid winning and earning a low yield. See Figure 2.8. In contrast, each of the winning bidders in uniform auctions earn the interest rate on the highest winning bid. Many researchers have argued that uniform auctions will encourage bids at lower interest rates and will result in lower interest cost for the Treasury. The consensus view seems to be that there is little difference in total interest cost for the Treasury between the two types of auctions.

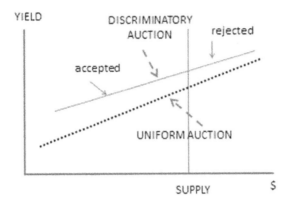

FIGURE 2.8 Impact of Uniform Auction on Demand Curve.

When-Issued Trading

Between the time a Treasury auction is announced and the time the securities are actually sold, trading in not-yet-issued, or *when-issued*, securities occurs. In the when-issued market, the buyers and sellers agree on a price to be paid in the future after the securities are sold at the auction. Since when-issued trading occurs before auction bids are submitted to the Treasury, auction bidders, who can observe prices in the when-issued market, have a good idea of market prices for the new securities. Figure 2.9 shows the timing of the announcement of an issue, auction date, and issue date.

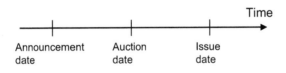

FIGURE 2.9 When-Issued Trading.

MUNICIPAL SECURITIES

State and local governmental units issue bonds called municipal bonds. The total amount of municipal bonds outstanding is enormous. For the majority of municipal bond issues, the interest payments are exempt from personal income taxes, although some municipal bonds are fully taxable as determined by the US tax code.

The issuers of municipal securities include state governments, local governments, state authorities, local authorities, and public colleges. A state or local authority is an entity set up for a specific purpose. For example, an authority may be set up to run a toll highway. While the majority of municipal securities issued in any year have maturities exceeding one year, a significant proportion of the municipal securities issued in any year may have maturities less than one year.

Some municipal bonds are *general obligation* (GO) bonds, which are backed by the full taxing power of the municipality. Other municipal bonds are *revenue bonds*, which are sold to finance a specific project. Typically, the revenues from that project are used to repay the revenue bonds. An example would be a toll highway; the revenues from the tolls are used to repay the bondholders. Revenue bonds typically have higher default risk and carry higher yields than general obligation bonds.

Municipal bonds are issued to finance many different projects, including schools, roads, government buildings, transportation facilities, electric power facilities, tunnels, sewage treatment plants, medical facilities, and low income housing.

The Primary and Secondary Markets for Municipal Bonds

The initial sale of securities is called the primary market. The resale market is called the secondary market. In the primary market, municipal securities may be sold by competitive bidding or by a negotiated sale to a group of underwriters. In a competitive sale, an auction occurs (similar to the auctions for Treasury securities). Groups, or syndicates, of municipal bond dealers will bid on the entire issue and then resell it to the public. The municipality will choose the bidding group that pays the highest price (lowest interest rate) for the securities.

In a negotiated sale, the issuer may have discussions with several underwriting groups and select a particular underwriting group to carry out the offering of securities. During the negotiation with the selected underwriter, the issuer and the underwriter devise the terms, conditions, and the timing of the issue. With a negotiated sale, the issuer has greater flexibility in setting the terms of the sale and the nature of the securities issued. In contrast, a competitive offering requires the terms to be set before the auction, and no changes are made afterwards.

The decision to have a competitive sale of securities or a negotiated underwriting is often the result of the laws of the state where the bonds are issued. Competitive sales have the advantage that many bidders are competing for the securities, and the issuer may be able to obtain a higher price and lower interest rate. In addition, competitive sales tend to have slightly lower underwriter fees than negotiated offerings. Negotiated underwritings have the advantage that the issue may be tailor made for market conditions and for potential buyers.

A number of municipal bond dealers make markets for municipal bonds over-the-counter. These dealers maintain an inventory of municipal bonds. They buy bonds at the bid price and sell bonds at the ask price. At a particular point in time, the ask price is higher than the bid price. The dealer hopes to profit by the difference in these two prices. However, a dealer may buy at a particular bid price and subsequently have to sell the security at a lower price. The difference between the ask price and the bid price is compensation to the dealer for the risk of taking a loss on a particular transaction, as well as the cost of tying up capital in bond inventory.

Because many municipal bonds are small issues, they are relatively illiquid. There is a "thin" market in them, meaning that trading is relatively infrequent. Many municipal bonds have serial issues. That is, a particular issue has staggered maturities. The staggered maturities allow the municipality to pay back the principal of the bonds over time. With staggered maturities, the principal amount of each maturity is often quite small, reducing liquidity further.

In contrast to public offerings of corporate debt, public offerings of municipal debt do not have to file registration statements with the Securities and Exchange Commission, and, therefore, the Securities and Exchange Commission does not verify the validity of the information. Buyers of municipal bonds depend upon accurate information being provided to them by the issuer and by the underwriter. Providing false or misleading information is a violation of the securities laws. Consequently, issuers and underwriters have a strong incentive to provide accurate information. Since registration with the Securities and Exchange Commission is expensive, the cost of issuing municipal bonds is typically lower than issuing corporate bonds, other things equal. On the other hand, the examination by the Securities and Exchange Commission for corporate bonds provides the bondholders with additional protection against false or misleading information.

Many years ago municipal bonds were typically *bearer* bonds. Whoever had physical possession of bearer bonds was the owner. Attached to bearer bonds were pieces of paper entitling the bondholders to coupon interest and principal payments, and these would be detached and cashed in at the appropriate dates. The identity of the holder of the bonds would remain anonymous. Allegedly, many individuals engaged in illegal activity or income tax avoidance wanted no record of their holdings. For these individuals, bearer bonds had a great advantage. However, the US government now requires all newly issued municipal bonds to be registered so that there is a formal record of the owners of individual securities. Increasingly, this registration process has become more electronically automated. The transfer of securities is also becoming more electronically automated over time.

Ratings for Municipal Bonds

Because there are so many municipal bonds outstanding and because information about these bonds is extremely difficult to obtain in many cases, bond rating agencies have developed to provide information about the relative probability of default. The three major rating agencies are Moody's, Standard & Poor's, and Fitch. These agencies are described in more detail in a later chapter.

The rating agencies indicate default probabilities by giving letter rankings to bonds. For municipal bonds, the highest ranking (with the lowest likelihood of default) is AAA. Bonds in the four highest ratings—AAA, AA, A, and BBB—are described as investment grade. Bonds with lower ratings are described as speculative or already in default.

In determining bond ratings, the ratings agencies try to determine the ability of the issuer to pay the debt obligation. The ability to pay depends materially upon the type of bond. General obligation bonds are backed by the full taxing authority of the issuer. For general obligation bonds, the rater will look at the economic well-being of the municipality, including the wealth and income of the community, the diversity of the local economy, and the anticipated future prospects of the major employers. The rating itself may depend upon the specific terms of the bond. For revenue bonds, the rating agencies will look at the economic prospects of the particular facility, including the stability of revenues, the anticipated future growth rate of revenues, competing facilities, and the expected prospects for the area served by the facility. For revenue bonds, the details of the bond issuer's obligations are quite important.

Municipal Bond Insurance

Some revenue municipal bonds have been insured against default. Before issuing the bond, the municipality approaches an insurance company and requests to be insured. The insurance company evaluates the likelihood that the bond issuer will default. If the default probability is reasonable, the insurer offers to insure the bond for an insurance premium paid by the issuer. In the event of nonpayment of interest or principal in a timely fashion, the insurance company is obligated to pay the bondholders. Since the insurance companies cover the risk of default, the interest rate on all insured bonds might be expected to be the same. However, this is not true. Insured bonds do sell at different interest rates because the features of these bonds may differ.

Taxation of Municipal Bonds

In the United States the interest paid on most municipal bonds is exempt from federal income taxes, but may be subject to state and local income taxes. In general, the interest for a bond issued by a municipality in the same state is not taxed for a resident. Thus, an investor living in New York State and buying municipal bonds issued in New York State will not pay income taxes on the interest. However, if the New York State resident held municipal bonds issued by the state of Wisconsin, the interest would be subject to New York State income taxes.

Because of the exemption from federal income taxes for interest on municipal bonds, the (before-tax) yields on municipal bonds are relatively low. If taxes were the only difference between municipal bonds and United States Treasury securities, the interest rate on the municipal bonds would be the interest rate on Treasury securities times 1 minus investors' tax rates. For example, if the interest rate on taxable Treasury securities is 10% and the tax rate for investors is 50%, the interest rate on municipal bonds would be $5\% = 10\% \ (1 - .50)$.

However, there are other differences between municipal bonds and Treasury securities. Municipal bonds may be subject to state income taxes, but Treasury securities are exempt from state income taxes. Municipal bonds may default, whereas Treasury bonds will not default as a practical matter. Treasury securities are also far more liquid than municipal bonds. Consequently, the interest rate observed on municipal bonds is higher than the Treasury interest rate times 1 minus the investors' tax rate. In addition, buyers of municipal bonds may be subject to taxes on capital gains or losses if they purchase the bonds at prices below or above par. For example, if a bond with $100 par value is purchased for $95, the bond buyer has a capital gain of $5 at maturity. The tax law requires the bondholders to pay federal taxes on this gain.

The legal reason for the tax exemption of interest on municipal bonds is quite complicated. In effect, this exemption has been granted by the United States government.

In the 1980s, the government began to restrict the types of municipal bonds that were eligible for this tax exemption. The general rule is that municipal bonds are tax-exempt if the purpose of the bonds is for the public benefit. Any bonds that are issued for private benefits are not tax-exempt. Previously, some private bonds were issued under the guise of municipalities. For example, a particular private firm might approach a municipality and ask the municipality to borrow money to be used to build a plant for this private firm. The municipality would benefit by creating local jobs and the private firm would pay much lower borrowing costs. Increasingly the government has restricted the use of municipal bonds for such private purposes.

The Tax Subsidy to Municipalities and Bond Investors

Because the interest on municipal bonds is exempt from federal income taxes, interest rates on municipal bonds are lower than on fully taxable bonds. This tax exemption represents a subsidy to municipalities. They can borrow money at much lower interest rates.

The merits of subsidizing municipalities in this way have been widely debated. According to some economists, a direct subsidy to municipalities would be more efficient. In other words, the federal government should make municipal bonds fully taxable and pay subsidies from tax revenues to deserving municipalities. This approach would involve allocations that might be motivated more by politics than by economic benefits.

Individual investors in high income tax brackets are the beneficiaries of the tax exemption for municipal bond interest. These investors are the wealthy members of society. Some economists argue that a subsidy to the wealthy is unfair. In spite of criticisms of the exemption of municipal bond interest from income taxes and the subsidy to wealthy investors who hold municipal bonds, a dramatic change in this tax exemption seems unlikely in the near future.

MORTGAGES

Mortgages are loans backed by real estate as collateral. The total amount of real estate loans outstanding is enormous. The Introduction provides some numbers showing the size of the mortgage market. In the United States, only the Treasury debt is larger in size than the total mortgage market debt.

Historically, thrift institutions and commercial banks were the major financial institutions involved in supplying funds to the mortgage market. Traditionally, thrifts and commercial banks made real estate loans and then held these loans as assets until the mortgage matured. Today, many mortgages are packaged together into *mortgage-backed securities* and sold in the secondary market. Claims on this mortgage pool are typically marketable and can be exchanged between investors. The institution which originates the securities in the pool no longer holds the mortgage but often continues to process the collection of mortgage payments for the pool. Besides thrifts and commercial banks, mortgage brokers also originate mortgages and sell them into mortgage pools.

This process of selling mortgages is called *securitization* because the mortgages are effectively changed into securities that can be bought and sold in the resale market. Mortgage-backed securities are one type of asset-backed security. Securitization has several important consequences that are discussed in the chapter on mortgages.

In recent years, so-called derivative mortgage products have expanded dramatically. In these mortgage derivative products, a pool of mortgages is broken up into slices or tranches that trade separately in the market. These individual tranches may be appealing to specific types of investors. Thus the total market value of the tranches may be greater than a pool of mortgages that is not subdivided into tranches. However, dividing a pool of mortgages into tranches reduces the size of each tranche and tends to reduce liquidity, other things equal.

CORPORATE DEBT

Corporations are large issuers of debt and equity. Corporate debt obligates the issuing firm to make fixed payments to debtholders. A fixed payment obligation may be advantageous or disadvantageous to stockholders depending upon the fortunes of the firm. If a corporation does extremely well, all incremental returns above the payments to the bondholders go to the stockholders, who earn high returns. If the corporation does poorly, there may be little or nothing left for stockholders after paying the fixed obligations to bondholders. The stockholders may lose everything invested. Consequently, use of debt financing tends to magnify the returns to stockholders. If the firm does well, stockholders do *very* well; if the firm does poorly, stockholders do *very* poorly. If the firm's returns are extremely poor, there are insufficient funds to pay the bondholders, resulting in defaults and losses suffered by the bondholders.

Textbooks on corporate finance devote considerable attention to the question of the optimal, or best, amount of debt financing for a firm. These texts do not provide any simple solution to the problem. Besides the question of the increased risk from magnification of stockholders' returns, a major controversy concerns the so-called tax advantage of debt. Because interest payments on corporation debt are deductible in computing corporate income taxes, there are possible tax advantages of debt. But expert opinions vary on measuring this possible benefit.

For some firms, the managers of the firms may have better information about the firm's prospects than the market. The decision to issue bonds or stock is affected by this difference in information, so-called *asymmetric information*. For example, if *only* the management knows of extremely attractive investment opportunities, the stock price of the firm does not reflect the profits from these opportunities and is relatively low. Sale of stock at this depressed price is a mistake; issuing debt is a better idea. In large corporations, the stockholders typically hire managers to act as agents on behalf of the stockholders. The gain to the agent from a particular corporate strategy may differ from the gain to the stockholders. Rational agents can be expected to act in their own personal interest, not in the stockholders' interest, creating an *agency problem*. This conflict of interest may affect the decision to issue stock or bonds.

SUMMARY

The US Treasury issues debt to finance federal budget deficits. Given the large cumulative total of the deficits over time, the total amount of debt is large. The Treasury has a serious task to issue debt to cover new deficits and roll over the maturing debt from previous deficits. Given the magnitude of Treasury operations, the impacts upon interest rates can be considerable. Other large issuers of securities include municipalities, mortgage issuers, and corporations.

QUESTIONS AND PROBLEMS

1. Since 1980, the market for Treasury debt has become increasingly important. Why?
2. What types of entities are the major holders of Treasury securities and why?
3. Explain the procedure by which the Treasury auctions securities. What are the pros and cons for a discriminatory auction versus a one-price auction?
4. The Treasury announces an auction of $54 billion par value of 52-week Treasury bills. $2 billion of noncompetitive bids are received. The competitive bids are as follows:

Price Per $1 of Par	Par Value
0.9950	$18 billion
0.9925	$20 billion
0.9901	$22 billion
0.9897	$28 billion
0.9894	$20 billion
0.9889	$18 billion

   Compute the price per dollar of par paid by noncompetitive bidders with a one-price auction. How would this price compared to the price paid by noncompetitive bidders with a discriminatory auction?
5. The Treasury auctions $47 billion of 10-year Treasury notes. Three billion dollars of noncompetitive bids are received. The competitive bids are:

Yield	Par Value
4.17%	$13 billion
4.15%	$17 billion
4.10%	$19 billion
4.07%	$21 billion

What is the interest rate on the lowest winning bid? What will be the coupon rate for this auction?

6. Suppose that the interest rate on taxable Treasury securities is 5% and that the tax rate for all investors is 25%. What should the interest rate be on a tax-free municipal bond assuming no default risk and no difference in liquidity?

7. The interest rate on fully taxable Treasury securities is 4% and the interest rate on tax-free municipal bonds is 2.75%. What is the tax rate of investors assuming all investors have the same tax rate, no default risk, and no difference in liquidity risk?

8. Explain the arguments for and against the tax-free status of municipal bonds. Who benefits from the existence of this tax-free feature?

CHAPTER 3

Financial Intermediaries

Many financial intermediaries play an important role in the debt markets. The purpose of this chapter is to describe the major financial intermediaries in the debt markets.

A long literature discusses the possible reasons for the existence of financial intermediaries. Basically, financial intermediaries exist because they expedite the flow of funds from economic sectors with surpluses to sectors with deficits. Financial intermediaries provide a number of advantages including the following: (1) pooling of small savings, (2) diversification of risks, (3) economies of scale in monitoring information and evaluating investment risks, and (4) lower transactions costs.

INITIAL SALE OF SECURITIES (PRIMARY MARKET)

When securities are issued, they may be sold directly to buyers, as in the case of the US Treasury. Alternatively, security issues are sold through investment banking firms that market the securities.

The original issuance of securities is classified as a public or private offering. The exact meaning of the term public is a technical legal question. In practical terms, a public offering has a sufficiently large size and a large number of buyers. Issues failing to meet the conditions for public offerings are considered private offerings.

In the United States, most public offerings of securities have to be registered with the Securities and Exchange Commission (SEC) before the securities can be sold, whereas private offerings are not registered. The purpose of SEC registration is to have the SEC verify the factual accuracy of the information about the securities to reduce the chance of fraud by issuers of securities. SEC endorsement does not indicate desirable investments but rather represents a confirmation of informational accuracy. Several types of public offerings of securities do not have to be registered with the SEC. These include US Treasury securities, municipal bonds, and debt with maturities of less than 270 days.

Investment Banking

Investment bankers are marketers of securities. They typically purchase securities from corporations or other issuers and then resell them. For finding buyers, investment bankers charge a fee, usually called the underwriting fee.

Public Offerings

Firm Commitments

Firm commitments involve the outright purchase of an entire security issue by an investment banker (or syndicate), which takes on the risks of reselling the issue to the public. The underwriter purchases the issue and tries to resell it publicly at a higher price, earning the difference minus costs as an underwriting fee or spread. The underwriter pays SEC registration expenses and other marketing costs. Since the resale price is not guaranteed, the underwriter runs the risk of being forced to sell the issue below the anticipated purchase price. Part of the underwriting fee is compensation for this risk.

A public registration may take several weeks or more. During this period, market conditions may change, and the underwriter may be exposed to considerable risks from a declining market.

To speed up the issuing process, a procedure called a *shelf registration* is now permitted. With a shelf registration, securities are effectively preregistered with the SEC. Once the registration is approved, the issue can be brought to market on very short notice. This may allow an issuer to time an issue as market conditions or the funding needs of the firm change. Investment banking fees are lower for shelf registration because the resale risk is lower. That is, the risk of price decline is small because the investment banker holds the debt for only one or two days.

Best Efforts

Public offerings may involve best-efforts selling. In this case, an investment banking firm tries to sell as much of an issue as possible. Any unsold amount reverts to the issuer. The investment banking firm does not bear much risk with best-efforts selling. Best-efforts selling is concentrated among low-risk and high-risk stock offerings. For low-risk offerings, the issuer does not need an underwriter to absorb the risk, since the risk is small. For high-risk offerings, underwriters are unwilling to absorb the risk. Moderate-risk offerings tend to be firm commitments.

Auctions

Some initial public offerings of stock are sold by uniform auctions in basically the same manner as US Treasury securities are sold. These public auctions are typically used only by firms that are well-known before their stock is sold to the public.

An example is the initial public offering of Google stock. At the time of this initial public offering, the name Google and the action of googling were well-known to the public. Therefore, it was very likely that Google stock could be sold by uniform auction at a fair market value. An advantage to the company was a lower underwriting fee.

Syndicates

Investment bankers typically use syndicates to sell securities. A syndicate is a group of investment bankers who combine their efforts to market an issue. A particular investment banker organizes the syndicate and is called the lead underwriter. A larger syndicate gives access to a larger group of potential buyers. Syndicates are usually employed for issues of common stock since the stock is often sold to many small buyers, who are more easily reached with more syndicate members. Syndicates are smaller, or nonexistent, for debt issues since bonds have relatively low resale risk for the investment banker.

Private Placements

Some corporate securities are sold to private buyers in what is called a private offering. Technically, private placements of securities are known as Rule 144 issues. An example would be the direct sale of a corporate bond issue to an insurance company. Insurance companies are large buyers of private offerings of bonds.

Private offerings may have advantages. First, the issuer does not have to bear the cost of registration of a public offering. Second, the issue can be tailor-made to the needs of the issuer and buyer. An insurance company may find a particular privately offered bond attractive because of its specific maturity, e.g. thirteen years, not easily found in the market.

Private offerings have disadvantages as well. First, private offerings cannot be widely traded; the resale market is limited, making private offerings relatively illiquid. Second, the interest rate on a private placement is higher than an otherwise identical public issue. The higher interest rate is a disadvantage to the issuer, although an advantage to the buyer.

Rule 144A Offerings

A Rule 144A offering is a sale of securities to qualified institutional buyers, typically insurance companies, mutual funds, or pension funds. A Rule 144A offering has characteristics of both a public offering and a private placement. Because institutional buyers of Rule 144A issues are assumed to be informed investors, these securities do not have to undergo a full public registration with the SEC. Rule 144A securities can be resold to other institutional buyers. Thus, they have somewhat more liquidity and somewhat lower yields than private placements. Rule 144A offerings are largely debt obligations.

The yields to maturity on Rule 144A offerings tend to be higher than the yields to maturity on public debt offerings. One reason for the higher yields is less information about the issuer because no detailed public registration with the Securities and Exchange Commission has to be filed for a Rule 144A offering. Rule 144A issuers are willing to pay somewhat higher interest rates in order to issue securities rapidly without any delay caused by public registration. Some firms issuing Rule 144A debt do not have any publicly traded securities and, therefore, do not file any financial information with the Securities and Exchange Commission. This type of firm has to pay considerably higher yields to maturity on its Rule 144A issues. In addition, many Rule 144A issues are converted to public issues within six to nine months after issue, consistent with the view that rapid issuance is important in many Rule 144A issues.

Cost of Public Offerings

Several factors affect underwriter costs. The percentage underwriter fee tends to be smaller for large security issues. For initial public offerings of stock, the underwriter fee tends to be 7% for small issues. For large issues, the fees may be smaller as a percent. The cost also depends upon the type of security issued; it is greatest for IPOs (initial public offerings of stock). SEOs (seasoned equity offerings) have lower costs; these are additional sales of stock by companies with existing publicly traded stock. The next lower cost is for convertible bonds. Finally, straight bonds have the lowest costs. For bonds, the underwriter fee is virtually the same for investment grade bonds (that is, bonds with ratings of BBB and above). For noninvestment grade bonds (with ratings of BB, B, CCC), the underwriter fee increases as the rating gets lower.

SECONDARY MARKET

Resale markets for securities have an important function. The opportunity for investors to buy or sell securities rapidly without affecting the price makes securities more liquid and the ownership of securities more desirable. Since investors are willing to pay higher prices and receive lower returns for liquid securities, liquidity in the resale market raises the initial purchase price and makes the costs of funds lower for business and governmental borrowers.

Organized Exchanges

For common stocks, a large proportion of security trading takes place on organized exchanges. Access to trading on organized exchanges is restricted to exchange members. Nonmembers pay commissions to member brokers to execute orders on the floor of the exchange.

The New York Stock Exchange (NYSE) is the largest organized stock exchange in the United States by volume of trading. Members of an exchange are described as having a seat. This is not a place to sit, but it represents the right to trade on the floor of the exchange. Exchange seats are traded, and their market value fluctuates as market conditions change. To trade on the floor of the exchange, one must purchase a seat and pass other standards set by the exchange. Members of the exchange may have more than one seat if they have a great deal of business on the floor of the exchange.

The organized exchanges have a set of requirements for a security to be traded, or, as it is usually called, listed. These requirements deal with a minimum size, a minimum number of shareholders, and a minimum period of existence. In the past, being listed on an exchange was considered an advantage. Some investigators believe that listing by itself raises the stock price. Currently, listing is regarded as less desirable. Many large and well-known firms are traded over-the-counter (discussed below) and some securities are traded on multiple exchanges.

Over time, transactions on security exchanges are becoming increasingly automated. Thus, small buy and sell orders are matched by computer. In addition, the stock exchange and the futures exchanges are linked by computer so that transactions on both exchanges can be executed simultaneously.

While most trading on the New York Stock Exchange is stocks, a number of corporate bonds are also traded. In general, the trading of bonds on the New York Stock Exchange involves small-volume transactions and may not be representative of larger-volume prices.

Over-The-Counter Trading

Over-the-counter (OTC) trading involves a network of dealers who make markets in individual securities. Apart from New York Stock Exchange corporate bond trading, the resale market for debt instruments is essentially an OTC market composed of dealers and brokers.

Electronic Trading Platforms

A variety of computerized trading systems have been developed for the trading of securities. These are often called electronic trading platforms. Access to these electronic trading platforms is typically restricted to financial institutions whose assets implicitly guarantee performance of a transaction. In contrast, for individual retail investors, performance of a contract is guaranteed by a broker since the broker will require individual investors to post collateral.

On electronic trading platforms, buyers and sellers carry out transactions anonymously. An institution wanting to sell securities can post an offer to sell the securities on the electronic trading platform. Another institution can then buy the securities. Institutional investors are able to search the posted quotes for desirable prices and consummate transactions electronically. The costs for these computerized systems are extremely low.

Security Dealers

Security dealers are market makers. They have an inventory of securities and buy for and sell from that inventory. Dealers quote bid prices, at which they are willing to buy, and ask prices, at which they are willing to sell. On average, the dealer hopes to make the difference between the bid and the ask prices minus operating costs.

Since bid–ask spreads differ for particular securities, an interesting and important question is the determination of these spreads. Dealer spreads have been found to be related to the risks borne by dealers.

First, spreads are inversely related to the volume of trading. For example, spreads tend to be large if trading is infrequent (a so-called thin market). An inactive resale market implies a longer holding period for dealer inventory. The longer the holding period, the greater is the chance of price change. The likelihood of an unfavorable event increases for longer holding periods, and the bid–ask spread increases.

In the bond market, US Treasury securities have active markets. In contrast, most corporate and municipal bonds are infrequently traded and have large bid–ask spreads. To a considerable extent, this difference between Treasury securities and corporate and municipal bonds results from the size of each issue. Individual Treasury issues have total par values in the billions of dollars, whereas corporate and municipal bond issues have total par values in the millions of dollars. In recent years, US Treasury security issues have been multibillion-dollars in size. Many issues have been in excess of $30 billion per issue, making these issues more than 100 times larger than the typical corporate bond issue.

Second, spreads are positively related to the inherent price risk of individual securities. Some securities can be expected to have a bigger percentage price change over a particular time interval compared to other securities. For example, short-term (30-day) US Treasury bills tend to have smaller percentage price changes than long-term (30-year) US Treasury bonds. As a consequence, the bid–ask spreads on bills will be much smaller than the bid–ask spreads on bonds. In the bond market, bid-ask spreads increase with bond maturity.

Third, the bid–ask spread should be a function of dealer financing costs. When rates of interest are high and other things are equal, bid–ask spreads are relatively high to compensate the dealer for the high cost of financing inventory.

Security Brokers

Security brokers act as agents for buyers and sellers. Brokers carry out transactions for a fee or commission. Many security brokers simply execute transactions for customers. Other security brokers provide advice to investors as well as execute transactions. This type of broker is called a full-service broker and charges higher fees as compensation for advice provided.

Large institutional investors often have "relationships" with brokerage firms. These institutional investors agree to send enough orders to a particular brokerage house to generate a minimum total dollar amount of commissions. In exchange, the institutions receive other services, such as investment reports, access to data, and investment suggestions. Consequently, the stated brokerage fee is higher than the cost of pure execution of orders. The added amount is payment for these other services and has been given the name *soft dollar payments*. The allowable soft dollar payments have been a subject of controversy, and the Securities and Exchange Commission has instituted rules prohibiting some types of services being included in the soft dollar payments.

MUTUAL FUNDS

A mutual fund is a pooling of the funds of many small savers. Each investor has a proportional claim on the assets of the fund. These funds are then invested by the managers of the mutual fund in stocks, bonds, and other financial claims, as allowed by the fund's prospectus. Mutual funds provide a clear example of the diversification role played by financial intermediaries.

The management charges a fee which varies with the investment objective of the fund. Funds requiring a great deal of managerial effort charge higher fees. Mutual funds are governed by the Investment Company Act of 1940 and various regulations imposed by the Securities and Exchange Commission.

Closed-End Funds

Closed-end mutual funds have an initial offering of shares, and no additional shares are sold. Existing shares cannot be redeemed. Thus, a closed-end fund typically has no new cash inflows or redemptions. Shares of closed-end funds represent a proportional interest in the fund and trade on the open market at prices that may differ from their net asset value. The net asset value (NAV) of a mutual fund is the liquidating value, or the amount available to distribute if all the fund's assets were sold off. Typically, closed-end fund shares trade at a discount from their net asset value. Closed-end fund discounts from net asset value cannot get too large since very large discounts would provide a profit opportunity to a large investor, who would buy all the shares of the fund at a discount and then liquidate the fund for a profit.

Sometimes closed-end mutual funds sell at a premium above the net asset value. Premiums may result from market imperfections because access to a particular market may be difficult or costly. The closed-end mutual fund may be able to access a particular market at lower cost than individuals can access this market. In some cases, closed-end mutual funds sell at unusually large premiums that appear to be the result of irrational behavior on the part of the buyers of these mutual funds.

Open-End Funds

Most mutual funds are open-end funds; the fund stands ready to sell new shares and redeem old shares on a daily basis.

Sales Fees

Many mutual funds have sales charges, which are called loads. Front-end loads are sales commissions that are deducted from the money invested. For example, a $10,000 investment with an 8.5% commission would result in a net investment of $9,150. Some mutual funds charge rear-end loads or redemption fees, payable when an investor liquidates shares in the fund. In general, rear-end loads decrease the longer that an investor holds shares in the fund. Many mutual funds charge annual loads, so-called 12b-1 fees.

Many load mutual funds allow investors a choice of the type of load. Typically, front-end load funds are called A shares; rear-end load funds are called B shares; annual load funds are called C shares. The expected holding period of the investor should affect the choice of load. Long-term investors might find front-end loads more appealing. Intermediate-term investors would tend to find rear-end load funds better. Short-term investors would prefer annual loads.

Many mutual funds are no-load funds. These funds charge no sales commissions. Other things being equal, an investor should clearly prefer a no-load fund to one with a load. Someone investing in a no-load fund must investigate the fund himself, since a security salesperson has a strong incentive to suggest a load fund. No-load funds can be purchased directly from the fund itself. In addition, brokers or other mutual fund families may carry out purchases.

Investment Objectives

Each fund specifies an investment objective. Some funds are *index funds*, which try to duplicate the performance of a particular index of securities, such as the S&P 500 Stock Index. Some index funds hold all of the securities in the index and others hold a sample that duplicates the results of the index. Many investors find index funds appealing because of evidence that the average mutual fund underperforms market indices by essentially the amount of the fees charged by the fund. Index funds charge very low fees allowing investors to earn higher average returns than actively managed funds, which have higher fees.

The investment objectives of non-index mutual funds vary. Some funds invest exclusively in stocks; some exclusively in bonds; some in a combination of stocks and bonds. Within these broader categories of funds, there are many specialized objectives. For stock mutual funds, specialized objectives include small company funds, growth funds, value funds, foreign funds, and global funds. In the area of bond funds, specialties include US Treasury securities, corporate bonds, high-risk corporate bonds, municipal (tax-free) bonds, foreign bonds, and money market funds. For many people and businesses, money market mutual funds have provided an attractive alternative to bank savings and time deposit accounts. Money market mutual fund accounts may provide a number of attractive services, including limited check-writing privileges and the ability to transfer funds easily between mutual funds or between the mutual fund and a bank.

Advantages of Mutual Funds

Mutual funds provide several advantages over direct investment by savers. First, because of its large size, a mutual fund can more easily diversify than individual investors. Second, mutual funds provide economies of scale, including efficient record keeping and economies in information search. For small portfolios, the amount of time required to monitor an efficient portfolio can be large relative to the absolute benefits of monitoring, implying significant advantages of having a mutual fund manager carry out the task.

Because mutual funds can trade securities in large quantities, brokerage commissions may be lower than for individual small investors. On the other hand, mutual funds trade in larger-size transactions. Larger transactions may result in price concessions. Large sellers may have to sell at lower prices and large buyers purchase at higher prices than small individual investors. These price concessions for large transactions are called market impact fees.

Fees Charged by Mutual Funds

Mutual funds charge investors a variety of fees.

1. The management fee is paid to the investment advisor for selecting investments. It is typically the largest fee for mutual funds. The typical range is between 50 basis points (0.50%) and 100 basis points (1.00%), although some mutual funds charge lower management fees and some charge higher management fees. For most mutual funds the management fee is a fixed

percent of assets, although some funds have a decreasing management fee for higher levels of total assets of the fund.

2. The administrator fees are the costs of running the back office of the mutual fund.

3. Servicing agent fees are payments for the cost of handling transactions with fund investors and dealing with correspondence between the fund and the investor, such as periodic reports, prospectuses, and proxies.

4. Custodian fees are paid to a third party to handle the securities held by the fund.

5. Several smaller fees include printing fees, registration fees, directors' fees, auditing fees, and legal fees.

The total percentage cost of the preceding fees is called the *expense ratio.* In addition, fund investors have to pay any brokerage commissions resulting from fund trading.

The fees charged by mutual funds, brokerage commissions from trading, and the market impact costs of trades tend to reduce the value of an investor's position unless these costs result in better selection of securities by the fund management. Suppose that the costs not compensated by improved performance are denoted by c. Then the wealth of the investor after n investment periods is proportionally less in the following way:

$$\text{Investor wealth after n-periods} = (1 - c)^n \qquad \textbf{3.1}$$

For example, if annually the mutual fund net costs after accounting for any improvement in returns from portfolio selection are 1.5%, investor wealth after 10-periods is 85.973% of its possible value if there were no costs at all. The investor's wealth has been reduced by 14.03% because of the net annual costs. If the number of periods involved is not very large, the reduction in an investor's wealth is approximately the cost per period times the number of time periods.

Exchange-Traded Funds (ETFs)

Exchange-traded funds are a hybrid between open-end and closed-end funds. Their shares are traded on the organized exchanges. Shares in an ETF represent a proportional interest in the securities held by the fund.

An ETF differs from a closed-end fund in that the size of the fund can be increased or decreased. Designated financial institutions are allowed to form *creation units.* For example, a financial institution might be able to create 50,000 shares of the particular ETF by purchasing the same securities in the same proportion as the ETF and having these designated as additional shares. The reverse can happen, permitting the size of the ETF total assets to decrease.

Most exchange traded funds are index funds, although the objective of most ETFs is to match a highly specialized index, such as an index of securities in a particular industry or in an individual country. Exchange traded funds have relatively low fees because they are index funds. Since they are traded on exchanges, purchases and sales of ETFs can be carried out any time during the trading day, although transactions involve paying brokerage commissions. There can be differences between the net asset value of the assets in an ETF and the price of the ETF shares on the exchange. If these differences get too large, creation units allow a change in the number of shares, tending to reduce any difference between the net asset value and the market price of the ETF shares.

Thus, exchange-traded funds have some of the features of closed-end funds and some of the features of open-end funds.

Hedge Funds

Hedge funds are investments designed for large investors. There is a high minimum amount of investment. Also, individual investors are required to have a sizable net worth, implying that they are able to make informed investment decisions. Hedge funds are not subject to restrictions included in the Investment Company Act of 1940. They are not required to file extensive reports with the Securities and Exchange Commission or provide investors with the periodic reports required of mutual funds.

The typical fees charged by hedge funds are quite high—a management fee of 2% plus 20% of profits. Mutual funds are prohibited from having fees that are a percentage of profits. Hedge funds also have lock-in periods, meaning that investors cannot redeem their investments before a specified time interval after investing in the fund.

Because hedge funds are not subject to the Investment Company Act of 1940 and other Securities and Exchange Commission rules, they are able to take extremely risky positions including short selling, borrowing money, speculating on foreign exchange rates.

Hedge funds are not required to report their results to any central depository, although some hedge funds voluntarily report their results. In contrast, mutual funds are required to file reports with the Securities and Exchange Commission. These SEC filings are open for public viewing.

The available empirical evidence suggests that the average hedge fund is not very profitable. A significant part of the reason for poor performance is the large fees of 2% annually and 20% of profits.

INSURANCE COMPANIES

In exchange for a periodic *premium*, an insurance company agrees to make a financial payment to insured individuals if a specified event occurs. Life and casualty are the major types of insurance. Life insurance is of two varieties, term insurance or permanent life insurance. Many term life insurance policies are for a relatively short time interval, such as ten years. Some term life insurance policies are for extended periods of time with a premium that increases with age.

Whole life insurance covers the entire life of a person and doesn't expire until death. The premium is paid over the person's entire life. The insurance company invests the premiums in the early years to earn enough to cover the added risks in later years. Whole life insurance incorporates an element of saving, whereas term insurance is pure insurance.

Property and casualty insurance companies insure against losses from fire, theft, flood, automobile accidents, and other types of loss. Because property and casualty insurance risks are harder to predict than life insurance risks, these companies make lower risk investments than life insurance companies.

Regulation of insurance companies is largely left to the states. Regulators curtail unfair sales practices, require liquid assets to meet loss payments, and limit investment in risky assets.

Insurance companies are rated by A.M. Best Company, Standard & Poor's, and other rating agencies. The ratings are designed to give the relative probability that the insurance company has sufficient reserves to make all of the likely payments in the total of all of its insurance policies written.

The insurance company charges a fee, called a premium. The premium is typically invested to provide a fund to meet future payouts. On the basis of statistical evidence, the insurance company can predict with a high degree of accuracy the likelihood of a particular event occurring to a large group of insured individuals. By spreading the risk over many insured individuals, insurance companies can protect people against the financial consequences of disastrous events. The insurance premium is the cost of this protection for the individual. The insurance premium is set at a level high enough to cover a risk premium, a profit margin, and the expected payments to the insured individuals.

The advantage of insurance to the insured is the payment of a relatively small, periodic, and stable amount. The insured prefers this small loss from paying an insurance premium to a possibly large, and potentially catastrophic, loss if there is no insurance. An uninsured entity can expect to occasionally suffer severe or catastrophic losses.

Life insurance typically involves a long-term dollar-denominated contract. Consequently, life insurance companies are large investors in fixed income securities.

Insurance companies face the problem of *adverse selection*. That is, individuals with the greatest risk to the insurance company are most likely to seek insurance. For example, someone with a known medical condition is more likely to purchase health insurance.

Insurance companies do several things to reduce the company's risk from adverse selection. The high-risk insurance applicants may be denied insurance. Also, the premium may be adjusted for the individual's risk. Restrictive covenants may be included in the insurance contract. Thus, life insurance typically does not cover death from skydiving. Coinsurance can be used to require the insured to bear some percentage of the losses. Coinsurance may be in the form of a deductible, meaning that part of a loss is not covered by insurance. Having deductibles is very common with medical insurance and other types of casualty insurance. Typically, a person with medical insurance is required to pay part of the charges. For automobile insurance, the insured person may have to pay the first $1000 of the losses from an accident. In addition, casualty insurance will frequently have an upper limit on the amount that the insurance company is obligated to pay to the insured party.

The existence of insurance may create the problem of *moral hazard*. The term moral hazard refers to the tendency of insured individuals or businesses to alter their behavior if they have insurance against adverse events. The result of failure of a major bank can be quite devastating to the entire financial system. As a consequence, governments may be essentially obligated to intercede if a large bank fails in order to prevent an economy-wide downturn. Thus, very large banks create a moral hazard since they may take on considerable risk because of the belief that the government implicitly ensures the bank won't fail.

PENSION FUNDS

Pension funds represent savings for payment of employee retirement benefits. Figure 3.1 illustrates the cash flows involved in pensions. Money is put into the pension fund while individuals are working. Then money is withdrawn when the individuals retire.

There are two basic types of retirement plans: defined contribution plans and defined benefit plans.

For *defined contribution plans*, the employer contribution is specified. 401(k) retirement plans are a defined contribution plan frequently used in the United States. For example, the employer may contribute 9% of an employee's salary. Frequently, the employee has a choice of mutual funds in which to invest. The payment received by the employee at retirement depends upon the investment performance of the funds. If the investment returns are high, the employee retirement benefit is high; if the returns are low, the payment is low.

Many defined contribution pension plans invest in diversified portfolios. However, a number of defined contribution plans concentrate their funds in the stock of the employer. Such concentrated pension plans are extremely risky. If the company does poorly, the employees' jobs as well as their pensions are at risk.

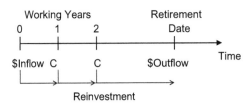

FIGURE 3.1 Pension Fund Cash Flows.

Defined benefit plans specify the amount to be paid to employees at retirement. For example, a defined benefit pension fund might specify the benefit to be 2% times the number of years employed times the average salary for the last five years employed. Someone employed for 20 years, earning $40,000 average salary for the last five years would receive $16,000 (0.02 × 20 × 40,000) annually.

Defined benefit plans may have vesting periods. Vesting periods require an employee to work some minimum number of years in order to receive any benefits from the defined benefit pension plan in the future.

Determining the appropriate amount of pension fund contributions for defined benefit plans is difficult. The employer uses an actuary to estimate the probable payments to employees at retirement. Then the current contributions to the plan are made. The current contributions necessary to achieve the actuarially determined payouts depend upon the rate of return assumed. For example, if interest rates are assumed to be high, lower current contributions are necessary.

Many employers fully fund their defined benefit plans. That is, current pension fund contributions are sufficient to meet likely contingencies. Other employers have underfunded their plans by contributing insufficient funds. Since pension fund contributions are a business expense reducing reported income, some firms with low earnings may reduce pension fund contributions to boost reported earnings. In some cases, firms with underfunded pension funds have gone bankrupt, leaving insufficient funds to make payments to retirees. Many defined benefit plans for government employees have underfunded their defined benefit plans. Underfunding keeps taxes low in the short run but creates a large tax liability for future taxpayers.

The Employee Retirement Income Security Act (ERISA) of 1974 sets minimum standards for corporate disclosure of pension fund information, contains rules for vesting and restrictions on underfunding, and controls pension fund investments. The act established the Pension Benefit Guarantee Corporation (PBGC) to insure private (i.e., nongovernment) pension funds against underfunding. All insured pension plans are required to make payments of premiums to the PBGC to increase the funds available to pay possible shortfalls in pension liabilities of private defined benefit plans. The Pension Benefit Guarantee Corporation does not insure the defined benefit plans of governmental units, such as states or municipalities. In the view of some experts, the Pension Benefit Guarantee Corporation has insufficient funds to cover expected underfunding from future corporate bankruptcies. Inadequate auditing of covered pension funds has contributed to the problem. Careful auditing by the Pension Guarantee Corporation should allow underfunded pension funds to be detected early so that funding adjustments can be made before the insurance company incurs losses.

The low interest rates in recent years have created a difficult investment situation for defined benefit pension funds. Many contracts have been written assuming relatively high interest rates compared to current rates, creating a likely shortfall in the funds that will be available to make payments to pensioners or insured individuals.

COMMERCIAL BANKS AND THRIFTS

Commercial banks and thrift institutions are the largest variety of financial intermediary. A commercial bank is an institution that has checking deposits and makes commercial loans. A thrift institution offers savings deposits. The thrift industry is composed of three types of savings institutions: savings and loan associations, mutual savings banks, and credit unions.

Regulation of Banks

Banks and thrifts have been heavily regulated for several reasons. One motive has been to try to guarantee the safety of bank deposits. Second, bank failures have had widespread negative effects on local or even national economies. Banks are regulated to reduce or eliminate these bank induced downturns in economic activity. The third motive for bank regulation has been the desire to have competition between lenders, but not excessive competition leading to bank failures.

The United States has a complicated system of regulation of commercial banks.[1] On a national level, there are three regulators: the Federal Reserve, the Federal Deposit Insurance Corporation (FDIC), and the Comptroller of the Currency (part

---

[1] We will focus on the regulation of commercial banks. Similar regulatory agencies serve the thrift industry.

of the US Treasury). In addition, each of the fifty states has a state bank regulator. These regulators share and coordinate the efforts.

Major areas of regulation of commercial banks include the following:

1. The granting of a charter, which is the right to operate a bank.
2. Branching activities. In the past the branching activities of banks were severely restricted. Until the 1980s, banks were restricted to operate in one state only. Now nationwide branching is permitted. The history of restricting banks to individual states has created a very large number of banks in the United States per capita as compared with most other industrialized countries. The United States has had a sizable number of small and relatively high cost and inefficient banks, with relatively high rates of bank failure of small banks.
3. Minimum equity or capital requirements are set by regulation. The Federal Reserve, the Comptroller of the Currency, and state banking authorities share the task of inspecting banks to make sure that they meet the capital requirements.
4. Insurance of deposits and bank closings. The Federal Deposit Insurance Corporation insures individual deposits in banks for up to $250,000 per person in an individual bank. The FDIC also has the job of determining when a bank has failed and needs to be closed. Then the assets of the bank are either sold as one unit to another bank or the assets are sold off individually. Any shortfall between the insured deposits and the funds received from liquidating the bank are to be paid by the FDIC. FDIC insurance has greatly reduced the probability of a bank run since individual deposits are insured.

FINANCIAL CRISIS OF 2007–2009

Throughout its history, the United States has experienced financial crises. One of the most severe was the Great Depression of the 1930s in which there was a major decline in production, a very large increase in the unemployment rate, and many bank failures. A consensus emerged that the Great Depression could have been prevented or mitigated if financial markets and banks had been regulated. As a consequence, the US government passed the Glass-Steagall act that separated commercial banking from activities such as underwriting, security dealing, security brokerage, and insurance. This separation was based on the belief that commercial banking should be a relatively stable business that should not be exposed to the inherent riskiness of these other activities. In addition, the government introduced the Securities and Exchange Commission (SEC) to regulate securities markets, as well as the Federal

Deposit Insurance Corporation (FDIC) to guarantee bank deposits and prevent "bank runs."

Origins of the Crisis

Beginning in the 1980s, several major factors significantly changed the commercial banking system and made the system much more susceptible to crises.

First, the US government began to deregulate or undo some of the regulations. For many years, banks had been restricted to operating in a single state in the United States. As a result, the United States has always had a very large numbers of banks per capita compared to other industrialized countries. A series of government actions gradually relaxed this single state restriction in the 1980s. The result was the merger of many banks. The number of banks declined from approximately 16,000 in 1985 to slightly less than 5,000 in 2018. Out of the approximately 5,000 commercial banks, a small number of banks became extremely large. Today, the twelve largest commercial banks in the United States control more than half of the assets of the banking system.

Second, the practice of *securitizing mortgages* began by the 1980s. With securitization, a bank puts a series of mortgages into a package and sells claims on this package of *mortgage-backed securities* to investors. Securitization contrasts with the previous practice of banks holding mortgages until they are paid off. With securitization, the bank earns a fee for originating mortgages and passes on the risks of changing interest rates to investors in the mortgage-backed securities. The bank may also be able avoid the mortgage default risk. Securitization of mortgages gives the bank more incentive to process larger numbers of mortgages and conceivably reduce lending standards. The result was an enormous increase in the amount of mortgage lending between 2000 and 2006.

Third, the US government deregulated all over-the-counter derivatives beginning in the late 1990s. The result was a very large increase in derivatives, which are simply securities based upon other securities. Derivative securities allow the transfer of risk from one party to another party, but do not eliminate the total risk in the system. With unregulated over-the-counter derivatives, there is no formal record of recent security prices or the volume of activity. Consequently, both the US government (including regulators) and individual financial firms had minimal information about these over-the-counter markets. No one had clear knowledge of the size of these markets.

Credit default swaps (CDS) became quite popular. A credit default swap insures against default of a specific debt instrument. In a credit default swap, one party might insure a pool of securitized mortgages against default, and another party buys this insurance. If there is a default, the buyer of insurance protection has the right to sell the debt instrument to the insurance writer at par value.

Fourth, the largest 10–12 banks in the United States became very active in the derivatives market including over-the-counter derivatives. These banks became market makers in these high-risk derivatives and also engaged in *proprietary trading* activities. Proprietary trading essentially constitutes speculating on potential future security price movements for the benefit of the bank.

As a result of these changes, the old distinction between commercial banks that make business loans and investment banks that engage in security underwriting, security market-making, and proprietary trading activities was eliminated.

The Crisis Begins

Between 2000 and 2006, the enormous increase in mortgage lending contributed to a speculative boom in housing prices throughout the United States. In some locations, prices of houses doubled or tripled within five years. This was a classic bubble.

The crisis began by 2007 as the number of defaults on mortgages began to increase significantly. The increased default rate precipitated an increase in the perceived default risk on mortgage-backed securities, resulting in declines in market prices of mortgage-backed securities. Many investors in mortgage-backed securities saw the prices of their securities decline. A significant proportion of mortgage-backed securities were held by the largest US banks, greatly weakening the financial positions of some banks.

Since the largest banks in the United States had very complicated balance sheets including positions in many different types of derivative securities, these large banks had difficulty measuring their total risk exposure.

Historically, many financial firms have had very little equity, and funded the majority of their operations by debt obligations. There was also a considerable reliance on very short-term financing, which had to be renewed on a daily or weekly basis.

The 2007–2009 crisis appears to have been precipitated by the failure of the number of two over-levered financial firms, Bear Stearns and Lehman Brothers. Each of these firms had taken large losses on some of their risky positions. When Bear Stearns failed, the government intervened, and other financial firms took over the viable assets of the firm. When Lehman Brothers failed in the fall of 2008, the government decided not to intervene. The result was a panic in the markets, with sharp declines in stock prices, rapidly declining housing prices leading to defaults by individual borrowers, declining prices of mortgage-backed securities and the inability of writers of credit default swaps to honor their obligations.

The US government took actions to reduce the impact of the crisis by injecting large amounts of money into the financial system and passing a fiscal spending plan to stimulate the economy. In addition, the Dodd-Frank Act was passed to introduce regulations to try to reduce the chances of a repeat crisis. The Dodd-Frank Act was an effort to increase the amount of equity capital in banks and to curtail the ability of commercial banks to take on risky security positions.

SUMMARY

Financial intermediaries expedite the flow of savings from savers to ultimate investors in physical assets. They offer some advantages, including pooling of savings, diversification of investment risks, economies of scale in monitoring information and evaluating investment risks, and lower transactions costs. In addition, individual types of intermediaries provide specialized services.

Investment bankers are engaged in the original sale of securities to the public. Dealers make markets in individual securities, trying on average to make a profit by buying at the bid price and selling at the ask price. Brokers match buyers and sellers of securities for a fee.

Mutual funds, insurance companies, and pension funds invest heavily in the debt markets. Mutual funds pool the funds of many investors and invest in stocks, bonds, or some combination, depending upon the stated investment objectives of the fund. Insurance companies charge premiums to cover financial losses. Pension funds invest retirement money.

Commercial banks play an important role in the financial system. Relaxation of regulations on commercial banks in the 1980s and 1990s resulted in consolidation of the banking system and the emergence of approximately ten extremely large banks controlling more than half the assets of the banking system. A large proportion of mortgages were securitized and sold off as mortgage-backed securities. In addition, over-the-counter derivatives were deregulated. In this regulation-free environment many over-the-counter derivatives were created including credit default swaps. In this low regulation environment, a great deal of speculation occurred and created a bubble in the housing market and in many financial derivatives. Eventually, the financial markets collapsed causing widespread losses in the financial system and in the real economy.

QUESTIONS AND PROBLEMS

1. Describe the reasons why financial intermediaries exist.
2. What role do investment bankers play in the financial system? What are the economic benefits of investment bankers? Why are the underwriter fees for high-yield bonds higher than the fees for investment-grade bonds?

3. Explain the economic reasons for the existence of bid-asked spreads. What are the major determinants of bid–asked spreads charged by security dealers? Compare the bid–asked on corporate bonds with US Treasury bonds and the spreads on short-term Treasuries with long-term Treasuries.

4. Describe the differences between a defined benefit and defined contribution pension plan. Which plan would likely be better for an individual likely to move?

5. Explain how insurance companies try to deal with the problems of adverse selection and moral hazard.

6. Describe the various types of mutual fund and other types of investment funds.

7. What are the roles of the major bank regulators?

8. What factors contributed to the financial crisis of 2007–2009?

CHAPTER 4

Time Values

Most securities involve cash flows at different points in time. To compare different securities, the cash flows on each security can be transformed into an equivalent value at the present time (i.e. present value) or at some future point in time (i.e. future value). Then, these present (or future) values can be compared and the best security chosen.

This chapter presents future value and present value computations assuming the same interest rate or discount rate for all periods. This assumption is usually called a flat term (or maturity) structure of interest rates. Later chapters extend the analysis to the case where the interest rate differs by maturity.

MEASURING TIME

Since cash flows for securities occur at different points in time, it is important for the reader to have a clear understanding of the timeline in Figure 4.1. Points in time are shown above the line, and periods in time are shown below the line. Point in time 0 is the present (or now). Point in time 1 is one period from now. Period 1 begins at time 0 and extends until time 1. The length of a period is arbitrary and depends upon the situation under consideration. The length of a period may be a day, a month, a half year, or a year.

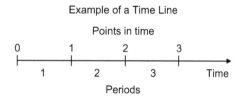

FIGURE 4.1 Example of a Timeline.

We will always assume that cash flows occur at the end of a period. Cash flows occurring at time zero are denoted with a subscript of 0, cash flows at time 1 have a subscript of 1, etc.

FUTURE VALUE

Suppose we have a dollar at time zero. That dollar can be invested and earn interest. If the interest rate is R, the dollar invested at interest has a total value of $1 + R$ dollars after one period. If R is 5%, a dollar invested for one period is worth $1.05.

If the dollar is invested for two periods, the future value is $(1 + R)^2$ if the first period's interest is reinvested. If the interest rate is 5%, the total value is $(1.05)^2$ or $1.0525. Formally,

$$\text{Future value at time } 2 = (1+R)^2 = 1 + 2R + R^2 \qquad \textbf{4.1}$$

$$(1.05)^2 = 1 + 2(.05) + (.05)^2$$
$$= 1 + .10 + .0025 = 1.1025 \qquad \textbf{4.2}$$

On the right, the 1 represents the original dollar. $2R$ $(2(0.05))$ is the interest on the original principal for each of the two periods. R^2 $((0.05)^2)$ is the interest-on-interest, i.e. the interest earned in the second period on the first period's interest.

If a dollar is invested for n periods, the total value at the end of n periods equals $(1 + R)^n$. The total value equals $1 principal plus the interest on original principal (n times R) plus many other terms for the interest on interest (compound interest).

PRESENT VALUE

Present value is the opposite (or reciprocal) of future value. Suppose an investor will receive a dollar at time 1. The present value at time 0 is $1 / (1 + R)$. For a 5% interest rate, the present value of a dollar is $1 / (1.05) = 0.9524$. Notice that $0.9524 at time 0 and $1 at time 1 represent equivalent values for investors with a 5% interest rate.

The present value of a dollar received n periods from now is $1 / (1 + R)^n$, which we will denote as PV_n. Figure 4.2 illustrates present value for several maturities. The present value gets smaller as the number of periods into the future increases because n is in the denominator. That is, a dollar received further into the future has a lower present value. The present value also decreases as the interest rate increases.

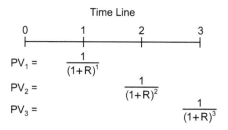

Time Line

$$PV_1 = \frac{1}{(1+R)^1}$$

$$PV_2 = \frac{1}{(1+R)^2}$$

$$PV_3 = \frac{1}{(1+R)^3}$$

FIGURE 4.2 Present Value Examples.

Adding Present Values

Present values of cash flows at different points in time are additive. Thus, the present value of a dollar at time 1, denoted by PV_1, and another dollar at time 2, denoted by PV_2, is the sum of the present values.

$$\text{Present Value} = \frac{1}{1+R} + \frac{1}{(1+R)^2} = PV_1 + PV_2 \qquad 4.3$$

$$\text{Present Value} = \frac{1}{1.05} + \frac{1}{(1.05)^2} = \$1.8594 \qquad 4.4$$

If the future cash flows are something other than one dollar, the present values are simply the cash flows times the present value of one dollar. Suppose we want to know the present value of $30 received one period from now and $40 received two periods from now. Then, the present values are:

$$\text{Present Value} = \frac{30}{1+R} + \frac{40}{(1+R)^2} \qquad 4.5$$

$$\text{Present Value} = \frac{30}{1.05} + \frac{40}{(1.05)^2} = \$64.85 \qquad 4.6$$

Present Value of an Annuity

An annuity is a stream of constant cash flows over a period of time. Suppose the cash flows are one dollar per period beginning at time 1 and continue until time n (i.e. a total of n payments of one dollar). See Figure 4.3. The present value of this annuity can be found by adding the present value of the individual dollars. We will abbreviate the present value of an annuity as PVA_n, where n is the number of periods.

FIGURE 4.3 A $1 Annuity.

$$\begin{matrix} \text{Present Value} \\ \text{of annuity} \end{matrix} = PVA_n = \frac{1}{1+R} + \frac{1}{(1+R)^2} + \ldots + \frac{1}{(1+R)^n}$$

$$= PV_1 + PV_2 + \ldots + PV_n$$

$$= \begin{bmatrix} PV \\ \$1 \\ at \\ time\,1 \end{bmatrix} + \begin{bmatrix} PV \\ \$1 \\ at \\ time\,2 \end{bmatrix} + \ldots + \begin{bmatrix} PV \\ \$1 \\ at \\ time\,n \end{bmatrix} \qquad 4.7$$

By the rules of algebra, this simplifies to:

$$PVA_n = \begin{bmatrix} \frac{1}{R} \end{bmatrix}\begin{bmatrix} 1 - \frac{1}{(1+R)^n} \end{bmatrix} \qquad 4.8$$

Suppose we have a two-period annuity of $1 per period and the interest rate is 5%. Then:

$$PVA_n = \frac{1}{1.05} + \frac{1}{(1.05)^2}$$

$$= \begin{bmatrix} \frac{1}{.05} \end{bmatrix}\begin{bmatrix} 1 - \frac{1}{(1.05)^2} \end{bmatrix} = \$1.8594 \qquad 4.9$$

If the annuity is $10 per period, the present value is simply $10 times the present value of a $1 annuity, or $18.59.

The present value of an annuity of $1 for n-periods can be found on a financial calculator by setting the payment (PMT) equal to 1, the number of prime periods (N) equal to n, and the yield to maturity (I / YR) equal to the value of R.

Annuities can be added or subtracted. As an example, suppose an individual will receive an annuity of one dollar per year for five years with the first payment starting five years from now. If the interest rate is 5%, this problem can be solved in the following way. If the first payment is received in five years and there are a total of five annual payments, the last payment will be received at the end of year 9. The present value of this annuity from the end of year 5 through the end of year 9 is simply the present value of a 9-year annuity minus the present value of a 4-year annuity that is $PVA_9 - PVA_4$. If the interest rate is 5%, the present value of this annuity can be found to be 7.1078 – 3.5460 = 3.5619. This type of problem has a practical application for individuals who will receive defined benefit retirement pensions that begin at some time in the future. The individual can find the present value of the pension.

Finding Future Value from Present Value

The future value of a stream of cash flows is often needed. In many situations, the future value can be most easily computed by first taking the present value and then bringing the cash flows forward by multiplying the present value by a future value factor, namely $(1 + R)^n$, where R is the interest rate and n is the number of periods. In the earlier problem, $30 is received at time 1 and $40 is received at time 2. The present value is $64.89 for an interest rate of 5%. To find the value at time 2, simply multiply $(\$64.89)$ $(1.05)^2 = \$71.50$.

Similarly, the future value of an annuity can be found by multiplying the present value of the annuity by $(1 + R)^n$. For a one-dollar annuity for two periods, the time 2 value is simply the present value times $(1 + R)^2$. If the interest rate is 5% as in the earlier example, the time 2 value is $(\$1.8594)$ $(1.05)^2 = \$2.05$.

PRICE OF A BOND

A bond is a loan for n periods. The cash flows from the lender's viewpoint are shown in Table 4.1. The lender pays the borrower the price (P) at time 0. From time 1 through time n, the borrower repays in the form of a coupon (c). (This is an annuity.) At maturity (time n), the borrower pays the par (face) value to the lender.

Table 4.1. Bond Cash Flows Received by Lender

Points in Time				
0	1	2	...	n
– P	+ c	+ c	...	+ c + par

The price of bond is the present value of the cash flows. Namely,

$$\text{Price} = P = \frac{c}{1+R} + \frac{c}{(1+R)^2} + \ldots + \frac{c + \text{par}}{(1+R)^n}$$

$$= \begin{bmatrix} PV \\ c \\ \text{time 1} \end{bmatrix} + \begin{bmatrix} PV \\ c \\ \text{time 2} \end{bmatrix} + \ldots + \begin{bmatrix} PV \\ c + \text{par} \\ \text{time } n \end{bmatrix} \qquad \text{4.10}$$

$$\text{Price} = P = c \left[\begin{array}{c} \text{present value} \\ \text{of annuity} \end{array} \right] + \frac{par}{(1+R)^n} \qquad \textbf{4.11}$$

$$P = c \left[\frac{1}{R} \right] \left[1 - \frac{1}{(1+R)^n} \right] + \frac{par}{(1+R)^n} \qquad \textbf{4.12}$$

Suppose we have a two-period bond with an annual coupon of $4 per period, a par value of $100, and interest rate of 5%. Then,

$$P = \frac{4}{1.05} + \frac{4+100}{(1.05)^2} = \$98.14 \qquad \textbf{4.13}$$

$$P = 4 \left[\frac{1}{.05} \right] \left[1 - \frac{1}{(1.05)^2} \right] + \frac{100}{(1.05)^2} \qquad \textbf{4.14}$$

Treasury strips have no coupons, but simply pay par value at maturity. They are often called zero-coupon bonds. The price of a strip is simply the present value of par.

$$\text{Price}_{strip} = \frac{par}{(1+R)^n} \qquad \textbf{4.15}$$

Bond Yield to Maturity

If the price of a bond, its coupon, par value, and maturity are known, the yield to maturity (y) can be computed by solving the following equation.

$$\text{Price} = P = \frac{c}{1+y} + \frac{c}{(1+y)^2} + \ldots + \frac{c+par}{(1+y)^n}$$

$$= \left[\begin{array}{c} PV \\ c \\ \text{time 1} \end{array} \right] + \left[\begin{array}{c} PV \\ c \\ \text{time 2} \end{array} \right] + \ldots + \left[\begin{array}{c} PV \\ c+par \\ \text{time } n \end{array} \right] \qquad \textbf{4.16}$$

Financial calculators are able to solve this equation rapidly. The procedure used by the calculator is trial and error. To illustrate how this works, suppose we have a two-period bond with price of $98.14, coupon of $4, and par value of $100. We need to solve the following equation for the yield to maturity, y:

$$\$98.14 = \frac{\$4}{1+y} + \frac{\$104}{(1+y)^2} \qquad \textbf{4.17}$$

Suppose we select a trial rate of 4% and compute the present value (PV).

$$PV = \frac{4}{1.04} + \frac{104}{(1.04)^2} = 100 \qquad \textbf{4.18}$$

This present value exceeds the price of the bond. Therefore, we need to try a higher rate to get the present value closer to the bond price. Try 5%.

$$PV = \frac{4}{1.05} + \frac{104}{(1.05)^2} = 98.14 \qquad \textbf{4.19}$$

Since the present value of the future cash flows from the bonds equals its price, we have found the yield to maturity. On a financial calculator, the yield to maturity is found with an algorithm that converges to the yield to maturity.

The yield to maturity on a Treasury strip can be found directly. For a strip,

$$\text{Price}_{\text{strip}} = \frac{\text{par}}{(1+y)^n} \qquad \textbf{4.20}$$

Solving this for yield to maturity,

$$1 + y = \left[\frac{\text{par}}{\text{Price}_{\text{strip}}} \right]^{\frac{1}{n}} \qquad \textbf{4.21}$$

To illustrate, suppose we have a two-period strip with $100 par value and price of $85.73. We need to solve the following equation.

$$1 + y = \left[\frac{\$100}{\$85.73} \right]^{\frac{1}{2}} = 1.08$$
$$y = .08 = 8\% \qquad \textbf{4.22}$$

Other Yield Measures

Bond investors typically compute two other yields. The current yield is the ratio of the coupon divided by the price, $c \, / \, P$. The current yield represents the return on the bond from coupon and overlooks any return from price change. The stated yield (or coupon rate) is the coupon divided by par, $c \, / \, \text{par}$. The yield to maturity, current yield, and stated yield are linked as we shall see shortly.

A bond selling at par is typically called a par bond. A bond selling below par is called a discount bond. A bond selling above par is called a premium bond. Figure 4.2 shows the relationship between bond price and coupon. Higher coupon bonds have higher prices. Thus, discount bonds have low coupons and premium bonds have high coupons.

In Figure 4.4, the relationship between bond price and coupon is linear. That is, each dollar of coupon adds a constant amount to price. When the coupon is zero, the bond is often called a zero-coupon bond. Treasury strips and Treasury bills are examples of zero-coupon bonds.

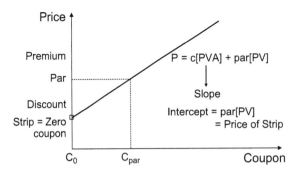

FIGURE 4.4 Bond Price Versus Coupon.

Bonds selling at par have the important characteristic that their yield to maturity, current yield, and stated yield are the same; i.e., $y = c / P = c /$ par. This follows from the mathematics of yield to maturity. The link between yield to maturity, current yield, and stated yield for nonpar bonds is shown in Table 4.2.

Table 4.2. Yield to Maturity (y), Current Yield (c / P), and Stated Yield $(c /$ par$)$

Discount bond
$P <$ par $y > c / P > c /$ par

Par bond
$P =$ par $y = c / P = c /$ par

Premium bond
$P >$ par $y < c / P < c /$ par

Finding the yield to maturity for a par bond is easy. Simply divide the coupon by par. Table 4.2 provides bounds on the yields to maturity for nonpar bonds. To find the yield to maturity for a discount bond, the lowest possible trial rate is c / P. Similarly, for premium bonds, the highest possible trial rate is c / P.

Most bonds are issued at par largely for tax reasons. They subsequently trade at a discount from par if interest rates rise after issue. If interest rates fall after issuance, the bond sells at a premium.

Table 4.3 illustrates the relationship between the yield to maturity, current yield, and stated yield for three two-period bonds with different coupons. The reader should verify the calculations. For the discount bond with $4 coupon, $y > c / P > c /$ par. For the par bond with $4 coupon, all three yields are equal. For the premium bond with $6 coupon, $y < c / P < c /$ par.

Table 4.3. Comparison of Yield to Maturity, Current Yield, and Stated Yield for Two-Period Bonds

Coupon	Maturity	Par	Price	Yield to Maturity (y)	Current Yield (c/P)	Stated Yield (c/par)
$4	2	$100	$98.14	5%	4.08%	4%
$5	2	$100	$100.00	5%	5%	5%
$6	2	$100	$101.86	5%	5.89%	6%

Perpetual Bonds

A perpetual bond never matures. It pays a periodic coupon indefinitely. The price of a perpetual bond in terms of its yield to maturity can be expressed as follows:

$$\text{Price} = P = \frac{c}{1+y} + \frac{c}{(1+y)^2} + \ldots \qquad 4.23$$

By the rules of algebra, this simplifies to

$$\text{Price} = P = \frac{c}{y} = \frac{\text{coupon}}{\text{yield}} \qquad 4.24$$

Thus, if a perpetual bond has an annual coupon of $4 and a yield to maturity of 5%, its price is:

$$\text{Price} = P = \frac{c}{y} = \frac{\$4}{.05} = \$80 \qquad 4.25$$

Only a small number of perpetual bonds exist. However, perpetual bonds are interesting because they serve as a limiting case. Long-term bonds approach perpetual bonds as the maturity gets longer. As in the case of par bonds, the yield to maturity for a perpetual bond equals the coupon divided by the price ($y = c / P$). Since a long-term bond is similar to a perpetual bond, the yield to maturity for a long-term bond is close to the yield to maturity for a perpetual bond. As an illustration, look up the prices of Treasury bonds and compare the current yield (i.e., c / P) for the longest-maturity Treasury bond (often called the "long bond") to the yield to maturity.

HOLDING PERIOD RETURNS

The yield to maturity is a measure of return if a bond is held until maturity. The holding period return can also measure return for a shorter period of time. We consider holding period returns for a single period.

$$\text{Holding Period Return} = \frac{\text{Ending Price} - \text{Beginning Price} + \text{Coupon}}{\text{Beginning Price}}$$

$$\text{HPR} = \frac{P_1 - P_0 + c}{P_0} \qquad\qquad 4.26$$

Where P_0 is the price at time 0 and P_1 is the price at time 1, one time period later. Notice that the holding period return can be decomposed into two parts.

$$\text{Holding Period Return} = \frac{\text{Ending Price} - \text{Beginning Price}}{\text{Beginning Price}} + \frac{\text{Coupon}}{\text{Beginning Price}}$$

$$\text{HPR} = \frac{P_1 - P_0}{P_0} + \frac{c}{P_0}$$

$$\text{HPR} = \left[\text{Percent Capital Gain (Loss)}\right] + \left[\text{Current Yield}\right] \qquad 4.27$$

The holding period return is the percentage capital gain or loss plus the current yield. Let's consider two cases: (1) constant interest rates over the holding period; (2) changing interest rates over the period.

Constant Interest Rates

Figure 4.5 shows the evolution of bond price over time for constant interest rates. The price of par bonds remains the same as time elapses. The prices of discount bonds and premium bonds approach par as time elapses.

For the case of constant interest rates, the holding period return is the same for all bonds and is equal to the yield to maturity. Discount bonds have a low current yield but have price appreciation, with the total return equaling the yield to maturity. Premium bonds have high current yields, but the price declines, with a net return equal to the yield to maturity.

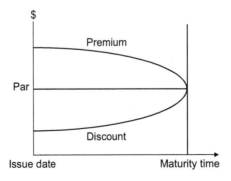

FIGURE 4.5 Bond Price and Maturity for Constant Interest Rates.

Using the information in Table 4.3, the holding period returns are computed in Table 4.4.

Table 4.4. Holding Period Returns with Constant 5% Interest Rates

Coupon	Price at Time 0 (P_0)	Price at Time 1 (P_1)	Holding Period Return $(P_1 - P_0 + c)/P_0$
$4	$98.14	$99.05	5%
$5	$100.00	$100.00	5%
$6	$101.86	$100.95	5%

Changing Interest Rates

If interest rates change, the holding period return has two components—the percent capital gain plus the current yield. If interest rates rise (fall), the percent capital gain is reduced (increased) and the holding period return is lower (higher). See Figure 4.6. The size of this impact depends upon the maturity of the bond and its coupon level and is discussed in the chapter on the risk of changing interest rates.

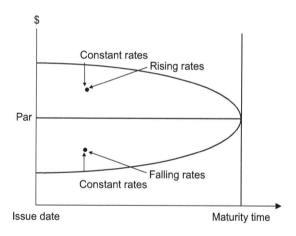

FIGURE 4.6 Bond Price and Maturity for Non-Constant Interest Rates.

To illustrate the impact of changing interest rates on holding period returns, assume the same example except that interest rates rise to 6% at time 1. The price of the bond at time 1 is $(c + par)/(1.06)$. See Table 4.5. The rise in interest rates to 6% at time 1 causes capital losses that reduce the holding period rates below 5%, the rate that would prevail if interest rates remain unchanged at 5%.

Table 4.5. Holding Period Returns with Interest Rates

Rising from 5% at Time 0 to 6% at Time 1.

Coupon	Price at Time 0 (P_0)	Price at Time 1 (P_1)	Percent Capital Gain (Loss)	Current Yield	Holding Period Return $(P_1 - P_0 + c)/P_0$
$4	$98.14	$98.11	−0.03%	4.08%	4.05%
$5	$100.00	$99.06	−0.94%	5%	4.06%
$6	$101.86	$100.00	−1.83%	5.89%	4.06%

SEMIANNUAL INTEREST PAYMENTS

The typical bond in the United States pays interest twice per year, or semiannually. The semiannual coupon is the annual coupon divided by two. The cash flows with semiannual coupons are shown in Table 4.6 for a two-year bond with a $4 annual coupon ($2 semiannually).

Table 4.6. Bond Cash Flows for Semiannual Coupons

Points in Time (Years)				
0	.50	1.00	1.50	2.00
−P	+$2	+$2	$2	+$102

With semiannual coupons, the interest rate is computed as a semiannually compounded rate that we will denote as i. By convention, everyone in the United States marketplace uses the semiannual yield to maturity, although this rate is usually called the "yield to maturity." The variable i is the solution to the following equation:

$$P = \frac{c/2}{\left[1+\dfrac{i}{2}\right]^1} + \frac{c/2}{\left[1+\dfrac{i}{2}\right]^2} + \ldots + \frac{c/2+\text{par}}{\left[1+\dfrac{i}{2}\right]^{2n}}$$

$$= \begin{bmatrix} PV \\ c/2 \\ \text{received} \\ \text{at time} \\ \text{6 months} \end{bmatrix} + \begin{bmatrix} PV \\ c/2 \\ \text{received} \\ \text{at time} \\ \text{1 year} \end{bmatrix} + \ldots + \begin{bmatrix} PV \\ c/2 + \text{par} \\ \text{received} \\ \text{at time} \\ n \text{ years} \end{bmatrix} \qquad \textbf{4.28}$$

In Equation (4.28), $i/2$ is the interest rate for half a year. The variable i is twice the half-year rate. Interest is compounded every half-year period.

The exponent for each term in equation (4.28) is the number of half-year periods until the cash flow is received. The first coupon of $c/2$ is received one six-month period from now and therefore its exponent is one. The second coupon is received in two six-month periods and has an exponent of two. In the last term, the last coupon and par value are received in n years or $2n$ six-month periods.

Suppose there is a two-year bond with $100 par value, coupons of $2 every six months, and yield to maturity (i) of 5%. Then the price is computed as follows:

$$P = \frac{2}{\left[1+\frac{.05}{2}\right]^1} + \frac{2}{\left[1+\frac{.05}{2}\right]^2} + \frac{2}{\left[1+\frac{.05}{2}\right]^3} + \frac{2+100}{\left[1+\frac{.05}{2}\right]^4}$$

$$= \$98.1190$$

4.29

Accrued Interest

Coupon interest on bonds is paid semiannually. By convention, holders of bonds earn a proportion of the next coupon for the length of time the bond is held. Thus, if the six-month period from the last coupon to the next coupon contains 183 days (in general k days) and 20 days (in general j days) have elapsed since the last coupon payment, the holder for those 20 days is entitled to a proportion of the next coupon equal to 20/183 or 10.93% (in general j / k). Thus,

$$\text{Accrued interest} = \left[\frac{j}{k}\right]\left[\frac{c}{2}\right] = \left[\frac{\text{days since last coupon}}{\text{days for 6 month period}}\right]\left[\frac{\text{semiannual}}{\text{coupon}}\right]$$

4.30

When a bond is sold, the buyer pays the accrued interest to the seller. If a person buys a bond in the middle of a period, the cash flows must be discounted for partial periods. If j days have elapsed and there are k days in a semiannual period, the proportion of a period that has elapsed is j / k. Figure 4.7 illustrates.

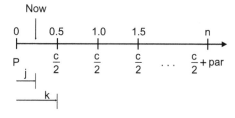

FIGURE 4.7 Bond Cash Flows for Purchase in Middle of a Time Period.

When there is accrued interest, the price of a bond is the following:

$$P + \left[\frac{j}{k}\right]\left[\frac{c}{2}\right] = \frac{c/2}{\left[1+\frac{i}{2}\right]^{1-\frac{j}{k}}} + \frac{c/2}{\left[1+\frac{i}{2}\right]^{2-\frac{j}{k}}} + \ldots + \frac{c/2 + \text{par}}{\left[1+\frac{i}{2}\right]^{2n-\frac{j}{k}}}$$

4.31

This equation says that the buyer of a bond must pay to the seller P plus the accrued interest $[j/k][c/2]$. The price plus the accrued interest is sometimes called the dirty price. The price without accrued interest (the flat price) can be found by rearranging this equation as follows.

$$P = -\left[\frac{j}{k}\right]\left[\frac{c}{2}\right] + \left[1+\frac{i}{2}\right]^{\frac{j}{k}}\left[\frac{c/2}{\left[1+\frac{i}{2}\right]^{1}} + \frac{c/2}{\left[1+\frac{i}{2}\right]^{2}} + \ldots + \frac{c/2 + par}{\left[1+\frac{i}{2}\right]^{2n}}\right]$$

4.32

To illustrate, assume a bond with \$100 par, semiannual coupon payments of \$2, and one and three-quarter years until maturity. In other words, the cash flows are as shown in Table 4.7.

Table 4.7. Bond Cash Flows for Bond Buyer

0	.25	.75	1.25	1.75
− P − Accrued Interest	+ \$2	+ \$2	\$2	+ \$102

Since one-half of a period has elapsed since the last coupon was paid, the accrued interest is one-half of \$2, or \$1. Suppose that i is equal to 5%:

$$P = -\left[\frac{1}{2}\right](2) + \left[1+\frac{.05}{2}\right]^{\frac{1}{2}}\left[\frac{2}{\left[1+\frac{.05}{2}\right]^{1}} + \frac{2}{\left[1+\frac{.05}{2}\right]^{2}} + \ldots + \frac{2+100}{\left[1+\frac{.05}{2}\right]^{4}}\right]$$

$$= -1 + (1.0124)(98.1190) = 98.33$$

4.33

BOND PRICE QUOTES

In the United States, bond prices are quoted per $100 of par value, although trading units are typically $10,000 or more. Coupons are quoted in eighths. Thus, 6 1/8 means a semiannual coupon of $6.125 / 2. The maturity date is the month and the last two digits of the year. Thus, Feb '10 means February 2010; the exact date in February has to be found from other sources, such as the *Monthly Statement of the Public Debt of the United States*, available online at the Treasury website, treas.gov. Prices are quoted in 32nds of a dollar.

In many other countries, bond prices are quoted in decimals. Thus, a quote of a French government bond might be €98.45. Quoting in decimals means that the difference in the asked price (the price at which bond dealers are willing to sell) and the bid price (the price at which bond dealers are willing to buy) is relatively small. For example, the ask price might be €98.46 and the bid price might be €98.44, a difference of 2 cents.

SUMMARY

Bonds involve cash inflows at future points in time. The price of the bond should be the present value discounted at the interest rate.

Bonds have three types of yields. The current yield is the ratio of coupon over price. The stated yield (coupon rate) is the coupon as a percent of par. The yield to maturity is the internal rate of return. For par bonds, the yield to maturity, current yield and stated yield are the same. For discount bonds, the yield to maturity is greater than the current yield which is greater than the stated yield. In other words, discount bonds have low coupons. For premium bonds the yield to maturity is less than the current yield which is less than the stated yield. Premium bonds have high coupons.

The one-period holding period return on a bond is the yield to maturity if interest rates remain constant. The holding period return is higher (lower) than the yield to maturity if interest rates decrease (increase).

In the United States, bonds pay half of the annual coupon every six months. Bonds accrue interest for every day that a bond is owned. In the United States, the yield to maturity is compounded at half year intervals (semiannually).

QUESTIONS AND PROBLEMS

1. Suppose you have $20 and are going to invest it for one year at 4%. What is the future value? What is the future value if you invest for two years? Decompose the future value into original principal, simple interest, and compound interest.

2. Suppose you are going to receive $50 in two years. What is its present value at a 4% interest rate?

3. Suppose you will receive $50 one year from now and $80 two years from now. What is the present value at 4%?

4. Repeat problem 3 using a 5% interest rate. Is the present value higher or lower? Explain why.

5. You will receive an annuity of $6 per year for two years. For a 4% interest rate, compute the present value of this annuity.

6. A two-year bond pays $5 coupons annually and has a $100 par value. Compute its price if the yield to maturity is 4%.

7. In problem 6, compute the stated yield and the current yield. What is the relationship between the current yield and the yield to maturity and why?

8. Using the information in problem 6, what is the holding period yield over the next year (a) if the yield to maturity remains at 4%, and (b) if the yield to maturity declines to 3% at time 1? In each case, decompose the holding period return into the current yield and the capital gain or loss.

9. A two-year bond with annual coupons of $5 and par value of $100 has a current price of $101.89. (a) What is its yield to maturity? (b) What are the current yield and stated yield?

10. In problem 9 part (a), suppose the holding period return over the next year is 6%. What would the yield to maturity at time 1 have to be for this to occur?

11. A Treasury strip with ten-year maturity and $100 par value has a current price of $67.56. Compute its yield to maturity.

12. In problem 11, suppose that the interest rate drops over the next year by 1%. What is the price of this strip in one year and what is the holding period return on this strip over the next year?

13. A two-year bond with a $4 annual coupon and $100 par value pays half of the coupon every six months. The yield to maturity (annualized semiannually compounded yield to maturity) is 4.5%. Find the bond's price.

14. A two-year bond with a $4 annual coupon pays half of the coupon semi-annually. Par value is $100 and the current price is $100.96. Compute the annualized semiannually compounded yield to maturity.

15. Suppose a bond has an annual coupon of $4, paid in two equal installments of $2. The par value is $100. Assume a semiannual period is 182 days and there are 100 days until the next coupon. Compute the accrued interest. Besides the next coupon in 100 days there will be three more coupons of $2 and a par value of $100 at final maturity. Compute the bond price if the annualized semiannually compounded yield to maturity is 4.5%.

16. You will receive an annuity of $15 per year for 20 years, with the first payment beginning 6 years from now. For a 6% interest rate, compute the present value of this annuity.

17. Suppose a 25-year bond has an annual coupon of c, par value of $100, a yield to maturity of 5.50%, and current yield of 5.5322%. What is the bond's coupon?

18. You will receive an annuity of $10 per period. The first payment is received immediately and then there are 19 more payments of $10. You invest these all at the interest rate x%. At time 19, the value of your investment is $511.60. What is the interest rate?

CHAPTER 5

Money Market Instruments and Rates

The most active market for securities as measured by daily volume of trading is the *money market*, which is defined as the market for securities with less than one year to maturity at the original issue date. Money market instruments include the following: Treasury bills, federal funds, repurchase agreements, certificates of deposit, commercial paper, and bankers' acceptances. Each of these instruments has slightly different characteristics, and thus each has a slightly different interest rate. Since many investors regard the individual money market instruments as close substitutes, changes in all the money market interest rates are highly correlated.

Money market instruments allow some issuers to raise funds for short periods of time at relatively low interest rates. These issuers include the US Treasury, which issues Treasury bills; corporations, which sell commercial paper; banks, which issue certificates of deposit; and security dealers, who finance their holdings in the money market. Simultaneously, many investors find money market instruments to be highly liquid investments with relatively low default risk. An investment is liquid if it can be bought or sold rapidly without affecting the market price and if the risk of price fluctuation is small. These money market investors include individuals, corporations, banks, other institutions with temporarily excess funds, and money market mutual funds. The money market is largely a wholesale (as opposed to retail) market, with the denominations of most transactions in the millions of dollars. The primary participants are financial institutions and large nonfinancial businesses. Consumers play a limited role in the money market; they are buyers of some money market securities and investors in money market mutual funds.

TYPES OF MONEY MARKET INSTRUMENTS

US Treasury Bills

Treasury bills are issued by the US Treasury to finance government expenditures. For practical purposes, Treasury bills are default-free since the Federal Reserve effectively has the power to provide sufficient funds to meet Treasury obligations. Treasury bills are highly liquid assets. They can be bought or sold rapidly without affecting the price. Therefore, the risk of price fluctuation is small. Consequently, Treasury bills have small bid–ask spreads.

In its weekly auctions, the Treasury issues large amounts of 13-week (91-day), 26-week (182-day), and 52-week Treasury bills. In recent years, individual issues of Treasury bills of $20 billion to $30 billion or more are quite common. Consequently, there are large numbers of Treasury bills outstanding, and each issue is of great size. This large supply of securities increases trading volume and substantially enhances Treasury bill liquidity. Because Treasury bills are short-term securities, their price fluctuations are small when interest rates change. Thus, the risk of price decline is small for Treasury bills, as is typical with money market instruments.

The interest earned on Treasury securities, including Treasury bills, is not subject to state and local income taxes. For this reason, Treasury bills may have a slightly lower interest rate than other money market instruments subject to these taxes. The default-free status of Treasury bills makes their yields lower than yields on otherwise identical money market instruments having some chance for default.

Federal Funds

Commercial banks in the United States are required to keep reserves on deposit at the Federal Reserve. Required reserves are a fraction of bank deposits, with the fraction varying for the type of deposit. For example, commercial banks might be required to keep 2% of their bank deposits on reserve at the Federal Reserve. The Federal Reserve uses a lagged system in which a bank computes the average bank deposits for a time period such as a week. Required reserves are a percentage of average bank deposits for the same length time interval. But the time interval for keeping deposits at the Federal Reserve is lagged by a few days, allowing banks that are short of reserves a few days to acquire more reserves to meet the average required reserves.

Banks with reserves in excess of required reserves can lend these funds to other banks. These interbank loans are called *federal funds* (abbreviated as *fed funds*) and are usually overnight loans. Large money center banks tend to be net buyers of fed funds, and small local banks tend to be net sellers.

The federal funds rate has historically has been a volatile interest rate and has fluctuated considerably from day-to-day. Daily fluctuations in the federal funds rate have sometimes been 4 or 5%. One reason for this rate volatility is that some banks may be suddenly forced to meet Federal Reserve requirements by borrowing fed funds. At the end of each quarter of the year, the federal funds rate has sometimes fluctuated dramatically. Annualized interest rates of 100% have been observed.

In recent years, the Federal Reserve Board has set precise targets for the federal funds rate in implementing monetary policy. At some earlier points in time, the Federal Reserve set the growth rate of money supply as its primary target, with federal funds as a secondary target. Because of difficulties measuring the money supply and its impact, the focus has shifted to federal funds.

Repurchase Agreements

Repurchase agreements (called *repos* or *RPs*) are generally overnight sales of US government securities with an agreement to repurchase on the next business day. The volume of transactions in overnight repos is huge.

To illustrate repos, imagine a bond dealer closing operations for January 15 with an inventory of $450 million of Treasury securities. Table 5.1 illustrates the sequence of events. These securities are held by the dealer in its role as a market maker, with the dealer hoping to profit by the average bid–ask spread. Suppose the equity of the dealer is $50 million. An additional $400 million is required to pay for these securities since the terms of purchase require same-day payment. One possible source of dealer financing is a bank loan with the securities used as collateral for the loan. A second (and slightly less expensive) method of financing is a repo. That is, the dealer sells the securities to a lender for $400 million (plus accrued interest) on the afternoon of January 15, agreeing to repurchase them the following morning of January 16 for $400 million plus one day's interest.

The price for the repurchase agreement is the current price plus interest. The interest rate on repos is typically slightly below the federal funds rate. Thus, repos allow nonbanks, which do not hold reserves at the Federal Reserve and consequently are unable to lend at the federal funds rate, to lend at a rate slightly below the fed funds rate. Repos are confined to large dollar amounts per transaction. Otherwise, the cost of carrying out the transaction would outweigh the overnight interest. Repos for longer than overnight (called term repos) are possible, although they are not as common as overnight repos.

Table 5.1. Financing Needs of a Bond Dealer

Points in Time		
2:00 PM January 15	5:00 PM January 15	9:00 AM January 16
Dealer buys $450,000,000 of bonds	Dealer sells $400,000,000 of bonds as repo	Dealer repurchases $400,000,000 and pays overnight interest

Repurchase agreements are extensively used as a means of short-term financing by government security dealers and by banks. Other money market securities (i.e., certificates of deposit, prime bankers' acceptances, and commercial paper) can be repoed. Dealers in these securities can use repos as a source of financing.

Repurchase agreements played a significant role in the 2007–2009 financial crisis. In 2008, a major securities firm, Lehman Brothers, incurred significant losses on its operations. This firm was relying on an enormous amount of overnight financing in the form of repurchase agreements. As Lehman Brothers' financial condition deteriorated, lenders became increasingly wary of lending money in the form of overnight repurchase agreements. Without sufficient funds, Lehman Brothers failed, setting off a panic in the security markets.

From the viewpoint of the lender of funds, a repo is called a *reverse*. Reverses are quite attractive to a number of lenders, including nonfinancial corporations, banks, municipalities, and thrift institutions. These lenders can invest their temporarily excess funds in reverses for very short periods of time with minimal risk. Municipalities are typically restricted in their investments to federal government securities; reverses provide an attractive investment in these securities. Some reverses are used as a means of borrowing securities; that is, the lender of funds is also a borrower of securities. These borrowed securities may be used in a short sale. In general, the amount lent in a repo is slightly less than the market value of the bonds. This discount from market value is called a *haircut* and provides some protection to the lender if the dealer goes bankrupt and the securities are liquidated at the prevailing market price. The size of the haircut depends upon the underlying price risk of the security, with riskier securities having bigger haircuts.

The risk of a repo depends upon its legal status. Depending upon the wording, a repo may constitute a sale or a collateralized loan. If the repo is a sale, the lender owns the securities; in the event of borrower default, the lender can sell the securities and use the proceeds if the lender has physical possession of the securities. If a repo is a collateralized loan, the borrower owns the securities; in the event of borrower default, the lender merely has a general claim upon the borrower. With this latter type of arrangement, the lender is at greater risk, and the interest rate is higher.

Commercial Paper

Commercial paper is a promissory note issued by firms as a source of short-term funds. The commercial paper market has existed because commercial paper can be a cheaper source of funds for financially sound firms than commercial bank loans.

The majority of commercial paper is issued by financial companies, including bank holding companies, finance companies, and insurance companies. Financial companies tend to use commercial paper as a regular source of funds. Nonfinancial firms tend to issue commercial paper on an irregular basis to meet special financing needs.

Commercial paper is not secured by specific assets of the issuing firm. In a secured loan, specific assets are pledged as collateral behind the loan. In the event of default, the secured lender has first claim upon the pledged asset. If this specific asset is insufficient to pay off the lender's claim, the lender then has a general claim upon the other assets of the borrower. An *unsecured* loan does not have specific assets pledged as collateral. However, the lender has a general claim upon the assets of the borrower rather than on a specific asset. Thus, the term unsecured is a type of misnomer.

Although commercial paper is unsecured, it is typically backed by lines of credit at commercial banks. A line of credit is essentially a prearrangement between a commercial bank and a borrowing firm that allows the firm to borrow up to some prearranged limit during a stated time interval. Lines of credit are not legally binding on the bank. Except during periods of extreme market turmoil, banks honor these lines of credit. In order to obtain a line of credit, a firm may be required to maintain compensating deposit balances at the bank of perhaps 10% or pay explicit fees to the bank for the line of credit. These costs are clearly part of the cost of issuing commercial paper.

Most commercial paper is issued with original maturities of less than 45 days. Commercial paper with maturities of less than nine months does not have to be registered with the Securities and Exchange Commission (SEC) as a public offering. This saves the considerable expense of SEC registration and may also avoid delays involved in the registration process.

Commercial paper may be sold directly by the issuer or may be sold to dealers who charge a placement fee. Firms regularly issuing commercial paper find it more economical to set up a department to issue commercial paper rather than use outside dealers. Since issues of commercial paper are heterogeneous, having many different issuers and many different maturity dates, there is no active secondary market for commercial paper. However, dealers may repurchase commercial paper for a fee.

Prime Rate

The prime interest rate is often said to represent the rate at which commercial banks lend to their most creditworthy (and, therefore, lowest-risk) customers. In practice, many loans are made at rates below the prime; the prime rate is not the rate for the most creditworthy firms. Nevertheless, the prime interest rate is a benchmark indicator of the level of interest rates.

Since the market for bank loans is highly competitive, all commercial banks quote a single prime rate. The prime rate changes for all banks simultaneously.

Bankers' Acceptances

Bankers' acceptances (BAs) are short-term debt obligations guaranteed by large commercial banks. Prime bankers' acceptances of the ten largest banks trade anonymously. They are highly liquid, low-risk, and low-return investments.

Bankers' acceptances typically arise out of international trade. Consider the following example illustrated in Figure 5.1. Assume an importer located in the United States and an exporter in Japan. The exporter would like to send goods to the US and receive payment in ninety days. In domestic transactions, trade credit is widely used to finance this transaction. With trade credit, a producer sends merchandise and allows the purchaser some time before payment is made. During this period of time, the purchaser attempts to sell the merchandise and generate the cash to make payment. In international transactions, the parties are located in different countries, implying that suppliers may not know the financial status of buyers. Legal remedies are more difficult and expensive in international transactions.

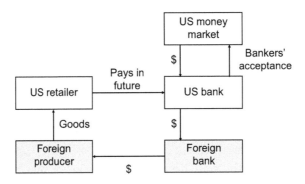

FIGURE 5.1 Bankers' Acceptances.

In a bankers' acceptance, the importer obtains a commercial letter of credit from his bank in the US. Through this commercial letter of credit, the US bank guarantees payment for the imported goods in ninety days. The letter of credit is sent to the exporter's bank in Japan. The exporter ships the goods and endorses the shipping documents. The documents and a time draft for the amount to be paid are presented to the exporter's bank. The Japanese bank then sends the draft and documents to the US bank, which "accepts" them. We now have a bankers' acceptance.

Frequently, the US bank pays the exporter's bank the present value of the purchase price. In turn these funds are paid to the exporter. The US bank can hold on to the bankers' acceptance and earn interest or sell it in the market. If the acceptance is sold in the market, the US bank has not lent any net funds. However, the US bank does guarantee payment. If the importer is unable to make payment on the due date, the US bank guarantees payment. In addition to any interest earned, the US bank also receives a fee from the importer.

Bank Certificates of Deposit

Large certificates of deposit (CDs) at commercial banks represent a major source of funds for commercial banks. These large certificates (with face values of over $100,000) are a significant source of funds for money center and large regional commercial banks. There are four basic types of large certificates of deposit: domestic CDs, Eurodollar CDs, Yankee CDs, and thrift CDs.

Large domestic CDs were first issued by the First National City Bank of New York in 1961 in order to regain deposits lost during a period of rising interest rates because of restrictions on the interest rates allowed on deposits. The domestic CD market continued to grow.

Negotiable domestic CDs of major banks are highly liquid investments. An active resale market exists for these CDs. A number of foreign banks have branches in the United States. Dollar-denominated CDs of these foreign banks are called Yankee CDs.

Eurocurrency Certificates of Deposit

A Eurocurrency deposit is defined as a deposit denominated in terms of a foreign currency. Thus, a deposit in US dollar terms made in London, England, is considered a Eurodollar deposit. A deposit of Japanese yen in London is also called a Eurodollar deposit, although technically it is a "Euroyen" deposit. Large US banks frequently raise funds through Eurodeposits in branches of the banks located outside the United States. The interest rate on Eurodeposits is typically slightly higher than the rate on domestic US deposits, making these rates attractive to depositors. These subsidiaries are typically free of regulatory restrictions, thus reducing the net cost of deposits to the bank. Freedom from regulation tends to benefit both the depositors and the banks.

Eurodollar CDs are dollar-denominated certificates of deposit issued by banks located outside the United States, with London being a common location. Common issuers of Eurodollar CDs are branches of US, Canadian, Japanese, and European banks. A US bank may decide to issue Eurodollar CDs through its London branch if the interest rate on a Eurodollar CD compares favorably with the rate on a domestic CD.

The interest rates on Eurocurrency CDs are quoted as LIBOR plus some markup. LIBOR is the London Interbank Offered Rate, which is the interest rate at which Eurobanks in London offer to lend to one another. Eurocurrency CDs have higher interest rates than US domestic CDs, partially because the foreign countries involved may impose exchange controls, possibly forbidding repayment of the CD. This risk is called *sovereign risk*.

Money Market Funds

As interest rates rose markedly during the 1970s, many small investors found themselves cut off from high money market rates of return. Because most money market instruments are in large denominations, small investors were typically restricted to savings deposits at commercial banks and savings banks. These savings deposits paid rates several percentage points less than the rates available on money market instruments.

To fill this gap and provide access for small investors to the money market, money market mutual funds developed. These funds pooled the resources of small investors and invested those resources at attractive money market rates. Figure 5.2 shows the impact of money market funds on the flow of funds.

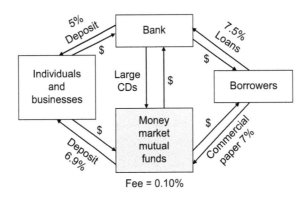

FIGURE 5.2 Money Market Mutual Funds.

Money market funds have caused large outflows of funds into them from savings accounts. Many depository institutions lost funds in a process called disintermediation. In effect, money market funds bypassed banks and let investors put their money directly into the money market. To permit banks to compete with money market mutual funds, banks are now allowed to offer depository accounts with rates competitive with money market rates. These new accounts are often called money market deposit accounts.

The typical money market fund holds a portfolio of one or more of the following: Treasury bills, bank certificates of deposit, commercial paper, and bankers' acceptances. Some money market funds specialize in particular instruments such as Treasury bills (for very-low-risk investors) or municipal notes, which are exempt from federal income taxes. Money market funds may allow investors to write checks on their accounts with some restrictions. Thus, in many ways, large money market funds are like banks, although money market funds are not insured by the FDIC.

The development of money market funds has helped to promote the growth of the commercial paper market. With money market funds as a ready market for commercial paper, many firms have issued commercial paper to take advantage of lower interest rates compared to commercial bank loan rates.

MONEY MARKET RATES

One of the peculiarities of the money market is its way of quoting interest rates. Some money market instruments (Treasury bills, commercial paper, and bankers' acceptances) are quoted on a discount basis. Other rates (fed funds, Federal Reserve discount rate, and repo rates) are quoted on an add-on basis. Each of these rates is different from the yield to maturity, the rate generally used for comparing coupon-bearing bonds. The following discussion explains discount rates, add-on rates, and bond equivalent yields.

Quoting Rates on a Discount Basis

Regardless what rate of interest is used to quote money market instruments, the cash flows are the same and are shown in Table 5.2. The buyer pays the price P at time zero. When the money market instrument matures in t days, the par value is received.

Table 5.2. Money Market Cash Flows

	Points in Time	
	0	t days
Cash Flows	$-P$	Par

The discount rate, d, is defined as the rate satisfying the following equation:

$$P = \text{par}\left[1 - \frac{d\,t}{360}\right]$$

5.1

Let us consider a simple example. A 90-day Treasury bill with a $100 par value has a discount rate of 4%. Its price is:

$$P = \$100\left[1 - \frac{(.04)(90)}{360}\right] = \$99$$

5.2

The buyer of this Treasury bill pays $99 and, in 90 days, receives $100. The interest received is $1 which is 1% of the par value. 1% for 90 days corresponds to an annualized rate of 4% for 360 days.

Several things are wrong with the discount rate. A 360-day year is used. Interest is computed as a percentage of the par value, which tends to understate the interest rate compared to interest as a percentage of the price. The apparent reason for this unusual way of quoting rates is the development of this market before hand-held calculators.

Add-On Rate Calculations

Federal funds, the Federal Reserve discount rate, and repos are quoted in terms of a rate called the add-on interest rate. Add-on interest rates relate the price and the par value in the following way:

$$P = \frac{\text{par}}{1 + \dfrac{at}{360}} \qquad \text{5.3}$$

The add-on rate is an improvement over the discount rate because the add-on rate computes the interest rate as a percent of the price. However, the add-on rate continues to use a 360-day year. The discount rate and the add-on rate are linked algebraically as follows:

$$a = \frac{d}{1 - \dfrac{dt}{360}} \qquad \text{5.4}$$

The denominator of this expression is the price of the money market instrument per dollar of par. Since this price must be less than 1.0, the add-on rate, a, must be bigger than the discount rate, d.

As an illustration, continue the earlier example with a discount rate of 4%, maturity of 90 days, price of $99, and par value of $100. Then:

$$a = \frac{.04}{1 - \dfrac{(.04)(90)}{360}} = .0404 = 4.04\% \qquad \text{5.5}$$

Bond Equivalent Yields

The bond equivalent yield is another money market rate that we will denote by r. The bond equivalent yield is the rate satisfying the following:

$$P = \cfrac{\text{par}}{1 + \cfrac{rt}{365}} \qquad 5.6$$

The bond equivalent yield is better than the add-on rate because it uses a 365-day year. The bond equivalent yield, add-on rate, and discount rate are linked as follows:

$$r = a\left[\frac{365}{360}\right] = \left[\cfrac{d}{1 - \cfrac{dt}{360}}\right]\left[\frac{365}{360}\right] \qquad 5.7$$

Since 365/360 is bigger than 1.0, the bond equivalent yield is bigger than the add-on rate (which is bigger than the discount rate). Continuing our earlier example with the discount rate equal to 4%, maturity in 90 days, a price of $99, and par value of $100, the bond equivalent yield is found as follows:

$$r = .0404\left[\frac{365}{360}\right] = .040965 = 4.10\% \qquad 5.8$$

The bond equivalent yield is widely used by market participants for comparing interest rates on money market instruments. The bond equivalent yield, r, is an approximation of the yield to maturity for a bond. Although the two are fairly close, they are not identical. For short maturities, the difference can be considerable. As maturity approaches 182.5 days, the two converge.

Yield to Maturity

The interest rate used for coupon-bearing bonds is the yield to maturity, i, using semiannual compounding. For a money market instrument, the semiannually compounded yield is defined as follows:

$$P = \cfrac{\text{par}}{\left[1 + \cfrac{i}{2}\right]^{\frac{2t}{365}}} \qquad 5.9$$

The semiannually compounded yield is larger than the bond equivalent if the maturity is less than 182.5 days. The two are equal at 182.5 days. The money market would be a lot simpler if the semiannually compounded yield to maturity was used for all debt obligations.

Some experts have advocated using the annually compounded yield to maturity, y, defined as follows:

$$P = \frac{\text{par}}{\left[1+y\right]^{\frac{t}{365}}}$$

5.10

The annually compounded yield to maturity compounds interest annually, while the semi-annual rate compounds interest twice per year. The annually compounded yield to maturity equals the semiannual rate plus the semiannual rate squared divided by 4 (i.e., $y = i + i^2 / 4$).

Comparing Money Market Rates

There are at least five different money market rates: the discount rate, the add-on rate, the bond equivalent yield, the semiannually compounded, and the annually compounded yields to maturity. Table 5.3 summarizes the previous results. The semiannually compounded yield compounds every six months; the annually compounded yield compounds every 12 months. The annually compounded yield is bigger than the semiannually compounded yield. Table 5.3 expresses price in terms of the five different rates and shows the five rates as a function of price.

Table 5.3. Comparing Money Market Rates

Discount rate (d):

$$P = \text{par}\left[1 - \frac{dt}{360}\right] \qquad\qquad d = \left[\frac{360}{t}\right]\left[1 - \frac{P}{\text{par}}\right]$$

Add–on rate (a):

$$P = \frac{\text{par}}{1 + \dfrac{at}{360}} \qquad\qquad a = \left[\frac{360}{t}\right]\left[\frac{\text{par}}{P} - 1\right]$$

Bond equivalent yield (r):

$$P = \frac{\text{par}}{1 + \dfrac{rt}{365}} \qquad\qquad r = \left[\frac{365}{t}\right]\left[\frac{\text{par}}{P} - 1\right]$$

Semiannually compounded yield to maturity (i):

$$P = \frac{\text{par}}{\left[1 + i/2\right]^{(2t/365)}} \qquad\qquad i = 2[\text{par} / P]^{(365/2t)} - 2$$

Annually compounded yield to maturity (y):

$$P = \frac{\text{par}}{\left[1 + y\right]^{(t/365)}} \qquad\qquad y = [\text{par}/P]^{(365/t)} - 1$$

To illustrate the relationships between the five rates, consider a case in which the discount rate, d, is 4% and the number of days, t, is 91.25. Since 91.25 days is one quarter of a year, the calculation of the semiannual and annually compounded yields is simple. First, compute the price, given these values of d and t and an assumed par value of $1:

$$P = \text{par}\left[1 - \frac{dt}{360}\right] = \left[1 - \frac{(.04)(91.25)}{360}\right] = .989861 \qquad \textbf{5.11}$$

The price per dollar of par is $0.989861. In Table 5.4, the formulas are used to compute the four remaining money market yields.

Table 5.4. Example of Money Market Rates

Add–on rate (a):

$$a = \left[\frac{360}{t}\right]\left[\frac{\text{par}}{P} - 1\right]$$

$$a = \left[\frac{360}{91.25}\right]\left[\frac{1}{.989861} - 1\right] = 4.04\%$$

Bond equivalent yield (r):

$$r = \left[\frac{365}{t}\right]\left[\frac{\text{par}}{P} - 1\right]$$

$$r = \left[\frac{365}{91.25}\right]\left[\frac{1}{.989861} - 1\right] = 4.10\%$$

Semiannually compounded yield to maturity (i):

$$i = 2[\text{par}/P]^{(365/2t)} - 2$$

$$i = 2[1/.989861]^{(365/182.5)} - 2 = 4.12\%$$

Annually compounded yield to maturity (y):

$$y = [\text{par}/P]^{(365/t)} - 1$$

$$y = [1/.989861]^{(365/91.25)} - 1 = 4.16\%$$

These money market yields for 91.25 days are shown graphically in Figure 5.3. The relationship between the five money market rates is shown in Figure 5.3 for maturities up to one-half year, that is, 182.5 days. Several tendencies are apparent from Figure 5.3. First, the biggest rate is the annually compounded yield, followed by the semiannually compounded yield, the bond equivalent yield, the add-on rate, and the discount rate. Second, the bond equivalent yield approaches the semiannually compounded yield to maturity as maturity approaches one-half year. Third, the differences between the bond equivalent yield and the semiannually compounded yield are sizable for shorter maturities. Bond equivalent yield is a poor approximation of semiannually compounded yield for the shorter maturities. Fourth, the differences between the discount rate and the other rates increase for longer maturities, suggesting that the discount rate is quite misleading for maturities close to one-half year.

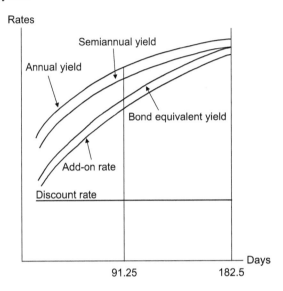

FIGURE 5.3 Comparing money market rates.

Figure 5.3 has a lesson for investors in the money market. Express all money market investments in terms of the same type of rate before selecting investments. Choosing between investments quoted in terms of different rates can lead to poor investment choices.

A more important implication of Figure 5.3 and the discussion of money market rates is that all money market institutions should quote rates by the same method. Money market institutions should confer and select one single rate for quoting all varieties of money market instruments. The annually compounded yield to maturity is the logical choice for a uniform rate for several reasons. First, the truth in lending law in the United States requires that consumer loans be quoted in terms of the annual percentage rate (APR), which is exactly the same as the annually compounded yield to maturity as defined above. Second, in some European countries, interest rates on bonds are quoted as the annually compounded yield to maturity. There would be much greater clarity if all countries agreed to quote interest rates as the annually compounded yield to maturity (APR).

SUMMARY

Money market instruments have maturities of less than one year. Trading in money market instruments is very active, and the total volume of transactions is huge. A variety of money market instruments exist. Each meets a special need of borrowers and lenders.

QUESTIONS AND PROBLEMS

1. Explain why each of the following money market instruments exists: commercial paper, bankers' acceptances, repurchase agreements, certificates of deposit, and federal funds. Why does each of these have an advantage over competing methods of financing?

2. Why did the market for Eurodeposits develop? What is the advantage of a Eurodeposit over a domestic deposit from a bank's viewpoint as well as a depositor's?

3. Find the prices of the following Treasury bills per dollar of par:
   (a) 40 days, discount rate of 1%.
   (b) 90 days, discount rate of 2%.
   (c) 80 days, discount rate of 0.50%.
   (d) 92 days, discount rate of 1.50%.

4. In problem 3, find the add-on interest rates, bond equivalent yields, semi-annually compounded, and annually compounded yields to maturity.

5. Determine Treasury bill discount rates, assuming the following information. Assume $1 par values:
   (a) $P = 0.995, t = 91$ days
   (b) $P = 0.993, t = 91$ days
   (c) $P = 0.998, t = 91$ days
   (d) $P = 0.998, t = 90$ days.

6. Compute the add-on rate, the bond equivalent yield, the semiannually compounded, and annually compounded yield to maturity for 30, 60, 90, 180 days. Graph these results.

7. Suppose that you are considering investing in one of two 91-day money market instruments: Treasury bills with a discount rate of 2% or commercial paper with a bond equivalent yield of 2.2%. Which investment is better?

8. Suppose that a 90-day Treasury bill has a bond equivalent yield of 2.75%. Compute the discount rate and the add-on interest rate.

9. Suppose a Treasury bill with a maturity of 90 days and par value of $100 has a discount rate of 3.25%. Determine the add-on rate.

10. Suppose a Treasury bill with a maturity of 100 days and par value of $100 has a price of $99.89. Determine its discount rate.

11. Suppose a Treasury bill with a maturity of 90 days has a semiannually compounded yield to maturity of 1.69%. Determine the discount rate.

CHAPTER 6

Duration and the Risks of Changing Interest Rates

The riskiness of bonds depends upon an investor's horizon. For investors with a very short horizon, changes in interest rates over the very near-term are important. The beginning of the chapter will deal with short horizon investors.

Investors with a long horizon are concerned with the value of their portfolio at some distinct date. For these long-horizon investors, the reinvestment rate for coupons and the interest rate at their horizon date are fundamental. The later part of this chapter will deal with long-horizon investors.

AN INTUITIVE INTERPRETATION OF DURATION

Figure 6.1 shows the relationship between bond price P and the interest rate y. As the interest rate increases, the bond price gets smaller at a decreasing rate. For any initial bond price P_0 and interest rate y_0, the new price P_1 can be computed for a new interest rate y_1. Since changes in interest rates are not predictable, the interest rate can go up or down with equal probability. Consequently, having a measure of the sensitivity of bond prices to changes in interest rates for both increases and decreases in interest rates is useful.

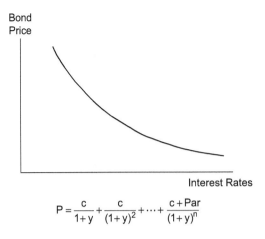

Bond Price

Interest Rates

$$P = \frac{c}{1+y} + \frac{c}{(1+y)^2} + \cdots + \frac{c+Par}{(1+y)^n}$$

FIGURE 6.1 Bond Price Versus Yield.

Calculus teaches us that the change in bond price as the interest rate changes can be estimated by moving along the tangent to a curve. The approximate change in bond price is the slope of the tangent times the change in the bond yield. The slope of the tangent is the derivative of price with respect to yield, dP/dy. Thus:

$$\text{Price Change} \approx \left[-dP/dy \right] \left[\text{Yield Change} \right] \qquad \textbf{6.1}$$

where the symbol $\approx$ indicates approximately equal to. Dividing $-dP/dy$ by price results in what is often called *modified duration*, $[-dP/dy]/P$.

$$\text{Percent Price Change} \approx \left[\text{Modified Duration} \right] \left[\text{Yield Change} \right] \qquad \textbf{6.2}$$

The first person to extensively discuss duration was Frederick Macaulay in the 1930s. He decided to multiply modified duration by $(1+y)$ which resulted in the following formula:

$$\text{DUR} = \frac{\dfrac{1c}{(1+y)^1} + \dfrac{2c}{(1+y)^2} + \ldots + \dfrac{n(c+\text{par})}{(1+y)^n}}{\text{price}} \qquad \textbf{6.3}$$

where y is the yield to maturity, c is the coupon, and n is the maturity.

Macaulay found this formula to have an intuitive interpretation, namely the weighted average maturity of the bond. Most practitioners however use what has become known as modified duration, Macaulay's duration times $(1+y)$. From now on, we shall simply call Macaulay's version "duration" and the modified version "modified duration."

Consider the following example, shown in Figure 6.2. The initial yield to maturity is y_0 and the interest rate changes to y_1. Suppose we have a perpetual bond with an interest rate of 5% and annual coupon of $5. Its price is 5 / 0.05 or $100. A perpetual bond's duration equals $(1 + y) / y = 1.05 / 0.05 = 21$. If the perpetual bond initially has a yield of 5% and a coupon of $5, the new price with an interest rate of 6% is $83.33.

$$P_0 = \frac{c}{y} = \frac{5}{.06} = 83.33 \qquad \textbf{6.4}$$

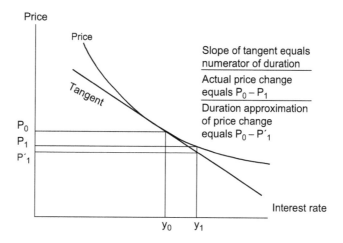

FIGURE 6.2 Change in Bond Price for Changing Interest Rate.

The percentage change in price is:

$$\%\Delta\ P = \frac{P_1 - P_0}{P_0} = \frac{83.33 - 100}{100} = -16.67\% \qquad \textbf{6.5}$$

where Δ indicates the change in a variable. The duration approximation is:

$$\%\Delta P \approx (\text{Duration})\ (\Delta y)$$
$$\approx (21)\ (.01) = 0.21 = 21\% \qquad \textbf{6.6}$$

The duration approximation suggests a price decline by approximately 21%, but the actual percentage changes 16.67%. Thus, the duration approximation has an error of about 4% of price. If the changes in interest rates are smaller, the duration approximation is more accurate. In fact, for infinitesimal changes in interest rates, the duration approximation is highly accurate.

As shown in Figure 6.2, the duration approximation overstates the price decline for interest rate increases. For interest rate decreases, the duration approximation understates the price increase.

Durations for Zero-Coupon, Par, and Perpetual Bonds

To help to understand duration, it's convenient to look at several special cases using Macaulay's formula. Durations for zero-coupon bonds, par bonds, and perpetual bonds are of special interest, and are shown in Table 6.1.

Table 6.1. Bond Price Volatilities for Special Types of Bonds.

Type of Bond	Duration
Zero-coupon	n
Par	$\dfrac{(1+y)[1-(1+y)^{-n}]}{y}$
Perpetual	$(1+y)/y$

A relatively easy and straightforward formula for computing Macaulay's duration is:

$$\text{DUR} = n - \left[n - \text{DUR}_{\text{par}} \right] \left[\frac{c/P}{y} \right] \qquad \textbf{6.7}$$

where DUR_{par} is the duration of a par bond and c/P is the current yield.[1] The duration of a par bond is simply $(1+y)$ (PVA), that is, one plus the interest rate times the present value of an annuity of $1.

This formula is an extremely easy method for computing duration. For a zero-coupon bond, c in the last term is zero, and the duration is simply the maturity, n. As the coupon increases, the last term gets bigger and the duration gets smaller since this term is negative.

PROPERTIES OF DURATION

The relationship between duration, maturity, and coupon level is shown in Figure 6.2, which assumes the same yield, y, for all bonds.[2] The duration of a perpetual bond is $(1+y)/y$. It is a horizontal line in Figure 6.3 and represents an asymptote or limiting case. For zero-coupon bonds, Macaulay's duration is the same as the maturity. It is shown as a straight line with a slope of 1.0. All bonds with maturities of 1 have duration of 1. The duration for premium and par bonds increases as maturity gets larger, eventually reaching the duration of a perpetual bond of $(1+y)/y$.

---

[1] This formula was derived by Caks et alia (1985).

[2] Proving these relationships requires taking the derivative of duration with respect to maturity.

For discount bonds, the duration increases as maturity gets larger until, at a long maturity, it reaches a maximum value; then the duration declines until it reaches the duration of a perpetual bond. In practice, discount bonds rarely have maturities beyond the peak in the curve shown in Figure 6.2. Therefore, we have two properties of duration (or the interest rate risk) of bonds.

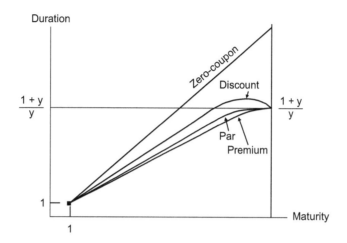

FIGURE 6.3 Duration Versus Maturity.

Property 1
The sensitivity of bond prices to changes in interest rates (i.e., duration) increases as maturity increases (with rare exceptions for very long maturity low coupon bonds). Longer maturity bonds have higher interest rate risk.

Property 2
The sensitivity of bond prices to changes in interest rates (i.e., duration) decreases as bond coupon increases. Higher coupon bonds (holding maturity constant) have lower interest rate risk.

Table 6.2 illustrates the relationship between duration and maturity assuming a 5% interest rate. Moving across the rows, the coupon gets bigger and duration decreases. Moving down the columns, maturity increases and the duration gets bigger.

Table 6.2. Duration for Various Coupons and Maturities

Yield to Maturity of 5%.

	Coupon Rate						
	0.02	0.03	0.04	0.05	0.06	0.07	0.08
Maturity				Par Bond			
1	1	1	1	1	1	1	1
5	4.79	4.70	4.62	4.55	4.48	4.41	4.36
10	9.01	8.66	8.36	8.11	7.89	7.71	7.54
15	12.62	11.89	11.34	10.90	10.54	10.25	10.00
20	15.58	14.47	13.68	13.09	12.62	12.25	11.95
25	17.93	16.48	15.50	14.80	14.27	13.86	13.52
30	19.71	17.99	16.90	16.14	15.59	15.16	14.82

The riskiest bonds are long-maturity, deep-discount (i.e., low-coupon) bonds, with zero-coupon bonds having the greatest price volatilities. High-coupon, short-maturity bonds have low volatilities. The greater price sensitivity of long-maturity bonds has important implications for bond portfolio managers.

Suppose that a manager believes in his ability to forecast changes in interest rates. If the manager forecasts rising interest rates, bond maturities should be shortened and coupons increased (although the maturity effect is usually more powerful and important). This is illustrated in Figure 6.4. If the manager believes interest rates are going to decrease in the future, the portfolio maturity should be increased and the coupons reduced.

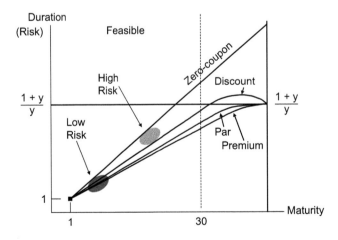

FIGURE 6.4 Interest Rate Forecasts and Portfolio Duration.

Duration of Portfolios

The duration of a portfolio of bonds is the price-weighted average of the durations of the bonds in the portfolio. To illustrate the calculation of the duration of a portfolio, suppose two bonds with prices P_1 and P_2 and durations DUR_1 and DUR_2. Then the portfolio duration is

$$DURATION_{portfolio} = \frac{(P_1)(DUR_1)+(P_2)(DUR_2)}{P_1+P_2} \qquad \textbf{6.8}$$

As example, consider the duration of a portfolio composed of two ten-year bonds: a 6% coupon bond with a price of $86.58 per $100 of par and an 8% coupon bond with a price of par. The portfolio duration is calculated as follows.

$$DURATION_{portfolio} = \frac{(86.58)(7.62)+(100)(7.25)}{86.58+100}$$

$$= 7.43 \qquad \textbf{6.9}$$

MORE ACCURATE APPROXIMATIONS

While modified duration provides reasonably accurate approximations of the change in bond price as interest rates change, the accuracy of the approximation can be improved by considering higher derivatives. Using a Taylor expansion, the total percentage change in bond price as yield changes can be expressed in terms of all the derivatives

$$\frac{\%\Delta P}{P} = \left[\frac{dP}{dy}\right]\left[\frac{1}{P}\right]\Delta y + \left[\frac{d^2 P}{dy^2}\right]\left[\frac{1}{P}\right]\left[\frac{(\Delta y)^2}{2!}\right]$$

$$+ \left[\frac{d^3 P}{dy^3}\right]\left[\frac{1}{P}\right]\left[\frac{1}{P}\right]\left[\frac{(\Delta y)^3}{3!}\right] + \dots \qquad \textbf{6.10}$$

where

$$\frac{dP}{dy} = \text{first derivative}$$

$$\frac{d^2 P}{dy^2} = \text{second derivative}$$

$$\frac{d^3 P}{dy^3} = \text{third derivative} \qquad \textbf{6.11}$$

The Taylor expansion expresses the percentage change in bond price ($\Delta P / P$) in terms of the first, second, and higher derivatives. The first derivative term incorporates minus modified duration divided by $1 + y$. That is,

$$\frac{-\text{modified duration}}{(1 + y)} = \left[\frac{dP}{dy}\right]\left[\frac{1}{P}\right]$$

6.12

The second derivative term incorporates what has been called convexity.

$$\text{Convexity} = \left[\frac{d^2P}{dy^2}\right]\left[\frac{1}{P}\right]\left[\frac{1}{2}\right]$$

6.13

In the Taylor expansion, the convexity is multiplied by the change in the yield squared (i.e., $(\Delta y)^2$). The impact of the second derivative or convexity term is shown in Figure 6.5 as the dotted line.

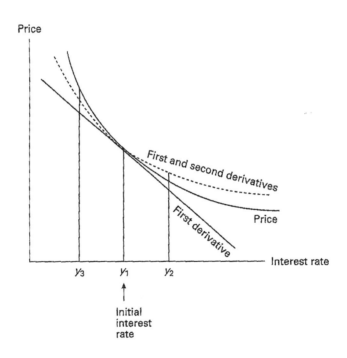

FIGURE 6.5 Duration Plus Convexity.

The second derivative makes the approximation more accurate. For increases in interest rates to y_2 the duration plus convexity approximation gives a high estimate of the bond price. For decreases in interest rates, the duration and convexity approximation give a low estimate of the new price. To see why an increase in yields gives high estimates, note that the odd-numbered derivatives (i.e., dP/dy) are negative. If the interest rate increases (decreases), then the odd-numbered derivatives are multiplied by a positive (negative) Δy, implying that the odd-numbered derivative terms are negative (positive). The second derivative is positive and multiplied by Δy squared, which is always positive. Consequently, the second derivative term is always positive. As each derivative is added to the Taylor expansion, the approximation converges to the true value.

When interest rates increase, the signs of the terms in the Taylor expansion are negative, positive, negative, and so on. The only way for the approximation to converge to the true value is for the approximation with the first term to lie below the true value, with the second term included to lie above, with the third term included to lie below, and so on.

When interest rates decline, all the terms in the Taylor expansion are positive. The first term gives a low estimate. As additional terms are added, the approximation gets closer, but never higher than the true value.

In the case of a perpetual bond, the Taylor expansion is[3]

$$\frac{\%\Delta P}{P} = \frac{-\Delta y}{y} + \frac{(\Delta y)^2}{y^2} - \frac{(\Delta y)^3}{y^3} + \ldots = \frac{-\Delta y}{y + \Delta y} \qquad \textbf{6.14}$$

In this equation, the first derivative term is $-\Delta y/y$, which is modified duration divided by $(1+y)(\Delta y)$. The second derivative term is $(\Delta y)^2/y^2$, which is the convexity (i.e. $1/y^2$) times $(\Delta y)^2$. The Taylor series has a simple sum for perpetual bonds, namely $-\Delta y/(y+\Delta y)$.

From the Taylor series, each term equals the previous term times $\Delta y/y$. As long as Δy is small relative to y, the additional derivatives add progressively smaller amounts to the total change. The example in Table 6.3 illustrates the importance of the terms in the Taylor expansion. Assume a perpetual bond with a \$5 annual coupon and an interest rate of 5%, implying a price of \$100 (i.e., 5 / 0.05 = 100). If the interest rate increases to 6%, the price becomes \$83.33 (i.e., 5 / 0.06). The decline in price is 16.67%. Compare this actual change with the individual terms in the Taylor expansion. The estimates in Table 6.3 get closer to the actual change as more terms are added.

---

[3] See M. Livingston, (1979).

Table 6.3. Taylor Expansion for a Perpetual Bond

First derivative $-\Delta y / y$	Second derivative $(\Delta y / y)^2$	Third derivative $-(\Delta y / y)^3$	Total change $-\Delta y / (y + \Delta y)$
$-.01 / .05 = -.20$	$(.01 / .05)^2 = +.04$	$-(.01 / .05)^3 = -.008$	$-.01 / (.05 + .01) = -.1667$
First term	Sum of first two terms	Sum of first three terms	Total change
-0.20	-0.16	-0.168	-0.1667

For perpetual bonds, the higher derivative terms are less important as the change in yield becomes smaller because each term in the Taylor expansion equals the previous term times $\Delta y / y$. The higher derivatives are also less important as the yield increases because the yield is in the denominator of each term of the Taylor expansion. The percentage error for perpetual bonds is

$$\%ERROR = \frac{\dfrac{-\Delta y}{y + \Delta y} - \dfrac{-\Delta y}{y}}{\dfrac{-\Delta y}{y + \Delta y}}$$

$$= \frac{-\Delta y}{y} \qquad \textbf{6.15}$$

If the absolute value of the change in yield is small relative to the level of yield, the percentage error from the modified duration (i.e., first derivative) approximation is close to zero. Adding the higher derivatives does not add much accuracy.

The preceding discussion of the Taylor expansion has been for perpetual bonds. Similar results apply for shorter-maturity bonds. In addition, for shorter maturities, the higher derivative terms are less important. Thus, for shorter maturities the modified duration approximation is more accurate than for perpetual bonds.

IMMUNIZING

Some investors are faced with a very specialized type of problem. The investor has money to invest today and must achieve a specific investment goal at a future date. Severe penalties are incurred if the investment goal is not attained; any excess beyond the desired goal brings no rewards. This type of investor is called an immunizer, because such investors would like to protect themselves against the chance of attaining less than the desired goal.

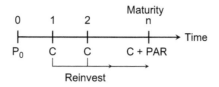

FIGURE 6.6 Immunization at the horizon date *n*.

Pension funds and life insurance companies are investors with this type of problem. Using actuarial tables, the pension fund can predict with considerable accuracy its obligations to the pensioners in a defined benefit plan. A defined benefit plan specifies the pension to be paid; the pension amount is typically specified by a formula. For example, the pension might be

[average salary] × [# years worked] × [2%].

A pensioner with an average salary of $50,000, who worked 30 years, would receive 60% of $50,000 or $30,000 per year. A typical defined-benefit plan provides a life annuity.

With a defined benefit pension, the pension fund manager has no direct incentive to attain more than the contractually-bound retirement benefits and a big incentive to avoid having too little money to make the contractually binding payments. Several strategies have been advocated for immunizers. We will discuss the pros and cons of each.

In recent years, interest rates have been extremely low in the United States as a result of the efforts of the monetary authorities to reduce interest rates and stimulate the economy. Low interest rates make immunization of a target dollar payout at specific future dates much more difficult. As a consequence of low interest rates, many defined-benefit pension plans are now underfunded, meaning that the assets in the fund today are not sufficient at current interest rates to meet the likely liabilities of the beneficiaries.

In addition, insurance companies normally rely heavily upon bond investments to earn sufficient funds to make future payouts on their policies. With low interest rates, insurance companies either have to raise their premiums or make riskier investments to try to earn sufficient funds to pay the likely contractual obligations at future dates. Since many insurance contracts are long-term arrangements in which the annual premiums are fixed at the beginning of the contract, insurance companies face serious problems as a result of low interest rates. Some long-term insurance contracts are now no longer available or have considerably higher premiums.

Zero Coupon Strategy

One simple strategy to lock in a dollar target is to buy zero coupon bonds. Since these bonds have no coupons, the risk of uncertain returns from investing the coupons is solved. The only cash flows occur at time 0 and at final maturity.

The US Treasury allows Treasury securities to be stripped. That is, the individual coupons and par value are sold separately. The resulting securities are called *strips* and are actively traded. With the growth of the market for strips, the need for more complicated strategies to immunize has been reduced. Nevertheless, an extensive literature has developed on procedures for immunizing with coupon-bearing bonds. In effect, these strategies try to create the equivalent of a zero coupon bond position from a portfolio of coupon-bearing bonds.

Maturity Strategy

Some investors use the so-called maturity strategy as a benchmark. In this strategy, an investor purchases a coupon-bearing bond with maturity equal to the investor's horizon.

An investor following this strategy is faced with the problem of reinvesting the coupons received in the future. For example, the coupon received at time 1 must be invested. If this coupon is invested in coupon-bearing bonds, then subsequent coupons must be reinvested.

Since the reinvestment rates are not known at time 0, the future total value of the bond portfolio is not known for certain. If interest rates at times 1 through $n - 1$ are lower than the initial interest rate at time 0, the future total portfolio value may be less than the amount required.

Duration Strategy

Another investment strategy is to invest in coupon-bearing bonds with maturity greater than the horizon date. The value of the bond portfolio using this strategy is uncertain for two reasons. First, the coupons from time 1 until time $n - 1$ have to be reinvested at uncertain future interest rates. Second, the bond portfolio is sold at the horizon date n. Therefore the market value of the portfolio at this horizon date is uncertain.

Two different adverse events could upset this strategy and make the liquidating value of the portfolio less than the required goal. First, interest rates might decline. Then, the reinvestment rate on the coupons is low, but the market value of the bonds at the horizon date is high; these two factors affect the liquidating value of the portfolio at the horizon date in opposite directions. A second possibility is a rise in interest rates. This would raise the reinvestment rate on coupons but lower the market value of the bonds on the horizon date. The higher reinvestment rate and the lower market value have opposite impacts upon the liquidating value of the portfolio. The net impact is not clear.

Investors can lock-in the liquidating value of their portfolio on the horizon date by setting the duration of the portfolio equal to the number of periods until the horizon date. This duration strategy is completely effective if two assumptions are met: (1) yield curves are flat, and (2) only one small change in interest rates occurs immediately after the portfolio is chosen.

Under the duration immunization strategy, if interest rates rise and the market value of the bonds in the portfolio declines, the bond coupons are reinvested at high rates of interest, exactly offsetting the decline in the bond's market value. If interest rates decline, offsetting effects occur in the opposite direction. The market value of the bond portfolio rises and the coupons are reinvested at lower rates of interest. The immunizer would be certain of the value of the portfolio at the horizon date for increases and decreases in interest rates.

The duration strategy assumes one change in interest rates and a flat term structure. Now, consider immunization strategies if these two assumptions are relaxed. If multiple changes in interest rates occur, the portfolio can be approximately immunized if portfolio rebalancing occurs after each small change in interest rates. After each change, the duration is set equal to the number of periods until the horizon date. If yield curves are not flat, the duration strategy works approximately if the portfolio is rebalanced each time a small change in interest rates occurs.

In practice, two major drawbacks limit the use of duration immunization strategies employing coupon-bearing bonds. First, the need to rebalance the portfolio frequently results in expensive transactions costs. Second, the biggest advantage of immunization occurs for long horizons. Since the maturity of a bond is larger than its duration, a portfolio with a long duration has a much longer maturity. The lack of long-term bonds limits the use of the strategy. For example, a portfolio with 20-year duration might require bonds with maturities of 40 years, depending upon the level of interest rates. Since bonds with maturities more than 30 years are rare, immunization is not practical in this case.

Dedicated Portfolio Strategy

Another strategy used by bond investors to lock-in a terminal value at their horizon date is called a dedicated portfolio strategy. This strategy assumes a very low reinvestment rate on coupons. In order to achieve the same terminal value with a lower reinvestment rate, the investor must initially invest more money. This will guarantee the minimum goal even under the worst-case scenario. However, the initial cost of the dedicated strategy is higher than a duration strategy. With a duration strategy, there are costs for rebalancing after the initial investment. If the strategy falls short of its goals, additional funds will have to be contributed.

OTHER BOND PORTFOLIO STRATEGIES

Some bond investors are concerned with the risk of short-term fluctuations in the value of their portfolio. In particular, if interest rates rise, the market value of the portfolio falls.

Several strategies are available for these investors. The simplest strategy is to invest in very-short-term securities. Then, the value of the portfolio is very stable. The disadvantage is the relatively low returns available on short-term bonds.

Two riskier strategies (with higher expected returns) are available. The so-called ladder strategy invests approximately equal proportions of the portfolio in a wide variety of maturities. If interest rates rise, the shorter-maturity part of the portfolio has only small price declines. When the shortest-maturity bond matures, the proceeds can be reinvested at the higher prevailing interest rate. The total portfolio risk is much lower than investing in a long-term bond exclusively.

The barbell strategy invests equal proportions of the portfolio in short-term and long-term bonds. A rise in interest rates causes the prices of long-term bonds to drop considerably, but those of short-term bonds to remain relatively stable. When the short-term bond matures, reinvestment at the new higher interest rate is available. The barbell strategy is higher-risk than the ladder strategy, but much lower-risk than 100% investment in long-term bonds.

IMMUNIZING ASSETS AND LIABILITIES

Some financial institutions such as banks may have assets and liabilities that are sensitive to changes in interest rates. For example, as interest rates increase, the value of the assets goes down, but so does the value of the liabilities. The interest rate risk is the net risk of assets and liabilities.

In the example of the bank balance sheet, the duration of the assets and the duration of the liabilities are calculated separately. Then the difference in the durations is calculated. As long as the difference in the durations is close to zero, the changes in the value of assets as a result of changing interest rates will be approximately offset by the changes in the values of the liabilities.

Bank Balance Sheet	
Assets	Liabilities & Equity
Cash	Deposits
Loan	Bonds
Buildings	Equity
DUR_A	DUR_L
$GAP = DUR_A - DUR_L$	

FIGURE 6.7 Duration Gap.

The duration gap provides some indication of the sensitivity of assets and liabilities to changes in the level of interest rates. However, the duration gap does not provide information about the default risk. For example, the government sponsored entities Fannie Mae and Freddie Mac had duration gaps that were very close to zero, but did not correctly estimate the default risk of their assets. In fact, the value of many of their assets went down because of defaults. The duration gap did not capture this default risk.

SUMMARY

Bond investors are interested in the sensitivity of their bond holdings to changes in interest rates. Duration shows that interest rate sensitivity declines as bond coupon gets larger and increases as maturity increases, except for some very-long-maturity discount bonds. Shorter-maturity, higher-coupon bonds are low-risk; and longer-maturity, lower-coupon bonds are high risk.

Some investors are immunizers who want to lock-in a terminal value at a particular horizon date. These investors can select from the zero coupon bond, maturity, duration, and dedicated strategies. Buying zero coupon bonds (strips) is an excellent strategy, if available.

APPENDIX

Maximum Value of Duration for Discount Bonds

For discount bonds, duration reaches its maximum for a maturity of

$$\frac{1+y}{y - c/\text{PAR}} + \frac{1}{\ln(1+y)} + \frac{y[\text{PAR}/c - 1/y]}{(1+y)^n \ln(1+y)} \qquad \textbf{6A.1}$$

This maximum value is

$$\frac{1+y}{y} + \frac{y[\text{PAR}/c - 1/y]}{(1+y)^{n^*}(1+y)} \qquad \textbf{6A.2}$$

where n^* is the maturity where duration has attained a maximum. Notice that this maximum value is only slightly larger than the duration of a perpetual bond. The first term is the duration of a perpetual bond; for large values of n^*, the second term is close to zero.

REFERENCES

Caks, John, William Lane, Robert W. Greenleaf, and Reginald Joules. 1985. "A Simple Formula for Duration." *Journal of Financial Research* 8, no. 3 (Fall): 245–49.

Hopewell, M., and G. Kaufman. 1973. "Bond Price Volatility and Term to Maturity: A Generalized Respecification." *American Economic Review* 63, no. 4 (September): 749–53.

Livingston, M. "Measuring Bond Price Volatility," *Journal of Financial and Quantitative Analysis* 14, no. 2 (June): 343–49.

Macaulay, F. 1938. *The Movements of Interest Rates, Bond Yields and Stock Prices in the United States since 1856*. New York: National Bureau of Economic Research.

QUESTIONS AND PROBLEMS

1. Assume a yield to maturity of 6%. Compute the duration for the following bonds. Assume $100 par values.
    (a) 10 years, zero coupon
    (b) 10 years, 6% coupon
    (c) 10 years, 8% coupon

2. In problem 1, assume that yields change from 6% to 8%. Work out the exact change in price and compare it with the change in price predicted by duration. Explain the difference. Assume $100 par values.

3. A perpetual bond has a coupon of $6 and a yield to maturity of 6%. Work out the actual percentage change in price and the duration approximation in the following three cases:
    (a) The yield decreases by 1%
    (b) The yield increases by 1%
    (c) The yield increases by 8%

4. Compute the duration of the longest-maturity Treasury bond and compare it to the yield to maturity.

5. Suppose that the interest rate on all bonds is 6%. You compute the duration on a 20-year bond and find it to be greater than 18. What can you say about the coupon on this bond?

6. Suppose that the interest rate on all bonds is 6%. Which is a correct statement?
    (a) The duration of a par bond can never be greater than 18 for any maturity.
    (b) The duration of a premium bond can never be greater than 17, even for long maturities.
    (c) The duration of a 15-year Treasury strip exceeds the duration of all par bonds.
    (d) The duration of a discount bond can never exceed 17.
    (e) None of the above.

CHAPTER 7

Spot and Forward Interest Rates

Earlier chapters assumed that the interest rates for all maturities are the same. In practice, interest rates differ by maturity. Most of the time, interest rates increase for longer maturities, but the pattern varies considerably. Therefore, this chapter will discuss time value computations assuming interest rates vary by maturity. We refer to this case as a non-flat term (or maturity) structure.

SPOT INTEREST RATES

An interest rate that begins today and continues until some future date is typically called a spot interest rate. We will denote spot interest rates by R. Each spot interest rate has two subscripts. The first subscript denotes the point in time when the interest rate is observed. The second denotes how long the interest rate lasts. Recall that time 0 is now. Future points in time are denoted by time 1, time 2, etc. Thus, $R_{0,1}$ is observed now and runs for one period. $R_{0,2}$ is observed now and lasts two periods. $R_{0,n}$ is observed now and lasts n periods. Figure 7.1 illustrates.

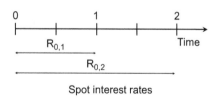

FIGURE 7.1 Spot Interest Rates.

In this chapter, we will stick to interest rates that are observed now, with a first subscript of 0. In later chapters, other cases are considered. As one example, $R_{1,1}$ is the interest rate observed one period into the future and lasting one period until time 2.

Present Values and Spot Prices

Suppose one dollar will be received one period from now. Its present value or spot price is $1 / (1 + R_{0,1})$. To simplify the notation, we call this PV_1. Thus,

$$\text{Present value of \$1 received at time 1} = PV_1 = \frac{1}{1 + R_{0,1}} \qquad \text{7.1}$$

Suppose that the one-period spot interest rate $R_{0,1}$ is 2%. Then,

$$PV_1 = \frac{1}{1.02} = .9804 \qquad \text{7.2}$$

One dollar received at time 1 has a present value of $0.9804. This is illustrated in Figure 7.2.

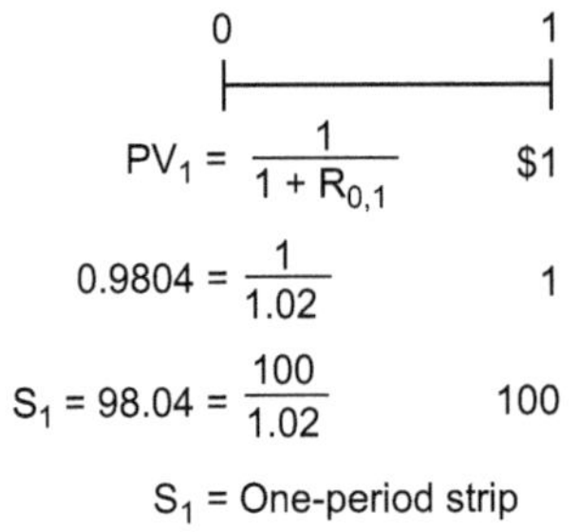

$$
\begin{array}{ccc}
0 & & 1 \\
\vdash & \!\!\!\!\!\rule{4cm}{0.4pt}\!\!\!\!\! & \dashv \\
\end{array}
$$

$$PV_1 = \frac{1}{1 + R_{0,1}} \qquad \$1$$

$$0.9804 = \frac{1}{1.02} \qquad 1$$

$$S_1 = 98.04 = \frac{100}{1.02} \qquad 100$$

$$S_1 = \text{One-period strip}$$

FIGURE 7.2 Present Value of $1 Received at Time 1.

The present value (or spot price) of one dollar received two periods from now is PV_2 or $1 / (1 + R_{0,2})^2$. Thus,

$$\text{Present value of \$1 received at time 2} = PV_2 = \frac{1}{(1 + R_{0,2})^2} \qquad \text{7.3}$$

If the two-period spot interest rate is 5%, the present value of one dollar received at time 2 is $0.9070. This is illustrated in Figure 7.3.

$$PV_2 = \frac{1}{(1.05)^2} = .9070 \qquad \text{7.4}$$

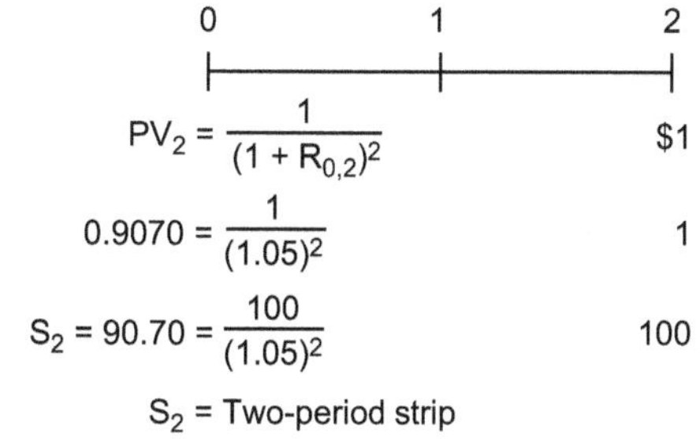

$$PV_2 = \frac{1}{(1+R_{0,2})^2} \qquad \$1$$

$$0.9070 = \frac{1}{(1.05)^2} \qquad 1$$

$$S_2 = 90.70 = \frac{100}{(1.05)^2} \qquad 100$$

$$S_2 = \text{Two-period strip}$$

FIGURE 7.3 Present Value of $1 at Time 2.

The present value (or spot price) of one dollar received n periods from now is PV_n or $1/(1+R_{0,n})^n$. Thus, *n-Period Present Value* is:

$$\begin{matrix} \text{Present value} \\ \text{of \$1 received} \\ \text{at time } n \end{matrix} = PV_n = \frac{1}{(1+R_{0,n})^n} \qquad 7.5$$

If n is 8 periods and $R_{0,8}$ is 10%, then,

$$PV_8 = \frac{1}{(1.10)^8} = .4665 \qquad 7.6$$

The reader should practice present value calculations on a financial calculator or in Excel.

Students often do not realize that an expression such as $1/(1+R_{0,n})^n$ simply means the present value of a dollar received n periods from now. Suppose you're asked which has greater value—one dollar received one period from now or a dollar received two periods from now. In algebraic notation, this question would be, "Which is bigger, $1/(1+R_{0,1})^1$ or $1/(1+R_{0,2})^2$?" If you think of these algebraic expressions as present values of a dollar at different points in time, it is clear that money received sooner has at least as much value as money received later.

In general, the present value of one dollar received at a near date should be at least as large as the present value of a dollar in the more distant future. That is,

$$PV_1 \geq PV_2 \geq \cdots \geq PV_n$$

$$\begin{bmatrix} \text{Present value} \\ \text{of \$1 received} \\ \text{at time 1} \end{bmatrix} \geq \begin{bmatrix} \text{Present value} \\ \text{of \$1 received} \\ \text{at time 2} \end{bmatrix} \geq \cdots \geq \begin{bmatrix} \text{Present value} \\ \textit{of \$1 received} \\ \text{at time } n \end{bmatrix} \qquad 7.7$$

In terms of the spot interest rates, we have:

$$\frac{1}{(1+R_1)} \geq \frac{1}{(1+R_2)^2} \geq \cdots \geq \frac{1}{(1+R_n)^n} \qquad 7.8$$

Notice that the present values or spot prices decrease for longer maturities in our examples.

$$PV_1 \geq PV_2 \geq PV_8$$
$$.9804 \geq .9070 \geq .4665 \qquad 7.9$$

TREASURY STRIPS

Treasury strips are zero-coupon bonds. Treasury strips are created by bond dealers from coupon-bearing Treasury bonds and notes. Technically, the term "strips" is an acronym standing for Separately Traded Interest and Principal Securities. It is frequently written in capital letters: *STRIPS*. The buyer purchases these zero-coupon bonds for a price P_n and receives the par value at maturity n. The cash flows are shown in Table 7.1.

Table 7.1. Cash Flows for Treasury Strip

	Points in Time			
	0	1	...	n
Cash Flows	$-P_n$	0	0	+ par

The price of a strip should be the par value discounted at the appropriate spot interest rate. This book will quote the price of a bond (including strips) assuming a par value of $100. Using our earlier to spot interest rates,

One-period strip:

$$\text{Price of one–period strip} = P_1 = [PV_1][\text{par}] = \frac{\text{par}}{1+R_{0,1}}$$

$$= \left[\frac{1}{1.02}\right] 100 = 98.04 \qquad 7.10$$

Two-period strip:

$$\begin{array}{c} \text{Price of} \\ \text{two-period} \\ \text{strip} \end{array} = P_2 = [PV_2][\text{par}] = \frac{\text{par}}{(1+R_{0,2})^2}$$

$$= \left[\frac{1}{(1.05)^2}\right]100 = 90.70$$

7.11

Finding Spot Interest Rates from Strips Prices

The spot interest rates can be found from the spot prices for Treasury strips. Suppose the prices of one-period and two-period strips are \$98.0392 and \$90.7029 per \$100 of par. The spot interest rates can be found as follows:

One-Period Strip

$$\text{Since } P_1 = \frac{\text{par}}{1+R_{0,1}}$$

7.12

$$1+R_{0,1} = \frac{\text{par}}{P_1} = \frac{100}{98.04} = 1.02$$

$$R_{0,1} = .02 = 2\%$$

7.13

Two-period strip

$$\text{Since } P_2 = \frac{\text{par}}{(1+R_{0,2})^2}$$

7.14

$$(1+R_{0,2})^2 = \frac{\text{par}}{P_2} = \frac{100}{90.7029} = 1.1025$$

$$R_{0,2} = .05 = 5\%$$

7.15

For an *n*-period Treasury strip, the *n*-period spot interest rate can be found as follows:

n-period strip

$$\text{Since } P_n = \frac{\text{par}}{(1+R_{0,n})^n}$$

7.16

$$(1+R_{0,n})^n = \frac{\text{par}}{P_n}$$

7.17

$$R_{0,n} = \sqrt[n]{\frac{par}{P_n}} - 1 \qquad \text{7.18}$$

FORWARD INTEREST RATES

In many financial transactions, borrowers and lenders agree right now to make a loan in the future. The conditions of the loan are set at time 0, but the transaction does not occur until a future date. These are called forward loans. Table 7.2 shows the timing.

Table 7.2. Timing of a Forward Contract

		Points in Time
	0	Delivery Date
Transaction	Sign Contract and Set Price	Pay $ and Receive Commodity or Deliver Commodity and Receive $

Individual consumers typically do not engage in forward transactions, but they restrict themselves primarily to spot transactions—that is, transactions where the goods or services are received and payment made immediately. A lease is an example of a forward contract. At time 0, a lease agreement is reached to provide some service in the future and make payments in the future.

Forward loans and forward interest rates are important to consider because there are many forward contracts in financial markets. In addition, an important theory of the maturity structure (or term structure) of interest rates is the *expectations hypothesis*, which focuses on forward interest rates.

Suppose we have a loan in which the cash flows to the lender (bond buyer) are shown in Table 7.3. Although the loan agreement is signed at time 0, there are no cash flows at time 0. The cash flows do not occur until the delivery date.

Table 7.3. Forward Contract Cash Flows for Lender (Bond Buyer)

		Points in Time	
	0	1	2
	0	Delivery Date	Maturity Date
Cash Flows	0	−F (Lend $F)	+ par (Receive par)

Let the forward interest rate for period 2 be denoted by $f_{0,2}$. The first subscript indicates that the rate is observed at time 0. The second denotes an interest rate for period 2. We will consider forward loans lasting one period; if loan maturities exceed one period, an additional subscript is needed to indicate when the loan begins and when it ends.

The forward interest rate discounts money from time 2 until time 1. Suppose $1 will be received at time 2. Its time 1 value is $1 discounted at the forward interest rate. The time 1 value of a dollar received at time 2 is:

$$\text{Time 1 value} = \frac{1}{1+f_{0,2}} \qquad \textbf{7.19}$$

Suppose $f_{0,2}$ is 8.09%. Then $1 received at time 2 has a time 1 value of $0.9252.

$$\text{Time 1 Value} = \frac{1}{1.0809} = .9252 \qquad \textbf{7.20}$$

Table 7.4. Forward Contract Cash Flows for Lender (Bond Buyer)

		Points in Time	
	0	1	2
	0	Delivery Date	Maturity Date
Cash Flows	0	$-1/(1+f_{0,2})$ $-.9252$	$+1.00$

The time 2 value of $1 received at time 3 is

$$\text{Time 2 value} = \frac{1}{1+f_{0,3}} \qquad \textbf{7.21}$$

See table 7.5.

Table 7.5. Forward Contract Cash Flows for Lender (Bond Buyer)

			Points in Time	
	0	1	2	3
			Delivery Date	Maturity Date
Cash Flows	0	0	$-1/(1+f_{0,3})$	$+1.00$

In general, the time $n-1$ value of \$1 received at time n is

$$\text{Time } n-1 \text{ value} = \frac{1}{1+f_{0,n}} \qquad \textbf{7.22}$$

Forward interest rates allow discounting for several periods. Thus, the time 1 value of \$1 received at time 3 is

$$\text{Time 1 value} = \frac{1}{(1+f_{0,2})(1+f_{0,3})} \qquad \textbf{7.23}$$

Suppose that $f_{0,2}$ is 8.09% and $f_{0,3}$ is 10%. The time 1 value of \$1 received at time 3 is as follows:

$$\text{Time 1 value} = \frac{1}{(1.0809)(1.10)} = \left[\frac{1}{1.0809}\right]\left[\frac{1}{1.10}\right]$$
$$= [.9252][.9091] = .8410 \qquad \textbf{7.24}$$

The present (time 0) value of \$1 received at time 3 is:

$$\text{Time 0 value} = \frac{1}{(1+R_{0,1})(1+f_{0,2})(1+f_{0,3})} \qquad \textbf{7.25}$$

Computing Forward Interest Rates

Forward interest rates can be computed from spot interest rates or from the prices of strips. The forward interest rate for time period 2 $(f_{0,2})$ can be computed as follows:

$$1+f_{0,2} = \frac{(1+R_{0,2})^2}{1+R_{0,1}} = \frac{\dfrac{\text{Par}}{1+R_{0,1}}}{\dfrac{\text{Par}}{(1+R_{0,2})^2}} = \frac{S_1}{S_2} \qquad \textbf{7.26}$$

Notice that the forward rate can also be computed by taking the ratio of the prices of strips. To illustrate, assume that the price of a one-period strip S_1 is \$98.04 per \$100 of par value and the price of a two-period strip S_2 is \$90.70 per \$100 of par value. Then the 1-period spot interest rate is 2% and a two-spot interest rate is 5%. Substituting, we see that the forward interest rate is 8.09%.

$$1.0809 = \frac{(1.05)^2}{1.02} = \frac{\dfrac{\text{Par}}{1+R_{0,1}}}{\dfrac{\text{Par}}{(1+R_{0,2})^2}} = \frac{98.04}{90.70} \qquad \textbf{7.27}$$

The forward interest rate for time period 3 can be computed as follows:

$$1 + f_{0,3} = \frac{(1 + R_{0,3})^3}{(1 + R_{0,2})^2} = \frac{S_2}{S_3} \qquad \textbf{7.28}$$

The n-period forward interest rate is computed as follows:

$$1 + f_{0,n} = \frac{(1 + R_{0,n})^n}{(1 + R_{0,n-1})^{n-1}} = \frac{S_{n-1}}{S_n} \qquad \textbf{7.29}$$

Link between Spot and Forward Interest Rates

Since the present value can be expressed in terms of both spot and forward interest rates, the two are linked. In particular,

Two periods

$$\frac{1}{(1 + R_{0,2})^2} = \frac{1}{(1 + R_{0,1})(1 + f_{0,2})} \qquad \textbf{7.30}$$

Take the reciprocal:

$$(1 + R_{0,2})^2 = (1 + R_{0,1})(1 + f_{0,2}) \qquad \textbf{7.31}$$

In words, the two-period spot interest rate is the geometric mean of the one-period spot interest rate and the forward interest $f_{0,2}$. Using our earlier numerical example,

$$(1.05)^2 = (1.02)(1.0809) = 1.1025 \qquad \textbf{7.32}$$

This equation indicates that an investor with $1 to invest at time 0 should end up with the same value at time 2 ($1.1025) if the money is invested at 5% for two periods or invested for one period at 2% and then reinvested forward at 8.09%. Since the forward interest rate is known at time 0, the investor can lock-in a return of 8.09% for the second period. The time 2 value ($1.1025) is known for certain in each case.

Equation **7.31** says that the two-period spot interest rate is the geometric mean of the one-period spot interest rate and the forward interest rate. This equation is approximately the same as saying that the two-period spot interest rate is the arithmetic mean of the one-period spot rate and the forward interest rate. To see this point, expand the equation:

$$1 + 2R_{0,2} + R_{0,2}^2 = 1 + R_{0,1} + f_{0,2} + R_{0,1}f_{0,2} \qquad \textbf{7.33}$$

Omit the squared term and the product term, resulting in the following approximation:

$$1 + 2R_{0,2} \approx 1 + R_{0,1} + f_{0,2} \qquad 7.34$$

This is rearranged to:

$$R_{0,2} \approx \frac{R_{0,1} + f_{0,2}}{2} \qquad 7.35$$

If the one-period spot interest rate is 4% and the forward interest rate is 12.15%, the arithmetic approximation of the two-period spot interest rate is 8.08%, whereas the actual interest rate (geometric mean) is 8%.

Three periods

$$\frac{1}{(1 + R_{0,3})^3} = \frac{1}{(1 + R_{0,1})(1 + f_{0,2})(1 + f_{0,3})} \qquad 7.36$$

Take the reciprocal:

$$(1 + R_{0,3})^3 = (1 + R_{0,1})(1 + f_{0,2})(1 + f_{0,3})$$
$$= (1 + R_{0,2})^2 (1 + f_{0,3}) \qquad 7.37$$

The three-period spot interest rate is the geometric mean of the one-period spot interest rate and the two forward rates, $f_{0,2}$ and $f_{0,3}$. An investor with \$1 to invest at time 0 should end up with the same wealth at time 3 if the investment is at the spot rate $R_{0,3}$ for three periods or at $R_{0,1}$ for the first period, $f_{0,2}$ for the second period, and $f_{0,3}$ for the third period.

n periods

$$\frac{1}{(1 + R_{0,n})^n} = \frac{1}{(1 + R_{0,1})(1 + f_{0,2})\dots(1 + f_{0,n})} \qquad 7.38$$

Take the reciprocal:

$$(1 + R_{0,n})^n = (1 + R_{0,1})(1 + f_{0,2})\dots(1 + f_{0,n})$$
$$= (1 + R_{0,n-1})^{n-1} (1 + f_n) \qquad 7.39$$

The *n*-period spot interest rate is the geometric mean of the one-period spot interest rate and the forward rates until period *n*. Someone can invest for *n* periods at the spot rate $R_{0,n}$ or invest for *n* periods at the sequence of rates $R_{0,1}, f_{0,2}, \dots, f_{0,n}$. In either case, the value after *n* periods is the same.

Equation (37) can also be used to solve for forward interest rates.

$$1 + f_{0,2} = \frac{(1 + R_{0,2})^2}{1 + R_{0,1}} \qquad 7.40$$

$$1 + f_{o,3} = \frac{(1 + R_{o,3})^3}{(1 + R_{o,2})^2}$$ 7.41

$$1 + f_{o,n} = \frac{(1 + R_{o,n})^n}{(1 + R_{o,n-1})^{n-1}}$$ 7.42

SHAPE OF THE TERM STRUCTURE

A rising (falling) term structure occurs when spot interest rates increase (decrease) for longer maturities. The shape of the spot rates is related to the forward rates. The case of two periods illustrates the link. If the two-period spot interest rate ($R_{o,2}$) is greater (less) than the one-period spot rate ($R_{o,1}$), the forward rate ($f_{o,2}$) must be greater (less) than the two-period spot interest rate. Figures 7.4, 7.5, and 7.6 illustrate these cases.

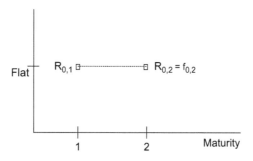

FIGURE 7.4 Flat Term Structure.

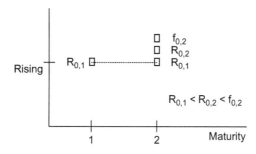

FIGURE 7.5 Rising Term Structure.

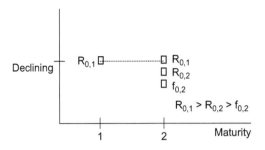

FIGURE 7.6 Declining Term Structure.

The important lesson is that rising (falling) spot interests imply rising (falling) forward interest rates. The reason is that $R_{0,2}$ is the geometric mean of $R_{0,1}$ and $f_{0,2}$. Since $R_{0,2}$ is the average of $R_{0,1}$ and $f_{0,2}$, $R_{0,2}$ must lie between them. For rising term structures, $R_{0,1} < R_{0,2} < f_{0,2}$. For falling term structures, $R_{0,1} > R_{0,2} > f_{0,2}$. In the n-period case, the link between the spot and forward interest rates is quite complicated since the n-period spot rate $(R_{0,n})$ is the geometric mean of the 1-period spot interest rate plus $n-1$ forward interest rates. Because the n-period spot interest rate is the average of the 1-period and $n-1$ forward interest rates, the spot interest rates will tend to be a smoother function of maturity than the forward rates.

ANNUITIES

Frequently, debt instruments involve constant cash flows over several periods. These constant cash flows are called annuities. For bonds, coupons are annuities, since the coupon payment is the same over a number of periods. For mortgages, the periodic payment is the same every period and is an annuity.

The present value of an annuity is simply the sum of the present values of the individual components of the annuity. The present value of an annuity of $1 at time 1 and $1 at time 2 is the sum of the present values. We will call this present value PVA_2. That is,

Two periods

$$\text{Present Value of Annuity} = PVA_2 = \frac{1}{1+R_{0,1}} + \frac{1}{\left(1+R_{0,2}\right)^2}$$

$$= PV_1 + PV_2 \qquad \qquad 7.43$$

Using our earlier numerical example,

$$\text{Present Value of Annuity} = PVA_2 = \frac{1}{1.02} + \frac{1}{\left(1.05\right)^2}$$

$$= .9804 + .9070 = 1.8874 \qquad 7.44$$

The present value of an annuity of $1 for two periods is $1.8874.

The present value of a dollar annuity for n periods is

n periods:

$$\text{Present Value of Annuity} = PVA_n = \frac{1}{1 + R_{0,1}} + \ldots + \frac{1}{\left(1 + R_{0,n}\right)^n}$$

$$= PV_1 + \ldots + PV_n \qquad \qquad 7.45$$

In the case of a flat term structure, the spot interest rate for all periods is R. Then the formula for the present value of an annuity simplifies:

n periods flat term structure:

$$\text{Present Value of Annuity} = PVA_n = \frac{1}{1 + R} + \ldots + \frac{1}{\left(1 + R\right)^n}$$

$$= \left[\frac{1}{R}\right]\left[1 - \frac{1}{\left(1 + R\right)^n}\right] \qquad \qquad 7.46$$

If the term structure is flat and the spot interest rates equal 5%, the present value of a ten-period annuity is computed as follows:

$$\text{Present Value of Annuity} = PVA_{10} = \left[\frac{1}{R}\right]\left[1 - \frac{1}{\left(1 + R\right)^n}\right]$$

$$PVA_{10} = \left[\frac{1}{.05}\right]\left[1 - \frac{1}{\left(1.05\right)^{10}}\right] = \frac{1 - .6139}{.05} = 7.7217 \qquad \qquad 7.47$$

PRICES OF COUPON-BEARING BONDS

An n-period coupon-bearing bond pays periodic coupons and par at maturity. The pattern of cash flows is shown in Table 7.6.

Table 7.6. Cash Flows for Coupon-Bearing Bond

	Points in Time			
	0	1	2 thru $n-1$	n
Cash Flows	$-P_n$	c	c	c + par

A coupon-bearing bond is essentially a portfolio of zero-coupon bonds or strips. Consider one-period, two-period, and n-period coupon-bearing bonds. The price of each bond is the present value of each of the coupons (c) and the par value.

One-period bond:

$$P_1 = \frac{c + \text{par}}{1 + R_{0,1}}$$

$$= [c + \text{par}]\, PV_1 \qquad 7.48$$

To illustrate, suppose the one-period spot interest rate ($R_{0,1}$) is 2%, and a bond has a coupon of \$4 and par value of \$100:

$$P_1 = \frac{4 + 100}{1.02} = 101.96 \qquad 7.49$$

Two-period bond

$$P_2 = \frac{c}{1 + R_{0,1}} + \frac{c + \text{par}}{(1 + R_{0,2})^2}$$

$$= [c][PV_1] + [c + \text{par}]PV_2$$

$$= [c][PV_1] + [c][PV_2] + [\text{par}][PV_2]$$

$$= [c][PVA_2] + [\text{par}][PV_2] \qquad 7.50$$

To illustrate, suppose the one-period spot interest rate ($R_{0,1}$) is 2%, the two-period spot interest rate ($R_{0,2}$) is 5%, and a bond has a coupon of \$4 and par value of \$100:

$$P_2 = \frac{4}{1.02} + \frac{4 + 100}{(1.05)^2} = 98.25 \qquad 7.51$$

n-period bond

$$P_n = \frac{c}{1 + R_{0,1}} + \ldots + \frac{c + \text{par}}{(1 + R_{0,n})^n}$$

$$= [c][PV_1] + \ldots + [c + \text{par}][PV_n]$$

$$= [c][PVA_n] + [\text{par}][PV_n] \qquad 7.52$$

The last line of this equation simply says that the price of a bond with n periods until maturity is equal to the coupon (c) times the present value of an n-period annuity (PVA_n) and the par value (par) times the present value of \$1 received n time periods from now.

YIELD TO MATURITY AND SPOT RATES

The yield to maturity on a coupon-bearing bond is a polynomial average of the spot interest rates. To see this point, consider the case of two-period bonds.

$$P_2 = \frac{c}{1+y} + \frac{c+\text{par}}{(1+y)^2} = \frac{c}{1+R_{0,1}} + \frac{c+\text{par}}{(1+R_{0,2})^2} \qquad 7.53$$

The yield to maturity is an average of $R_{0,1}$ and $R_{0,2}$. The precise average depends upon the size of the bond coupon and the maturity in the general case. For short maturities, the yield to maturity is close to the n-period spot interest rate. For longer maturities, the yield to maturity is heavily influenced by all the spot interest rates.

The following two examples show that yield to maturity is an average of spot rates. See Figures 7.7 and 7.8. The examples assume that the one-period spot rate is 2% and the two-period spot rate is 5%. The bond with the 6% coupon has a yield to maturity of 4.91%. The bond with a 1% coupon has yield to maturity of 4.98%. You should check the calculations on a financial calculator or in Excel. Each of these bonds is fairly priced. Although the bond with the 1% coupon has a higher yield to maturity, it is not a better purchase. The yield to maturity for 1% coupon bonds is higher simply because the proportion of the cash flows occurring in the second time period is larger and the spot interest rate of 5% for the second period has a larger impact on the yield to maturity compared to the bond with the 6% coupon.

This example shows that higher yield to maturity does not necessarily mean a better investment vehicle. In some cases, bonds with higher yields to maturity will be better investments. In other cases, a higher yield to maturity merely reflects the relative size of the cash payments on a bond and the spot interest rates for all of the maturities.

0	1	2

$$102.03 = \frac{6}{1.02} + \frac{106}{(1.05)^2}$$

$$102.03 = \frac{6}{1+y} + \frac{106}{(1+y)^2}$$

$$y_6 = 4.91\%$$

FIGURE 7.7 Example with Coupon of $6.

$$0 \quad\quad\quad 1 \quad\quad\quad 2$$

$$92.59 = \frac{1}{1.02} + \frac{101}{(1.05)^2}$$

$$92.59 = \frac{1}{1+y} + \frac{101}{(1+y)^2}$$

$$y_1 = 4.98\%$$

FIGURE 7.8 Example with Coupon of $1.

These examples also illustrate that there is a two-stage process to determine the yield to maturity. First, the spot interest rates are used to find the present value of the cash flows (i.e., the price). Second, given the price, coupon, maturity, and par value, the yield to maturity can be computed using a calculator or Excel.

Par Bonds

In the case of a bond with a price of par, the yield to maturity can be explicitly expressed as a function of the spot interest rates. In the two-period case, we have:

$$y\text{par}_2 = \frac{1 - \dfrac{1}{\left(1 + R_{0,2}\right)^2}}{\dfrac{1}{1 + R_{0,1}} + \dfrac{1}{\left(1 + R_{0,2}\right)^2}} \qquad 7.54$$

If the one-period spot interest rate is 2% and the two-period spot rate is 5%,

$$y\text{par}_2 = \frac{1 - \dfrac{1}{\left(1.05\right)^2}}{\dfrac{1}{1.02} + \dfrac{1}{\left(1.05\right)^2}} = 4.93\% \qquad 7.55$$

In practice, coupons are quoted in units of 1/8 of a dollar. In the case of n-period par bonds,

$$y\text{par}_n = \frac{1 - \dfrac{1}{\left(1 + R_{0,n}\right)^n}}{\dfrac{1}{1 + R_{0,1}} + \ldots + \dfrac{1}{\left(1 + R_{0,n}\right)^n}} \qquad 7.56$$

The numerator is 1 minus the present value of $1 received at time n. The denominator is the present value of an annuity of $1 per period for n periods. This expression shows that the yield to maturity for par bonds can be calculated in one stage. For nonpar bonds, the price must first be computed given the spot rates. Then the yield to maturity can be computed from the price.

METHODS FOR ESTIMATING THE TERM STRUCTURE OF INTEREST RATES

A variety of methods have been proposed for estimating the term structure of interest rates.

Coupon Strips

One method for estimating the term structure is to use the prices and interest rates for Treasury strips. An example was shown earlier in this chapter. The method is relatively straightforward and simple.

A major advantage of using coupon strips to estimate the term structure is very strong evidence that interest rates estimated from coupon strips reproduce the prices of coupon-bearing bonds. That is, a portfolio of strips with the same cash inflows as a coupon-bearing bond or note has virtually the same market value as the underlying Treasury bond or note. The chapter on arbitrage will show that arbitrage by bond dealers makes this property hold.

Recursive or Bootstrapping Method

Another method for estimating the term structure has been called the recursive or bootstrapping method. With this method, the one-period interest rate can be estimated from a one-period coupon bearing bond because there is one equation and one unknown.

$$P_1 = \frac{c + \text{par}}{1 + R_{0,1}} \qquad 7.57$$

Next, the 2-period interest rate can be computed from the price of a 2-period coupon bearing bond.

$$P_2 = \frac{c}{1 + R_{0,1}} + \frac{c + \text{par}}{(1 + R_{0,2})^2} \qquad 7.58$$

The equation for this bond's price contains two unknowns, the one-period spot interest rate and the two-period interest rate. Since the one-period interest rate has already been found, there is one equation and one unknown. The two-period interest rate can now be computed. For longer maturities the process is repeated over and over again. One problem with this approach is that some maturities may be missing. For example, if there is no two-period bond, then the three-period interest rate and all longer maturity interest rates cannot be estimated. However, interpolation can be used to estimate the rates for the missing maturities as an average of one-period and three-period spot interest rates. Another problem with this approach is that the estimation errors for a particular maturity may get compounded into the estimation errors for all longer maturities.

The following example illustrates the bootstrapping approach.

1-Period Bond

$$P = \frac{c + Par}{1 + R_{0,1}}$$

$$99.52 = \frac{104}{1.045} \qquad R_{0,1} = 4.5\%$$

2-Period Bond

$$P = \frac{c}{1 + R_{0,1}} + \frac{c + Par}{(1 + R_{0,2})^2}$$

$$99.09 = \frac{4.50}{1.045} + \frac{104.50}{(1 + R_{0,2})^2} \qquad R_{0,2} = 5\%$$

FIGURE 7.9 Bootstrapping-Recursive Method.

Bond Pairs

If two bonds with same maturity but different coupon levels exist, the price of a zero-coupon bond or strip can be derived algebraically as follows. The proof is technical and is included in the appendix.

$$PV_n = \frac{c_2 P_1 - c_1 P_2}{c_2 - c_1} \qquad 7.59$$

From the price of a zero-coupon bond, the spot interest rate for that maturity can be computed. A major difficulty of this approach is that it works only for maturities for which there are two or more bonds with different coupons. While there are a number of maturities with multiple coupon bonds, many maturities have only one bond of that maturity date.

Curve Fitting

A variety of authors have suggested various methods of fitting mathematical functions to the prices of coupon bearing bonds by regression analysis. These methods assume a particular relationship between observed bond prices or interest rates and coupons and taxes. The methods have the advantage that they use many different bonds and thus errors of estimation may average out. They have the disadvantage that the estimated term structure may be significantly affected by the type of mathematical functions used in estimation.

QUESTIONS AND PROBLEMS

1. Assume that the one-period spot interest rate is 2% and the two-period spot interest rate is 4%. Answer the following questions:
   (a) What is the present value of $100 received one year from now?
   (b) What is the present value of $100 received two years from now?
   (c) You are going to receive $100 two years from now. What is its time 1 value? What is the forward interest rate?
   (d) Suppose you invest $1 today at the two-period spot interest rate; what is its value at time 2? Alternatively you invest $1 at the one-period spot rate and reinvest at the forward interest rate; what is the value at time 2? How do these two investments compare?

2. Treasury strips with $100 par values have the following prices: one-period, $98; two-period, $95. Answer the following questions:
   (a) What are the one-period and two-period spot interest rates?
   (b) What is the forward interest rate?
   (c) If you invest $1 in one-period strips, what is the value after one period?
   (d) If you invest $1 in two-period strips, what is the value after two periods?
   (e) If you invest $1 at time 1 at the forward interest rate implied by the strips, what is the value of this dollar at time 2?

3. Treasury strips with $100 par values have the following prices: one-period, $98; two-period, $95. You are going to receive an annuity of $100 for the next two-periods.
   (a) What is the present value of this annuity?
   (b) What is the time 1 value of this annuity?
   (c) What is the time 2 value of this annuity?

4. An annuity of $100 per period for two periods has a present value of $178.33. If the term structure of interest rates is flat, compute the interest rate.

5. Suppose the term structure in problem 1 applies. A two-period coupon-bearing bond has an annual coupon of $5 and par value of $100. Answer the following questions:
   (a) What is the bond's price?
   (b) What is the bond's yield to maturity?
   (c) Suppose you arrange (at time 0) to buy this bond in the forward market for delivery at time 1 immediately after the coupon is paid. What should the forward price be?

6. As a reward for reading this book, you are given a choice between $100 received one year from now and $107 received two years from now. How should you go about deciding which of these choices is better?

7. Suppose that the prices of one- through three-period strips per $100 of par are $98, $95, and $91. Compute the spot and forward interest rates and show these on a graph.

8. Compute the spot and forward interest rates if the prices of one-period and two-period strips are each $96 per $100 of par value.

9. Using the information in problem 7, compute the yield to maturity on a two-period par bond.

10. Suppose that the one-period spot interest rate is 5%. What is the minimum value for the two-period spot interest rate? (Hint: Express the two-period spot rate in terms of the one-period spot rate and the forward rate.)

11. There are two two-year bonds. One bond has an annual coupon of $4.50, par value $100, current price of $97.37. The other bond has an annual coupon of $5.00, par value of $100, and price of $98.30.
    (a) Find the present value of two-year annuity of one dollar per year.
    (b) Compute the price of a two-year strip and the two-year spot interest rate.
    (c) Compute the price of a one-year strip and the one-year of spot interest rate. Hint: the present value of a two-year annuity of one dollar per year equals the price of a one-year strip divided by $100 plus the price of a two-year strip divided by $100.

12. Assume that the one-period spot interest rate is 4% and the two-period spot interest rate is 6%. A two-year bond with annual coupon of $5 and par value of $100 is traded. You make a forward purchase for delivery in one year of this bond. What is the forward price of this bond?

13. Suppose a four-year Treasury strip with $100 par value has a price of $85 and a five-year Treasury strip with $100 par value has a price of $80. What is the forward interest rate for period five?

14. Suppose that a one-period Treasury strip with $100 par value has a price of $97.05 and a two-period strip has a price of $93.75. A two-period coupon

bearing bond has an annual coupon of $7.50 and par value of $100. Determine the yield to maturity on this coupon-bearing bond.

15. Suppose that the price of one-, two-, and three-year strips are $97, $93, and $88 per $100 of par. A three-year bond has an annual coupon of $5 and par value of $100. Determine its yield to maturity.

APPENDIX

The following table shows how to create a zero-coupon bond and an annuity from two bonds with the same maturity but different coupon levels. Short selling is explained in detail in the chapter on arbitrage.

Table A.1. Creating a Zero-Coupon Bond and an Annuity

Creating a Zero-Coupon Bond			
	Time		
Action	0	1 . . .	n
Short sell $c_1/(c_2 - c_1)$ units of bond 2	$\dfrac{+c_1\,P_2}{c_2 - c_1}$	$\dfrac{-c_1\,c_2}{c_2 - c_1}$	$\dfrac{-c_1(c_2 + \text{par})}{c_2 - c_1}$
Buy $c_2/(c_2 - c_1)$ units of bond 1	$\dfrac{-c_1\,P_1}{c_2 - c_1}$	$\dfrac{+c_2\,c_1}{c_2 - c_1}$	$\dfrac{+c_2(c_1 + \text{par})}{c_2 - c_1}$
Net	$\dfrac{-(c_2\,P_1 - c_1\,P_2)}{c_2 - c_1}$	0 . . .	par

Creating an Annuity from Two Bonds			
	Time		
Action	0	1 . . .	n
Buy $1/(c_2 - c_1)$ units of bond 2	$\dfrac{-P_2}{c_2 - c_1}$	$\dfrac{+c_2}{c_2 - c_1}$	$\dfrac{+(c_2 + \text{par})}{c_2 - c_1}$
Short sell $1/(c_2 - c_1)$ units of bond 1	$\dfrac{+P_1}{c_2 - c_1}$	$\dfrac{-c_1}{c_2 - c_1}$	$\dfrac{-(c_1 + \text{par})}{c_2 - c_1}$
Net	$\dfrac{-(P_2 - P_1)}{c_2 - c_1}$	1 . . .	1

CHAPTER 8

Arbitrage for Bonds

An important idea in finance is the concept of *arbitrage*. In frictionless markets, arbitrage forces the same asset to have one price at a particular instant in time, no matter where it is traded. In some cases, arbitrage forces there to be a boundary on the price of one security relative to the price of another security.

As a simple example, consider a common stock traded on both the New York Stock Exchange and the NASDAQ at exactly the same point in time. If the stock has a price of $50 on the New York Stock Exchange and $53 on the NASDAQ, an arbitrager can simultaneously buy the stock at $50 and sell (short sell) it at $53 for an immediate and risk-free profit of $3. The purchase at $50 and the sale at $53 drive the prices together. Since the transactions are simultaneous, the arbitrager does not need capital to make arbitrage profits. Therefore, one arbitrager who repeatedly and rationally exploits price differences is able to drive the prices together.

Arbitrage is clearest in a world of frictionless financial markets, when the following assumptions will hold: (1) no taxes, (2) no default risk, (3) no transactions costs or storage costs, and (4) unrestricted short selling (defined below) is allowed. In practice, markets are not frictionless. Frictions can create differences between the prices of the same thing in different markets. Thus, a stock trading on the New York Stock Exchange and on the NASDAQ may have slightly different prices because of the transactions costs of buying in the lower-priced market and selling in the higher-priced market.

This chapter presents several examples of risk-free arbitrage linking the prices in fixed income markets. Fixed income markets have the feature that contractually binding cash flows for multiple periods are involved. We focus on default free Treasury securities.

Participants in financial markets often use the term arbitrage to refer to risky positions. For example, when a possible merger between two firms is being negotiated, some investors may buy the securities of one of the firms and short sell the securities of the other firm expecting to make a profit when the merger is finalized. This type of position is risky because the merger may not go through, and the position may result in losses. In contrast, profits are certain with risk-free arbitrage.

SHORT SELLING

An important aspect of some arbitrage positions is short selling. In a *short sale,* an investor sells a security that they do not own. Short sales may occur if an investor believes the price of security is going to decrease in the future. By short selling at the current higher price and purchasing at the expected lower future price, the investor hopes to make a gain. To carry out the short sale, the short seller borrows certificates of ownership from another investor who owns the security (see Figure 8.1). The short seller must pay the lender of the certificates any dividends due on the securities. When the short seller closes out the short sale by buying the security in the market, the new certificates are returned to the individual who lent the securities to the short seller. The short seller makes a profit (loss) if the securities are repurchased at a lower (higher) price. A short sale has no time limit. Short positions can remain in effect indefinitely as long as collateral requirements (discussed below) are met.

FIGURE 8.1 The Process of Short Selling.

In an *unrestricted short sale,* the short seller can use the proceeds from the sale. In practice, most short sellers are not able to use the proceeds because of the possibility of a short seller absconding with the funds. In addition, short sellers usually have to post *collateral* to guarantee against default. For example, if someone short-sold a security at $100 and the price moved up to $120, the short seller has an unrealized loss of $20. Unless collateral of at least $20 has been posted, the short seller might be tempted to default by simply walking away from the transaction. The lender of the securities has legal recourse, but at considerable expense.

The availability of securities to borrow for a short sale varies widely. There are typically fees paid to the certificate lenders. Sometimes these fees are low and sometimes much higher for securities not widely available. For example, for common stocks of large firms with active trading, fees paid to certificate lenders are low. For the stocks of smaller companies with limited availability, fees are higher and certificate lenders are hard to find. A similar pattern prevails in the bond markets. In some cases, borrowing certificates to short sell is impossible, and short sales are not possible.

Short sellers of stock must pay the dividend to the lender of the securities for two reasons. First, the lender of the securities is entitled to the dividend. Second, the holder of record of the stock at a particular point in time is entitled to the dividend. After this point in time, the holder of the stock is not entitled to the dividend. This point in time is called the ex-dividend point. When the stock goes ex-dividend, the stock price falls by the after-tax value of the dividends. If the short seller did not pay the dividends, the short seller could capture the value of the dividends by short selling immediately before the ex-dividend point in time and covering the short sale immediately after.

In the bond markets, bond prices are automatically adjusted daily for accrued interest. There is no sudden jump in the total price paid for a bond on the coupon payment date, and consequently no special payments have to be made by the short seller of a bond.

Short selling a bond is the equivalent of borrowing money. Table 8.1 illustrates the case when a two-period strip is shortsold. The short seller receives $90.70 immediately and pays back $100 two years later. The interest is $9.30 at the interest rate of 5% per annum for two periods. The opposite of short selling is buying. Buying a bond is the equivalent of lending money.

Table 8.1. Short Selling a Bond Equals Borrowing

	Points in Time		
	0	1	2
Cash Flows	+ $90.70	0	− $100

CONDITIONS FOR ARBITRAGE

In cases where the entire position can be closed out immediately, the arbitrage is straightforward. For example, if a stock sells for different prices in two markets, the stock can be purchased in the lower-priced market and immediately sold in the higher-priced market. The transaction is closed immediately and there are no future obligations.

In cases of multi-period cash flows such as bond markets, the existence of a profitable arbitrage is not as clear-cut. The following rule identifies an arbitrage opportunity. The logic of this is discussed in the Appendix to this chapter.

ARBITRAGE RULE: If the cumulative net cash flows from a position are never negative and may be positive in at least one period, an arbitrage opportunity exists.

The cumulative net cash flows are found by adding the cash flows starting from the present until the future date. Thus, the cumulative cash flows for time 1 are the sum of the time 0 and time 1 cash flows. The cumulative cash flows for time 2 are the sum of the time 0, time 1, and time 2 cash flows.[1]

In the case where the net cash flows in every period are 0 or positive, the cumulative cash flows need not be considered to test for the existence of an arbitrage opportunity. However, if the net cash flows during any time interval are negative, the cumulative cash flows need to be considered. A variety of examples are presented below to illustrate the operation of this rule about cumulative cash flows.

Arbitrage and Present Values

Arbitrage has many important applications in financial markets. In the following example, arbitrage is shown to constrain present values. Arbitrage guarantees that the present value of a dollar received later cannot have a value greater than a dollar received sooner. To prove this result by arbitrage, consider the following counter-example. Suppose a one-period strip with $100 par value has a price of $95.24 and a two-period strip with $100 par value has a price of $97. That is, the present value of $100 received at time 1 is $95.24 and the present value of $100 received at time 2 is $97.

The following arbitrage opportunity is available. Buy the one-period strip at a price of $95.24 and short sell the two-period strip at a price of $97. The cash flows are shown in Table 8.2.

---

[1] If future interest rates were known, positive cumulative cash flows might be reinvested. However, since there is no precise information about future interest rates, we assume no interest earned on cash flows carried forward into the future.

Table 8.2. Arbitrage Cash Flows

Action	Points in Time		
	0	1	2
Buy 1-Period Strip	− $95.24	+ $100	
Short sell 2-Period Strip	+ $97.00		− $100
Net Cash Flows	+ $1.76	+ $100	− $100
Cumulative Net Cash Flows	+ $1.76	+ $101.76	+ $1.76

The arbitrager makes a sure profit of $1.76 immediately. The $100 net cash inflow at time 1 can be used to pay off the cash outflow of $100 at time 2. Conceivably, interest might be earned from time 1 to time 2.

The cumulative net cash flows are found by adding net cash flows as we move from the present to the future. In Table 8.2, the cumulative net cash flows are always positive, indicating a sure profit. The sure profit from arbitrage is immediate and requires no collateral. Therefore, one arbitrager without any collateral can repeatedly engage in this arbitrage transaction until the profits from arbitrage disappear.

Arbitrage operations drive prices toward their equilibrium values. That is, purchase of the one-period strip by the arbitrager drives its price up; sale of the two-period strip forces its price down. Arbitrage profits cease to exist when the price of the one-period strip is greater than or equal to the price of the two-period strip, or when the present value of $1 received in one period is greater than or equal to the present value of $1 received in two periods.

In contrast, suppose that the price of a one-period strip is higher than the price of the two-period strip as shown in Table 8.3. Buying one two-period and short selling one one-period does not result in an arbitrage opportunity since the cumulative net cash flows are not always positive.

Table 8.3. A Non-Arbitrage Position

Action	Points in Time		
	0	1	2
Short 1-Period Strip	+ $95.24	− $100	
Buy 2-Period Strip	− $90.00		+ $100
Net Cash Flows	+ $5.24	− $100	+ $100
Cumulative Net Cash Flows	+ $5.24	− $94.76	+ $5.24

Arbitrage and Coupon-Bearing Bonds

Arbitrage guarantees that a bond with a higher coupon and the same maturity must have a higher price. In order for no arbitrage opportunities to exist, a linear relationship between bond price and bond coupons should exist. This is illustrated in Figure 8.2.

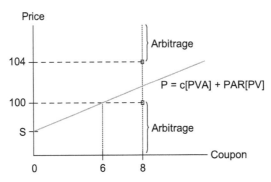

FIGURE 8.2 Several Arbitrage Possibilities.

Consider the counterexample in Table 8.4. Bonds G and H are two-period bonds with par values of $100 and prices of $100. Bond G has a coupon of $3 and bond H has a coupon of $4. The higher-coupon bond has the same price as the lower-coupon bond.

Table 8.4. Two-Period Bonds

		Points in Time	
	0	1	2
Bond G	– $100	+ $3	+ $103
Bond H	– $100	+ $4	+ $104

These prices present an arbitrage opportunity: short sell bond G and buy bond H. The cash flows are shown in Table 8.5.

Table 8.5. Arbitrage for Two-Period Bonds

		Points in Time	
	0	1	2
Short sell Bond G	+ $100	– $3	– $103
Buy Bond H	– $100	+ $4	+ $104
Net Cash Flows	0	+ $1	+ $1
Cumulative Net Cash Flows	0	+ $1	+ $2

At time 0, the net cash flow is zero; the net cash flows at times 1 and 2 are $1. The cumulative net cash flow is always zero or positive, resulting in a risk-free arbitrage profit. The actions of arbitragers push the price of bond H higher relative to bond G.

The arbitrage in Table 8.5 no longer results in a risk-free profit when the price of the higher-coupon bond exceeds the price of the lower-coupon bond. For example, if bond H has a price of $101, the cash flows from short selling one unit of bond G and buying one unit of bond H are shown in Table 8.6. There is a cash outflow of $1 at time 0 and cash inflows of $1 at times 1 and 2. This position is not a risk-free arbitrage since the cumulative net cash flows are negative in one period.

Table 8.6. Two-Period Bonds: No Arbitrage Profit

	Points in Time		
	0	1	2
Short sell Bond G	+ $100	– $3	– $103
Buy Bond H	– $101	+ $4	+ $104
Net Cash Flows	– $1	+ $1	+ $1
Cumulative Net Cash Flows	– $1	0	+ $1

Given the prices in Table 8.6, there are other arbitrage opportunities available. For example, an arbitrager can short sell 1.01% of bond G and buy one unit of bond H. This results in the arbitrage profit shown in Table 8.7.[2]

Table 8.7. Two-Period Bonds: Arbitrage Profit

	Points in Time		
	0	1	2
Short sell Bond G	+ $101	– $3.03	– $104.03
Buy Bond H	– $101	+ $4	+ $104.00
Net Cash Flows	– 0	+ $0.97	– $0.03
Cumulative Net Cash Flows	– 0	+ $0.97	+ $0.94

The arbitrage opportunity shown in table 8.7 will exist as long as the price of bond H is less than the price of bond G times 108 / 106 (= 1.018868). At this point, the forward interest rate implicit in the two bonds is zero. To see the logic, consider the case where the forward rate for period 2 reaches its lowest value of zero. Then the cash flows in Table 8.6 would be equivalent to the following cash flows.

---

[2] This example considers one arbitrage position. However, there may be multiple possible arbitrage positions.

Table 8.8. Two-Period Bonds Cash Flows Equivalent to One-Period Bonds

	Points in Time		
	0	1	2
Short sell Bond G	+ $100	− $106	
Buy Bond H	− $101	$108	

Since both of these bonds must be discounted at the one period spot rate $R_{0,1}$, the ratio of the price of H to the price of G must be at least equal to the ratio of the cash inflows at point in time 1. Thus, a lower bound of zero for the forward interest rate implies a lower bound for the price of bond H relative to bond G.

Discovering arbitrage opportunities requires finding the relatively underpriced and relatively overpriced securities. There is no simple formula for discovering arbitrage opportunities in the general case. Arbitrage opportunities can be discovered in the general case by using linear programming as discussed in the appendix to this chapter.

It is tempting to assume that higher yield to maturity indicates an arbitrage opportunity between two bonds. Although in some cases higher yield to maturity may indicate an arbitrage opportunity, a higher yield to maturity does not by itself imply an arbitrage opportunity.

Another Arbitrage Example

Table 8.9 contains an example in which bond G has a price of $100 and bond H has a price of $103. There is an arbitrage from buying bond G and short selling bond H. The net cash flows are negative in periods 1 and 2, but the net cash flow at time 0 is sufficiently large to create an arbitrage opportunity. The cumulative cash flows show unambiguously that an arbitrage opportunity exists, whereas the negative cash flows for periods 1 and 2 do not by themselves show an arbitrage opportunity.

Table 8.9. Two-Period Bonds: No Arbitrage Profit

	Points in Time		
	0	1	2
Buy Bond G	− $100	+ $3	+ $103
Short sell Bond H	+ $103	− $4	− $104
Net Cash Flows	+ $3	− $1	− $1
Cumulative Net Cash Flows	+ $3	+ $2	+ $1

REPLICATING PORTFOLIOS

Arbitrage occurs if a particular security can be created from a portfolio of other securities at a lower price (the replicating portfolio). Assume a particular investment with price of P_0 has a set of future cash inflows. A replicating portfolio (or combination of securities) has the same future cash flows and current value of P_R. The prices of the investment and the replicating portfolio should be the same (i.e., $P_0 = P_R$). Otherwise there will be arbitrage opportunities.

The concept of replicating portfolios can be illustrated by a counterexample, a case where arbitrage opportunities exist. Assume a two-period bond with price of $100, annual coupon of $4, and par value of $100. There are Treasury strips with $100 par values: a one-period Treasury strip with price of $96 and a two-period Treasury strip with a price of $90. These three bonds are shown in Table 8.10.

Table 8.10. Cash Flows from Three Bonds

Bonds	Points in Time		
	0	1	2
2-Period Bond	$100	$4	$104
1-Period Strip	$96	$100	
2-Period Strip	$90		$100

Assuming that strips are divisible, there is an arbitrage opportunity between the coupon-bearing bond and a combination of strips, as shown in Table 8.11. Suppose we try to duplicate the future cash flows on the coupon bearing bond from a combination of strips. In order to have a cash inflow of $4 at time 1, 4% of a one-period strip can be purchased for a time 0 cost of (0.04)($96), but with a cash inflow of (0.04)($100) at time 1. To receive a $104 cash flow from strips at time 2, 104% of a two-period strip must be purchased. The purchase price of this strip is (1.04)($90) at time 0. Thus, by buying 4% of a one-period strip and 104% of a two-period strip, the time 1 and time 2 cash flows on the coupon-bearing bond are replicated, but the total purchase price of the strips is $2.56 less than the sale price of the coupon-bearing bond shown in Table 8.11.

Table 8.11. Arbitrage between Coupon-Bearing Bond and Strips

	Points in Time		
	0	1	2
Short Two-Period Bond	+ $100	– $4	– $104
Buy 4% of a One-Period Strip	– $3.84	+ $4	
Buy 104% of a Two-Period Strip	– $93.60		+ $104
Net Cash Flows	+ $2.56	0	0
Cumulative Net Cash Flows	+ $2.56	+ $2.56	+ $2.56

Because the prices of strips are too low relative to the price of the coupon-bearing bond, the actions of arbitragers will force the prices to adjust until there is no arbitrage opportunity. Arbitrage by itself does not tell us which of the prices will change. However, there would be no arbitrage profit if the price of the two-period strip becomes $92.46, as shown in Table 8.12.

Table 8.12. Cash Flows in Equilibrium if the Price of a 2-Period Strip is $92.46

	Points in Time		
	0	1	2
Short Two-Period Bond	+ $100	– $4	– $104
Buy 4% of a One-Period Strip	– $3.84	+ $4	
Buy 104% of a Two-Period Strip	– $96.16		+ $104
Net Cash Flows	0	0	0
Cumulative net Cash Flows	0	0	0

In practice, Treasury bond dealers look for arbitrage opportunities by comparing the prices of strips and strippable coupon-bearing bonds. If a bond is worth more as strips, bond dealers will purchase coupon-bearing bonds and strip them, selling off the individual parts as strips. If a coupon-bearing bond has a greater value than individual strips, bond dealers purchase a portfolio of strips and reconstitute it into a coupon-bearing bond. Dealer arbitrage between strips and coupon-bearing bonds can be carried out rapidly and at almost no cost. If the dealer buys a bond and sells it off as strips or if the dealer buys a portfolio of strips and reconstitutes these as a bond, the dealer is left with an immediate profit and no future cash flow obligations, resulting in a powerful arbitrage.

In some other arbitrage positions, the positions cannot be closed out immediately for a profit but must be held for some period of time. In these cases, collateral may need to be posted to guarantee performance, creating a possible divergence in prices. One such example is the case of coupon strips versus par strips. When a bond is stripped, the coupon and principal in the last time period are decomposed into two separate securities, coupon strips and par strips, which are not interchangeable in reconstituting a bond. These two strips may sell at different prices although they each pay exactly the same amount at maturity. If collateral is required for arbitrage, there is no risk-free arbitrage between them, and the prices of principal strips and coupon strips do not have to be identical.

CREATING FORWARD CONTRACTS FROM SPOT SECURITIES

This section discusses the link between spot and forward markets, laying the groundwork for the link between spot and futures markets. The primary lesson of this section is that arbitrage provides a fundamental link between the spot and forward markets. Market activity in forward markets is often limited, but there is enormous trading in futures markets. Futures and forward markets are very similar with the primary difference being the requirement of posting of collateral in futures markets. This difference is discussed in detail in the chapter on futures markets.

An investor can create a forward position from spot securities in a frictionless market. The two-period case for strips provides the basic insight. A long forward position has a zero cash flow at time 0, an outflow at time 1, and an inflow at time 2, as shown in Table 8.13.

Table 8.13. Long Forward Position

	Points in Time		
	0	1	2
Long forward	0	− Forward price	+ Par

Creating a forward position requires finding some combination of one-period and two-period spot securities having the same cash flows as a forward position in Table 8.13. The necessary positions are shown in Table 8.14. Go long (buy) a single two-period strip and simultaneously short sell x percent of a one-period strip, with the constraint that the net cash flows at time 0 are zero. Algebraically, find a value of x such that $xS_1 = S_2$, implying that x must equal S_2 / S_1. The time 0 net cash flows have a sum of zero; the time 1 net cash flows are an outflow equal to S_2 / S_1, which is the forward price; at time 2 there is a cash inflow of $1. This set of cash flows is defined as a long forward position—that is, a loan of funds in the forward market.

Table 8.14. Creating a Long Forward Position

		Points in Time	
Actions (at time 0)	0	1	2
Long 1 two-period strip	$-S_2$		$+\$100$
Short S_2 / S_1 one-period bonds	$+S_1 \left[\dfrac{S_2}{S_1}\right]$	$-\left[\dfrac{S_2}{S_1}\right]100$	
Net = long forward	0	$-\left[\dfrac{S_2}{S_1}\right]100$	$+\$100$

The amount S_2 / S_1 is a forward price; it represents the time 1 value of $1 received at time 2. Denote this forward price as $F_{0,DEL=1}$, the forward price observed at time 0 for delivery at time 1. The definitions of forward price, forward rate, and of S_1 and S_2 imply that:

$$F_{0,DEL=1} = \frac{S_2}{S_1} = \frac{1}{1+f_{0,2}} \qquad 8.1$$

To illustrate the relationship between spot and forward interest rates, consider the following example. Assume $R_{0,1} = 0.02$, $PV_1 = 0.9804$, $R_{0,2} = 0.05$, $PV_2 = 0.9070$, $f_{0,2} = 0.0809$, $F_{0,DEL=1} = 0.9252$. The price of a one-period strip is $98.04 and a two-period strip is $90.70. Then the operations shown in Table 8.15 create a long (lend) forward position from a spot position. Table 8.16 shows the operations to create a short forward position, which is the equivalent of borrowing in the forward market.

Table 8.15. Creating a Long Forward Position

		Points in Time	
Actions (at time 0)	0	1	2
Long 1 two-period strip	$-\$90.70$		$+\$100$
Short .9070 / .9802 one-period bonds	$+\$90.70$	$-\$92.53$	
Net = long forward	0	$-\$92.53$	$+\$100$

Table 8.16. Creating a Short Forward (Borrowing) Position

Actions (at time 0)	Points in Time		
	0	1	2
Short 1 two-period strip	+ $90.70		– $100
Long .9071 / .9802 one-period bonds	– 90.70	+ $92.53	
Net = short forward	0	+ $92.53	– $100

The forward interest rate is the discount rate for which $100 at time 2 has a value of $92.53 at time 1. That is, the forward rate $f_{0,2}$ satisfies the following equation: $92.53 = \$100 / (1 + f_{0,2})$. The resulting forward interest rate is 8.06%. The two-period spot interest rate of 5% is the geometric average of the one-period interest rate of 2% and the forward rate of 8.06%. That is, $(1.05)^2 = (1.02)(1.0806)$.[3]

ARBITRAGE AND FORWARD INTEREST RATES

Arbitrage forces a precise relationship between actual forward interest rates and the forward interest rates implied by the spot interest rates. In our example, the implied forward rate is 8.06%. If the actual forward interest rate is different, arbitragers will enter the market and force the actual interest rate and the interest rate implied by spot prices to become equal.

What happens if the market for actual forward loans has an interest rate of 15% at the same time that the forward interest rate implied by spot prices is 8.06%? Arbitragers are able to profit and, by their exploitation of profit opportunities, drive all interest rates toward equilibrium values.

The arbitrage operation to profit from the price disparity is to borrow at 8.06% and lend at 15%. To borrow at the implied forward rate of 8.06% requires the short forward position in Treasury strips shown in Table 8.16. The arbitrage is shown in Table 8.17. This arbitrage is completely risk-free since the investor taking this position has a certain profit at time 1. The arbitrage operations force interest rates toward their equilibrium values. That is, lending at 15% forces this rate down; borrowing at 8.06% forces this rate up. Arbitrage ceases to be profitable when the two rates are identical.

---

[3] The preceding analysis for strips can logically be extended coupon bearing bonds.

Table 8.17. Arbitrage Position: Lend at 15% and Borrow (Short forward) at 8.06%.

Actions (at time 0)	Points in Time		
	0	1	2
Lend forward at 15% Short 1 two-period strip and	0	− $100/1.15 = −$86.96	+ $100
Long .9070 / .9804 one-period strips	0	+ $92.53	− $100
Net	0	+ $5.57	0

Suppose the market for actual forward loans has an interest rate of 5% at the same time that the implied forward interest rate is 8.06%. The arbitrage operation is to borrow at 5% and lend (long forward) at 8.06%. The arbitrage is shown in Table 8.18. Borrowing at the 5% actual forward interest rate forces this rate up; lending at 8.06% forces this rate down until the two rates are identical.

Table 8.18. Arbitrage Position: Lend at 8.06% and Borrow (Short forward) at 5%

Actions (at time 0)	Points in Time		
	0	1	2
Borrow forward at 5% Long 1 two-period strip and	0	+ $100/1.05 = +$95.24	− $100
Short .9070 / .9804 one-period strips		− $92.53	+ $100
Net	0	+ $2.71	0

ARBITRAGE PROOF OF LINEAR RELATIONSHIP BETWEEN BOND PRICE AND COUPON

In frictionless markets, arbitrage guarantees a linear relationship between bond coupon level and bond price for bonds with the same maturity, i.e., $P = c\,(PVA_n) + (PAR)\,(PV_n)$. To prove this, consider a case where a linear relationship does not exist. Consider three bonds with coupons and prices such that $c_1 < c_2 < c_3$ and $P_1 < P_2 < P_3$.

There are two nonequilibrium cases to examine shown in Figure 8.3. In the first case, the price of a bond with coupon c_2 is above the straight line joining P_1 and P_3. We call this price P_2^{high}. Then an investor can create a portfolio of bonds 1 and 3 with the same coupon and face value as bond 2. Assume that the arbitrager invests $w\%$ in bond 1 and $(1-w)\%$ in bond 3, with the constraint that the total coupon is equal to c_2. That is, $c_2 = (w)(c_1) + (1-w)(c_3)$. Solving for w leads to

$$w = \frac{c_3 - c_2}{c_3 - c_1} \qquad 8.2$$

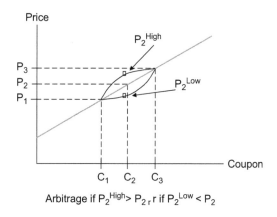

An arbitrager can short sell bond 2 for P_2^{high} and buy $w\%$ of bond 1 and $(1 - w)\%$ of bond 3. The portfolio of bonds 1 and 3 will have a coupon equal to c_2, a face value of PAR [that is, $wPAR + (1 - w)PAR = PAR$], and a portfolio price of $wP_1 + (1 - w)P_3$. From the geometry of the figure, the portfolio price must be less than P_2^{high}. The arbitrager profits by the difference. This is illustrated by the example in Figure 8.3.

Second, if the bond price P_2^{low} is below the straight line joining bonds 1 and 3, the investor can buy bond 2 and short sell a combination of bonds 1 and 3 with a higher present value but identical coupon and face value as bond 2. The arbitrager makes a profit from this difference. If there are taxes, the relationship between price and coupon becomes more complicated.

As an example, suppose that $PV_1 = \$.95$, $PV_2 = \$.90$, and therefore $PVA_2 = \$1.85$. Since the price of a bond in a perfect market would be the present value of the annuity of coupons plus the present value of par, the prices of two-year bonds with par values of $100 and coupons of $3, $4, and $5 should be $95.70, $97.40, and $99.10, respectively. Suppose that the bond with the coupon of $4 has a price of $98. Then the arbitrager should short sell one unit of the $4 coupon bond and should buy a portfolio composed of one-half of a unit of the $3 coupon bond and one-half of a unit of the $5 coupon bond. The one-half is found by plugging the coupons into equation (8.2), that is $(\$5 - \$4)/(\$5 - \$3) = 1/2$. The arbitrage operations are shown in Table 8.19. Arbitragers continue to make profits until their actions force the prices of the three bonds to be in line.

If the bond with the $4 coupon sold for less than $97.40, the arbitrage is to buy this bond and short sell a portfolio composed of half of each of the other bonds. Arbitrage will continue until the prices of the three bonds are in line.

Table 8.19. Two-Period Bonds: Arbitrage Profit

	Points in Time		
	0	1	2
Buy 0.50 units of bond with $3 coupon	− $95.70 / 2	+$3 / 2	+$103 / 2
Buy 0.50 units of bond with $5 coupon	− $99.10 / 2	+ $5 / 2	+ $105 / 2
Short sell 1.0 units of bond with $4 coupon	+ $98.00	− $4	− $104
Net Cash Flows	+ $.60	0	0
Cumulative Net Cash Flows	+ $.60	0	0

SUMMARY

Arbitrage is the simultaneous purchase and sale of securities to benefit from price disparities. The arbitrager buys at the relatively low price and sells at the relatively high price. These actions force the prices to be in equilibrium. In some cases, arbitrage puts bounds on the relative prices of securities.

A replicating portfolio has the same future cash flows as a particular security. If the future cash flows are the same, the prices should be the same. If not, arbitrage opportunities are available and drive prices together.

QUESTIONS AND PROBLEMS

1. A one-period strip has a price of $96.50 and par value of $100. A two-period strip has a price of $97 and par value of $100. Show the arbitrage opportunity.
2. A two-period bond has an annual coupon of $3, par value of $100, and price of $98.50. Another two-period bond has an annual coupon of $3.50, par value of $100, and price of $98.50. Are there any arbitrage opportunities?
3. In problem 2, is there an arbitrage opportunity if the $3.50 coupon bond has a price of $98.75?
4. In problem 2, suppose the $3.50 coupon bond has a price of $101, are there arbitrage opportunities?
5. The coupon on a two-period par bond is $5. A one-period strip has a price of $96.45 and a two-period strip has a price of $92.75. Are there arbitrage opportunities? Explain.

6. Suppose that $R_{0,1}$ is 3% and $R_{0,2}$ is 6%. For one-period and two-period strips with $100 par values, show the operations to create: (a) a long forward position, (b) a short forward position.

7. Assuming the term structure in the preceding problem, show the arbitrage operations if the actual forward interest rate is:

    (a) 15%

    (b) 5%

8. Suppose that you buy a three-year bond with annual coupons of $7 and par value of $100 for a price of $102. One-year, two-year, and three-year strips with $100 par values sell for $95, $90, and $85 respectively. Suppose that you short sell 7% of the one-period strip, short sell 100% of the three-period strip, and short sell 11.50% of the two-period strip. Is this an arbitrage position? What would describe this position?

9. A five-year bond has a price of $100, annual coupon of $5, and par value of $100. An eight-year bond has a price of $100, annual coupon of $3, and par value of $100. Are there any arbitrage opportunities?

10. Suppose there are three two-year bonds with par values of $100 and with coupons of $3, $4, $5 and that the prices of one-year and two-year strips are $97 and $93. In a perfect market, what should be the prices of bonds with coupons of $3, $4, and $5? If the bond with the $4 coupon sells for $101, describe the arbitrage opportunities. If the bond with the $4 coupon sells for $100, describe the arbitrage opportunities.

11. Suppose that there is a spot market for Treasury strips and a forward market. A one-period strip with $100 par value sells for $95.50 and a two-period strip sells for $92.25 per $100 of par in the spot market. In the forward market for strips for delivery in one year, strips have quotes of $97.00 per $100 of par. Are there any arbitrage opportunities available?

12. A one-period strip has a spot interest rate of 8% and par value of $100. A two-period strip has a spot interest rate of 3.80% and par value of $100. Are there any arbitrage opportunities?

APPENDIX: FINDING ARBITRAGE OPPORTUNITIES

Finding arbitrage opportunities requires comparing the prices and future cash flows of different securities or combinations of securities. The underpriced security should be purchased and the overpriced security should be (short) sold. In some cases an arbitrage opportunity can be found by inspection. A general solution requires the use of linear programming. Linear programming searches through all feasible combinations of securities and determines whether there is a combination of purchases and short sales that result in an arbitrage opportunity. The following three-year and three-security example illustrates the procedure.

Table A8.1. Finding Arbitrage Opportunities for 3 Bonds

	Points in Time		
0	1	2	3
$-P_1 x_1$	$+c_1$	$+c_1$	$+c_1 + P_1$
$-P_2 x_2$	$+c_2$	$+c_2$	$+c_2 + P_2$
$-P_3 x_3$	$+c_3$	$+c_3$	$+c_3 + P_3$
SUM_0	SUM_1	SUM_2	SUM_3

In Table A8.1, the prices of securities are denoted by P, the coupons by c, the par value by par. Each of the three securities in the example has a subscript to differentiate it from the other securities. The arbitrager purchases or short sells x_j % of each security, assuming x_j is constrained to be larger than –1 and less than +1. The sum of the cash flows at each point in time is denoted by SUM with a subscript for the point in time. The linear programming solution maximizes the sum of the cash flows at time 0 subject to constraints that the cumulative sum of cash flows at each point in time is never negative and that each of the x variables lies between –1 and +1. If the sum of the cash flows at time 0 is positive and the constraints hold, there is an arbitrage opportunity. Otherwise, there is no arbitrage opportunity.

The problem is as follows:

Objective Function: Maximize SUM_0

Subject to the following constraints:

$$SUM_0 + SUM_1 \geq 0$$

$$SUM_0 + SUM_1 + SUM_2 \geq 0$$

$$SUM_0 + SUM_1 + SUM_2 + SUM_3 \geq 0$$

$$-1 \leq x_j \leq +1, \text{ for } j = 1, 2, 3 \qquad \textbf{A8.1}$$

The objective function of the linear programming solution tries to maximize the sum of the cash flows at time zero subject to the constraints that the cumulative net cash flows at each point in time are never negative and the amount invested in each bond is between –1 and +1. There is an arbitrage opportunity if the linear programming solution finds the sum at time zero to be positive. Otherwise there is no arbitrage opportunity.

The linear programming solution in equation A8.1 maximizes the time zero cash flow. It is possible that maximizing the cash flow at a later point in time with the constraint that all cumulative net cash flows are nonnegative will result in an arbitrage realized at some future date.

A method for discovering the existence of an arbitrage opportunity at some future date is to maximize the cumulative sum of the cash flows at the most distant point in time subject to the constraints that the cumulative net cash flows at every prior point in time (including time 0) are nonnegative. There will be an arbitrage opportunity if the cumulative sum of the cash flows at the most distant point in time is positive. This is the rule that was presented earlier in this chapter.

Maximizing the cumulative sum of the cash flows at the most distant point in time allows for the possibility that an arbitrage opportunity is available at some future point in time, but not at time 0. This more general rule allows for this possibility.

CHAPTER 9

Term Structure of Interest Rates

This chapter focuses upon the reasons why interest rates differ by maturity, or *term*. A schedule of spot interest rates by maturity is called the *term structure of interest rates*. The term structure can be rising, flat, declining, or humped.

The first part of the chapter focuses on historical patterns observed for the term structure. The second part of the chapter deals with theories explaining the term structure of interest rates.

PATTERNS IN YIELD CURVES

The most frequent shape for yield curves is upward-sloping. Downward-sloping yield curves have occurred at the end of the expansion phase of business cycles, especially when the Federal Reserve is tightening monetary conditions. This business cycle pattern for the term structure is illustrated in Figure 9.1.

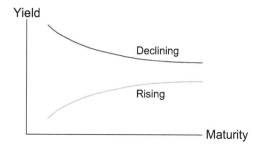

FIGURE 9.1 Business Cycle Patterns for the Term Structure.

This pattern implies the following three empirical regularities for term structures:

1. The most common yield curve shape is upward-sloping.
2. Declining yield curves occur when interest rates are historically high.
3. Short-term interest rates are more variable than long-term interest rates.

Historical evidence indicates another empirical regularity of the term structure:

4. The prices of long-term bonds are more variable than the prices of short-term bonds.

Although the prices of long-term bonds are more variable than those of short-term bonds, the yields on short-term bonds are more variable. These are not contradictory statements as is shown by the following simple example. Consider a one-year bond and a thirty-year bond, each with a price and par value of $100 and coupons of $5, implying yields to maturity of 5% on each of the bonds. Suppose the yield on the one-year bond increases by 2% to 7% and that the yield on the thirty-year bond increases by 1% to 6%. Then, the new prices are

One-year bond

$$P = \frac{\$105}{1.07} = \$98.13 \qquad \textbf{9.1}$$

Thirty-year bond

$$P = \$5 PVA_{30,5\%} + \$100 PV_{30,5} \qquad \textbf{9.2}$$

Where $PVA_{30,5\%}$ is the present value of a $1 annuity for thirty periods at 5% and $PV_{30,5\%}$ is the present value of $1 receives thirty periods from now and discounted at 5% interest rate.

Although the change in the interest rate on the thirty-year bond is one-half the change in rate on the one-year bond, the percentage change in price for the thirty-year bond is many times as large. For the longer-term bond, the change in interest rates compounded over thirty periods causes a large price reaction.

In general, the percentage change in bond price is approximately equal to the duration times the change in yield. Formally,

$$\% \Delta Price = [\,Modified\ Duration\,][\,\Delta y\,] \qquad \textbf{9.3}$$

For long-term bonds, the duration is very large. Although the change in yield is relatively small for long-term bonds, the duration effect is big enough to dominate. Thus, the total change in price for long-term bonds is bigger than for short-term bonds.

Any complete theory of the term structure should predict all of the preceding regularities. No single theory described below predicts all of the empirical regularities. Thus, no single theory is a complete explanation of the term structure. However, each theory provides some interesting insight into the term structure.

SEGMENTED MARKETS THEORY

In the segmented markets theory, a separate market exists for each maturity. Interest rates for each maturity are set by demand and supply for funds for that maturity. In this theory, investors do not shift between different maturities. In the segmented markets theory, some investors (for example, commercial banks) confine their holdings of bonds to short maturities, whereas other investors (such as life insurance companies) purchase long-term bonds exclusively and hold these to maturity. Thus, short-term and long-term markets exist independent of the other maturities.

The segmented markets theory is consistent with any shape of yield curve, but it does not predict any of the empirical regularities of the term structure. Researchers have found some evidence that the demand for bonds and the supply of bonds of different maturities affects the yields for those maturities.

INCREASING LIQUIDITY PREMIUMS

In the theory of increasing liquidity premiums, yields increase as maturity increases. This theory makes several implicit assumptions. First, bond investors are risk-averse (i.e., they prefer lower variability of return) and prefer the shortest maturity bond. Second, bond prices for longer-term bonds are more variable. Third, borrowers are ignored. Under these assumptions, bond investors require higher yields to maturity on longer-term bonds to compensate for the higher risk.

If all investors are risk-neutral, the expected rate of return on all investments equals the risk-free interest rate, implying a flat term structure. If investors are risk-averse, the required rate of return should equal the risk-free interest rate plus a risk premium for the higher return variability of longer-maturity bonds. Figure 9.2 illustrates the increasing liquidity premium theory.

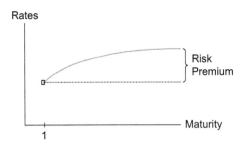

FIGURE 9.2 Increasing Liquidity Premium Theory.

Empirically, longer-maturity bonds have a larger percentage price changes than shorter maturity bonds. This empirical pattern provides logical support for the increasing liquidity premium theory. However, the theory of increasing liquidity premiums, by itself, implies yield curves that are always rising. The empirical evidence contradicts this implication since sometimes the yield curve is downward sloping or has a humped back shape. Nevertheless, since yield curves are upward sloping most of the time, the increasing liquidity premium theory has substantial credibility.

The liquidity premium theory overlooks bond issuers. Some bond issuers may prefer long-term funds, locking in a fixed interest rate. Other bond issuers may prefer short-term or intermediate-term funds. A complete term structure theory should account for the maturity needs of all borrowers.

In summary, the increasing liquidity premium theory has the ability to explain the fact that yield curves are rising most of the time but does not explain all yield curve shapes.

EXPECTATIONS HYPOTHESIS

A widely discussed theory of the term structure of interest rates is the expectations hypothesis. In the expectations hypothesis, the current forward interest rates are determined by the market's anticipations of future spot interest rates. For the two-period case, the forward rate for period 2 is a predictor of the one-period spot interest rate one period into the future. In mathematical terms:

$$f_{0,2} = E\,[R_{1,1}] \qquad \textbf{9.4}$$

Where:

$f_{0,2}$ = forward interest rate for period 2.

$E[R_{1,1}]$ = the expected one-period spot interest rate observed one period from now.

In other words, the forward interest rate is determined by people's anticipation of the average spot interest rate next period. The unbiased expectations hypothesis links the forward rates observed today to expectations of future spot interest rates. Figure 9.3 illustrates that the forward interest rate for time period 2, $f_{0,2}$, is the mean of the spot rates expected one period from now, $R_{1,1}$. If today's spot rates are the geometric mean of today's forward rates, this hypothesis ties today's spot interest rates to spot interest rates expected to prevail in the future.

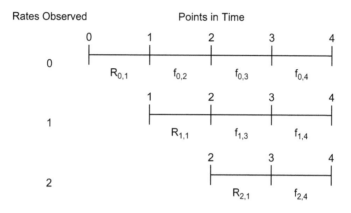

FIGURE 9.3 Forward Rate $f_{0,2}$ is the Expected Spot Interest Rate One Time Period from Now, $R_{1,1}$.

In the general case

$$f_{0,j} = E\,[R_{j-1,1}] \qquad 9.5$$

Where:

E = the expectation.

$f_{0,j}$ = the forward rate observed at time o (presubscript) for period j (postsubscript).

$R_{j-1,1}$ = the spot rate observed at time j-1 (presubscript) and lasting one period (postsubscript).

Figure 9.4 shows the link between anticipated future spot interest rates and today's forward interest rates.

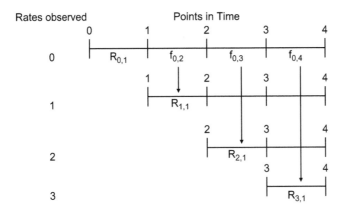

FIGURE 9.4 Forward Interest Rates and Expected Future Spot Rates.

Figure 9.5 shows that the forward interest, $f_{0,2}$, is the mean of the anticipated future spot rate, $R_{1,1}$, observed one period later. In the expectations hypothesis, the forward interest rate on average, equals the subsequent spot rate. In the theory, the forward rate $f_{0,3}$ is an unbiased predictor of the spot rate $R_{2,1}$ observed two periods later, and so on.

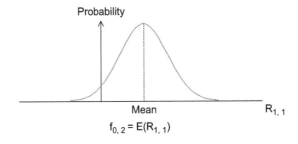

FIGURE 9.5 Expectations Hypothesis: Forward Rates Predict Future Spot Rates.

The unbiased expectations hypothesis is consistent with any yield curve shape. Under this hypothesis, a flat yield curve occurs if the market expects all future interest rates to equal the current one-period spot rate. For example, if the current spot rate is 6% and all expected future spot rates are 6%, all current forward and spot rates are 6%. See Figure 9.6.

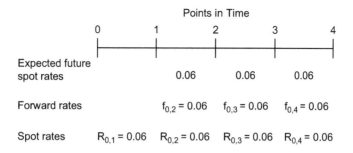

FIGURE 9.6 Example of a Flat Term Structure.

If the market anticipates higher future interest rates, the yield curve rises. In Figure 9.7, the market expects rising future interest rates, and the current spot rates also rise.[1]

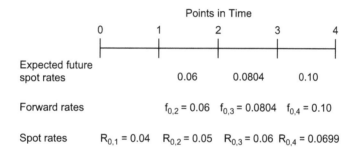

FIGURE 9.7 Example of a Rising Term Structure.

If the forward interest rates decline monotonically, the spot rates decline also. One of the empirical regularities mentioned above is the tendency for declining yield curves to occur when interest rates are high by historical standards. The unbiased expectations hypothesis is consistent with this pattern if the market is forecasting interest rates to decline from their current levels. Figure 9.8 illustrates how a declining yield curve can occur.

---

[1] The spot rates are computed from the following formula:

$$(1 + R_{o,n})^n = (1 + R_{o,1})(1 + f_{o,2}) \ldots (1 + f_{o,n}).$$

For example, for the four-period case:

$$(1 + R_{o,4})^4 = (1 + R_{o,1})(1 + f_{o,2})(1 + f_{o,3})(1 + f_{o,4}).$$

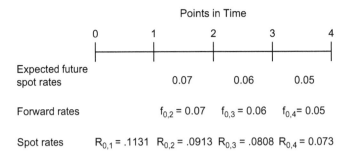

FIGURE 9.8 Example of a Declining Term Structure.

An unusual and interesting yield curve shape is the humped (or humpbacked) yield curve. Humped yield curves occur when interest rates are high by historical standards. Under the unbiased expectations hypothesis, humped yield curves occur if the market expects interest rates to rise for a while and then to decline. Figure 9.9 presents an example where the current spot rate is 5.01%. Then the forward rate rises to 7% and subsequently declines to 6% and 5%.

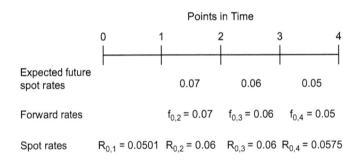

FIGURE 9.9 Example of a Humpbacked Term Structure.

A humpbacked yield curve occurred in 1979 when the Federal Reserve began a policy of tightening interest rates that would eventually lead to very high interest rates and a recession with declining interest rates. The bond market correctly foresaw that interest rates would go up for a while and then decline when the recession began. This real-life case is clearly consistent with the expectations hypothesis.

The expectations hypothesis has been criticized by some observers for making the unrealistic behavioral assumption that investors can forecast very distant future interest rates. These distant forecasts are essential for setting the forward interest rates in the expectations hypothesis. How can investors be expected to forecast interest rates 10, 15, 20, or 25 years into the future when there is so much uncertainty about events over these long horizons?

Testing the Expectations Hypothesis

One way of testing the expectations hypothesis is to compare forward rate forecasts with actually observed subsequent spot rates. The evidence indicates that forward interest rates are on average higher than the subsequently observed spot rates. In addition, the difference between forward rates and subsequently observed spot rates increases for longer maturities. The upward bias of forward rates suggests that forward rates incorporate risk premiums that increase with more distant maturities.

Another way of testing the expectations hypothesis is to compare the holding period returns for bonds of different maturities. If the expectations hypothesis is correct, the holding period returns for bonds of all maturities will be the same. Empirical studies have found that the holding period return for bonds increases as bond maturity gets longer. These results also indicate a risk premium built into forward rates. The appendix to this chapter provides formal proof that these two forms of testing are essentially equivalent.

Pros and Cons of the Expectations Hypothesis

The expectations hypothesis has a number of positive aspects. This theory relates the shape of the current yield curve to anticipations of interest rates in the future. Both borrowers and lenders should logically consider future borrowing and lending alternatives. The expectations hypothesis considers the impact of these forecasts of the future on the shape of the current yield curve. The expectations hypothesis can explain in a logical fashion why declining yield (or humpbacked) curves might occur. The expectations hypothesis is consistent with any shape of the yield curve.

On the negative side, forward rates tend to be relatively high forecasts of subsequent spot rates with the forecast error increasing as the maturity gets more distant. Since most of the time the yield curve is upward sloping, if the expectations hypothesis were true, market participants would be forecasting higher rates most of the time. This would be inconsistent with the fact that, at least in the short run, interest rates follow a random walk with increases and decreases being equally likely.[2] In addition, forecasting interest rates at distant dates may not be practical.

---

[2] There is evidence that over long periods of time security prices and interest rates tend to follow mean reverting process.

COMBINED THEORY

Combining the unbiased expectations hypothesis with the liquidity premium theory results in a more powerful theory.[3] This theory says that the forward rate of interest depends upon the expected spot rate in the future and a liquidity premium. The liquidity premium is assumed to increase for longer maturities (that is, L_j is greater than or equal to L_{j-1}).

$$f_{o,j} = E\left[R_{j-1,1}\right] + L_j \qquad \text{9.6}$$

where L_j is the liquidity premium for maturity j.

The combined theory is consistent with any shape of the yield curve and predicts upward sloping yield curves most of the time. Both of these are consistent with observed yield curves.

Since the forward rate in the combined theory equals the expected future spot rate plus a liquidity premium, rising term structures will be observed even if the market forecasts that the average interest rate in the future will remain constant For example, suppose the market expects the future spot interest rate to be 5% indefinitely into the future. In addition, there is a liquidity premium that increases with maturity, specifically a liquidity premium of 1% for period 2, 1.5% for period 3, and 2% for period 4. Then, the forward and spot rates are as shown in Figure 9.10. The spot interest rates increase with maturity, although the market expects future spot rates to be unchanged from the current one-period spot rate.

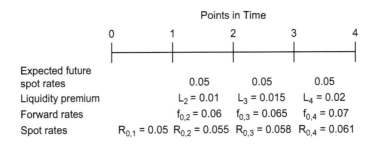

FIGURE 9.10 Rising Term Structure and Constant Expected Rates.

SUMMARY

Yield curves exhibit several empirical regularities: (1) the most common yield curve shape is upward-sloping; (2) declining yield curves occur when interest rates are

---

[3] Some authors call this the liquidity premium theory.

historically high; (3) short-term interest rates are more variable than long-term interest rates; and (4) long-term bond prices are more variable than short-term bond prices.

Major theories of the term structure are the segmented markets theory, the increasing liquidity premium theory, and the expectations hypothesis. Each of these theories provides some insights, but none provides a complete explanation of yield curves.

Combining the increasing liquidity premium theory and the expectations hypothesis results in a theory implying that interest rates for different maturities depend upon expected future interest rates and risk premiums that increase with maturity. This combined theory can explain any shape of the term structure and is also consistent with the tendency for the term structure to slope upward most of the time.

QUESTIONS AND PROBLEMS

1. Describe the major empirical regularities of the term structure of interest rates.
2. Explain each of the major term structure theories.
3. To what extent are the theories consistent with the empirical regularities?
4. Which of the term structure theories are consistent with rising, flat, declining, or humped yield curves?
5. Suppose an initially flat term structure with all interest rates equal to 6%.
   (a) Compute the price change for a one-year par bond if the interest rate increases by 2%. Then compute the price change on a perpetual par bond if the interest rate on this bond increases by 1%.
   (b) Compute the durations of each bond. Which bond has a greater percentage price change and why?
6. Suppose the one-period spot interest rate is 2% and the forward interest rate is 4%. Compute the holding period return over the next period for a two-period zero-coupon bond for each of the following values for next period's spot interest rate: 2%, 4%, and 6%.
7. You observe the following spot interest rates. What structure theories are consistent with this pattern?

Maturity (Years)	Spot Rate
1	8%
2	4%
3	2%
4	1%

8. Assume the combined theory explains the term structure. The one-period spot rate is 2%, the expected spot rate next period is 5%, and the liquidity premium is 2%. Compute the forward interest rate.

9. Suppose that we observe the following prices on strips with $100 par values: $S_1 = \$97.09$; $S_2 = \$94.00$; $S_3 = \$90.00$; $S_4 = \$85.00$. Which term structure theories are consistent with these strips prices?

10. Suppose that we observe the following prices on strips with $100 par values: $S_1 = \$97.09$; $S_2 = \$94.00$; $S_3 = \$90.00$; $S_4 = \$90.85$. Which term structure theories are consistent with these strips prices?

11. Suppose that the combined theory explains the term structure of interest rates. The current one-period spot interest rate is 4.5%. The market expects interest rates next period to increase by x%. There is a liquidity premium of 1.5%. The two-period spot interest rate is current 5.74%. What is the expected increase in the spot interest rate over the next period?

APPENDIX: FORWARD RATES AS PREDICTORS VERSUS HOLDING PERIOD RETURNS

This appendix shows that testing the ability of forward rates to predict subsequent spot rates is essentially equivalent to comparing holding period returns for bonds of different maturities. The analysis focuses on zero-coupon bonds (strips). Essentially, the same results should apply for coupon bearing bonds, but with a great deal more algebra.

The holding period return (or realized return) depends upon the current spot interest rate and changes in forward rates over time. Let

$P_{0,n}$ = the price observed at time 0 of a strip (zero-coupon bond) maturing at time n.

$P_{1,n}$ = the price observed at time 1 of a strip (zero-coupon bond) maturing at time n.

HPR = holding period return.

The holding period return is defined as follows

$$HPR = \frac{P_{1,n}}{P_{0,n}} - 1 \qquad \textbf{A9.1}$$

By substituting the prices expressed in terms of forward interest rates, we have

$$HPR = \frac{(1+R_{0,1})(1+f_{0,2})(1+f_{0,3})\cdots(1+f_{0,n})}{(1+R_{1,1})(1+f_{1,3})\cdots(1+f_{1,n})} - 1 \qquad \text{A9.2}$$

The holding period return equals the one-period spot rate $(R_{0,1})$ if the forward rates come true, that is if

$$f_{0,2} = R_{1,1}$$

$$f_{0,3} = f_{1,3}$$

through

$$f_{0,n} = f_{1,n} \qquad \text{A9.3}$$

Equation A9.2 is approximately the same as

$$HPR = R_{0,1} + [f_{0,2} - R_{1,1}] + [f_{0,3} - f_{1,3}] + \cdots + [f_{0,n} - f_{1,n}] \qquad \text{A9.4}$$

Thus, the holding period return is approximately the one-period spot interest rate plus the sum of the differences between the forward rates and the subsequent forward rates. For example, if all interest rates fall, the holding period return is approximately equal to the one-period spot rates plus the sum of the declines in the forward interest rates.

The expected holding period return is

$$E(HPR) = R_{0,1} + [f_{0,2} - E(R_{1,1})] + [f_{0,3} - E(f_{1,3})]$$
$$+ \cdots + [f_{0,n} - E(f_{1,n})] \qquad \text{A9.5}$$

The expected holding period return equals the current spot interest rate if the forward rate for period 2 equals the expected spot rate next period, and the more distant forward rates equal the expected forward rates next period. The terms with the differences between the forward rates and the expected future rates represent risk premiums. If these terms are positive, there are risk premiums and then the expected holding period return is higher than the current spot rate. In the expectations hypothesis, the forward rates equal the expected future rates, the expected holding period return equals the one-period spot interest rate $(R_{0,1})$ for all bonds, and there are no risk premiums. In contrast, in the increasing liquidity premium theory, longer-term bonds have forward rates higher than the expected future rates, and the expected return exceeds the current spot interest rate.

Two-Period Examples

In the case of two periods, the holding period return is approximately

$$HPR = R_{0,1} + [f_{0,2} - R_{1,1}] \qquad \text{A9.6}$$

The holding period return is the one-period spot rate plus the difference between the forward rate and the spot rate next period. This difference is often called the forecast error.

The expected holding period return is:

$$E(HPR) = R_{0,1} + [f_{0,2} - E(R_{1,1})] \qquad \text{A9.7}$$

The expected holding period return is the one-period spot rate plus the difference between the forward rate and the expected future spot rate. This difference is called the liquidity premium, L_2. If the expectations hypothesis holds, the forward rate equals the expected future spot rate. Then the liquidity premium is zero. If the combined theory applies, the forward rate equals the expected future spot rate plus a liquidity premium.

CHAPTER 10

Ratings and Default Risk

The chance of default is an important consideration for bond buyers. Since there are many thousands of different bond issues, gathering information to assess the chances of default of individual issues is a difficult process. Bond rating agencies have been developed to help provide this information to the market. Moody's, Standard & Poor's (S&P), and Fitch are the three largest rating agencies.

Ratings exist for many types of debt instruments including sovereign debt (bonds issued by countries), municipal debt, asset-backed debt, and money market debt. The rating agencies use different scales for each of these types of debt.

CORPORATE BOND RATINGS

We will focus on corporate bond ratings. Table 10.1 lists the ratings of the three agencies and their interpretations. Notice that there are letter ratings of AAA, AA, A, BBB, etc. Beginning with AA, the letter ratings have subratings, often called notch ratings. For example, within the rating category of A, there are subcategories (or notches) of A+, A, A−. Each of these subcategories represents slightly different probabilities of default. Bonds with lower ratings have higher default risk and higher yields to maturity. Ratings of BBB- and higher are often called *investment grade* and ratings below BBB- are called *high-yield* or *junk bonds*.

Table 10.1. Bond Ratings

Moody's	Fitch and S&P	Interpretation
Aaa	AAA	Highest-Quality
Aa1	AA+	
Aa2	AA	High Quality
Aa3	AA–	
A1	A+	Strong Payment
A2	A	Capacity
A3	A–	
Baa1	BBB+	Adequate Payment
Baa2	BBB	Capacity
Baa3	BBB–	
Ba1	BB+	Likely to Fulfill
Ba2	BB	Obligations; Ongoing
Ba3	BB–	Uncertainty
B1	B+	
B2	B	High Risk Obligations
B3	B–	
	CCC+	Current Vulnerability
Caa	CCC	To Default
	CCC–	
Ca	CC	In Bankruptcy or
C	C	Default or Other
D	D	Marked Shortcomings

Ratings are good relative predictors of default. The highest rating category has the smallest frequency of default. The second-highest rating category has a slightly larger frequency of default, and so on. Moody's and Standard & Poor's have long histories of rating corporate bonds and have documented a close link between bond ratings and subsequent default rates.

Because the default rates of bonds rated BB+ and below increase dramatically as the rating decreases, many financial institutions (insurance companies, pension funds, and mutual funds) are restricted in their ability to buy these bonds.

Determinants of Corporate Bond Ratings

Since the ratings of corporate bonds are good predictors of default frequency, the next logical question is what determines the ratings. The ratings agencies do not reveal the exact procedure used to derive ratings. Statistical studies have shown that for corporate bonds, the ability to pay depends upon debt levels, profitability, and firm risk levels. A bond will tend to have a higher rating if the following are true:

1. The firm has lower debt ratios (debt/assets, debt/equity).
2. The firm has higher interest coverage ratios (earnings before interest and taxes divided by interest).
3. The firm has higher rates of return of assets (profit/assets, profit/equity).
4. The firm has lower relative variation in earnings over time.
5. The firm is of larger size.

BOND RATINGS AND YIELDS

Because there is a strong link between rating and default probability, bonds with lower ratings and higher default probabilities have higher yields. This relationship is shown in Figure 10.1. The yield spread is the bond yield minus the yield on a similar maturity, default-free Treasury security. In the figure, the yield spread increases at an increasing rate as the bond rating gets lower because the probability of default increases at an increasing rate as bond ratings decrease.

Bond yields also depend upon the likely recovery rate in the event of a bankruptcy. Firms with highly marketable assets should have lower bond yields, other things equal.

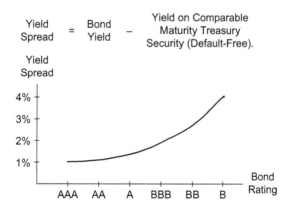

FIGURE 10.1 Bond Yield Spreads Versus Bond Ratings.

Bond Ratings and Underwriter Spreads

Figure 10.2 shows the relationship between underwriter spreads (i.e. the fee paid to underwriters) and bond ratings. Investment grade bonds tend to pay the same underwriter fee even though the bond ratings differ. As the bond rating falls below investment grade, buyers are harder to find because many financial institutions are restricted in their ability to buy bonds below investment grade, making it more difficult for the underwriter to find buyers. The underwriter fee goes up because of the additional difficulty of marketing bonds below investment grade.

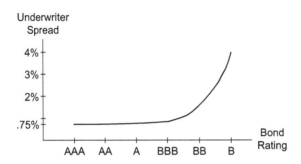

FIGURE 10.2 Underwriter Spreads Versus Bond Ratings.

Changes in Bond Ratings

A number of research papers have compared the timing of changes in bond ratings by the rating agencies versus changes in the prices of bonds or stocks of the bond issuing company. If bond rating changes contain new information not available to the public, there should be a change in bond and/or stock prices at the time of the rating change. While the empirical evidence is mixed, most evidence indicates that ratings changes are coincidental with changes in stock and/or bond prices. This evidence suggests that rating agencies are able to obtain or perceive information that is not available to investors. One logical explanation is that rating agencies are allowed to meet privately with the management of individual companies and be given private information. The evidence is consistent with rating agencies having valuable information for corporate bonds.

Although the average rating for corporate bonds is a relatively good predictor of default, there have been a number of highly publicized cases where the rating agencies have not foreseen defaults. In addition, rating agencies have been criticized as being slow to adjust their ratings to changes in the financial position of firms. Since rating agencies provide ratings to so many different securities, some of the time their changes in ratings will lag behind changes in values.

Fees Charged by Rating Agencies

Rating agencies charge fees for providing bond ratings. The fees charged might be for individual issues and involve an initial fee plus an annual fee. For bond issuers that frequently issue bonds, the rating agencies will typically charge a *relationship fee* that covers all of the bond issues. The rating agency then provides a company rating as well as ratings for the individual issues. Because individual bonds of a particular bond issuer may have slightly different features (such as being subordinated versus unsubordinated), the ratings may vary by issue for the same issuing company.

For publicly issued corporate bonds, the policy of Moody's and Standard & Poor's is to rate all issues of bonds. Moody's and S&P request a fee for providing this rating. If the issuer agrees to pay the fee, Moody's and S&P will meet with the issuer and give the issuer the opportunity to discuss the firm's prospects and possibly divulge private information.

Fitch provides ratings only if requested. Fitch also has a two-stage process. In the first stage, an issuer requests a preliminary rating for a relatively small fee. Then issuing firms have the choice to proceed with a full rating or stop the process and not reveal any rating. This two-stage process tends to result in the average released Fitch rating being slightly higher than the average bond ratings for Moody's and/or S&P. Some critics have argued that this two-stage process causes so-called "inflated ratings." However, the empirical evidence indicates that bond yields are lower when Fitch has higher ratings than Moody's and/or S&P, meaning that Fitch ratings contain additional valuable information.

In the market for mortgage-backed-securities, all ratings are solicited. Perhaps this practice of having all solicited ratings has contributed to excessively optimistic ratings for mortgage-backed securities. This point is discussed more extensively in the chapter on mortgage-backed securities.

Split Ratings

In the corporate bond market, virtually all public bond issues are rated by Moody's and S&P. About 40% of all public bond issues are also rated by Fitch. The three rating agencies do not always agree on the rating for a particular bond issue. Moody's and S&P disagree with each other about 50% of the time at the notch level, for example, A versus A–. When the two disagree, approximately 50% of the time Moody's has a higher rating than S&P and 50% of the time the reverse happens. Fitch ratings disagree with both Moody's and Standard & Poor's about 30% of the time. In addition, split ratings often persist over time. They do not necessarily converge.

The disagreements between the three rating agencies suggest that providing ratings is an imprecise task. Rational rating agencies might provide different ratings with the same information. Figure 10.3 shows that the range of rational ratings for a particular opaque bond issue may cover several different rating categories. The reason is that information about firms may be opaque or ambiguous. For companies with relatively opaque information, rational bond rating agencies can have different ratings for the same issue, resulting in split ratings. In the case of relatively transparent companies, the range of rational ratings is much narrower, and split ratings are less likely to occur. If the range of rational ratings is extremely narrow, all the rating agencies will tend to agree on the rating.

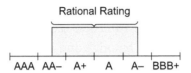

FIGURE 10.3 The Range of Rational Ratings for an Opaque Issuer.

High-Yield (Junk) Bonds

Bonds with lower ratings (i.e., BB+ and below) are called high-yield (junk) bonds. There are two types of high-yield bonds: "fallen angels" and "original-issue." "Fallen angels" are bonds originally issued with higher ratings, which have declined as the firm has fallen on hard times.

Since 1977, many "original-issue" high-yield bonds have appeared. Some are issued by firms with very high business (operating) risk. Others are issued by highly levered firms. Some highly levered mergers have been financed with high-yield bonds. Because these mergers had a very small proportion of equity financing, the bonds carried a high risk of default and high yields.

The role of original issue high-yield bonds has been controversial. Traditionally, the market for investment-grade public debt has been restricted to larger firms. Smaller firms have been forced to finance with bank debt or possibly private placements of debt with insurance companies. Original issue high-yield debt has opened up a new source of funds to many smaller and high-risk firms. In one view, high-yield debt has been a stimulus to economic expansion because firms were removed from the straitjacket of highly restrictive bank loans. In the opposing view, high-yield debt issuers escaped the close monitoring function provided by commercial banks and consequently suffer from unwise financing and investment decisions.

In the 1930s, there were many bond defaults. As a result, original issue junk bonds disappeared until they were reintroduced by Drexel, Burnham & Lambert, led by Michael Milken. Several authors have argued that the junk bond market was monopolized by the underwriter firm of Drexel, Burnham & Lambert in the 1970s and 1980s. In this view, Milken was able to sell junk bonds at low yields with high underwriter fees. The evidence supports this view. After Drexel went bankrupt in the early 1990s, the underwriter fees for original issue high-yield bonds dropped dramatically, suggesting that Drexel's very large market share of over 50% of high-yield bond issues kept underwriter fees quite high. When Drexel exited, there apparently was more competition between bond underwriters, and underwriting fees for high-yield bond issues declined significantly.

THE BANKRUPTCY PROCESS

Every corporate bond issue has an *indenture*—a formalized contract between the issuing firm, the bondholders, and a trustee. The indenture specifies the obligations of the firm to the bondholders, including the coupon payments, the maturity, the call feature, call prices, and sinking fund requirements. The bond trustee is appointed to act on behalf of the bondholders, who might otherwise find it difficult to protect their own interests. Consequently, the trustee must be independent of the issuing firm. Typically, the trustee will be the trust department of a large bank. The firm pays the trustee a fee as stated in the bond indenture.

The management of a corporation is the agent for the stockholders and is supposed to act in their best interest. In this agent role, the management may seek out ways to benefit the stockholders at the expense of the bondholders. Consequently, there is a natural conflict between stockholders and bondholders. One way for bondholders to protect themselves against stockholders is to require the inclusion of protective covenants (i.e., restrictions) in the bond indenture. Protective covenants make it difficult for the stockholders to expropriate the wealth of bondholders.

The American Bar Association has prepared a document entitled *Commentaries on Model Debenture Indenture Provisions*. This book lists standard bond indenture provisions. These protective covenants are written by legal experts and are based upon previous case law—i.e., cases in which bondholders sued firms that had acted against the interests of the bondholders. These model indentures are specifically designed to prevent repetition of these actions. The indenture provisions in the *Commentaries on Model Debenture Indenture Provisions* are widely used by corporate bonds and are often called *boilerplate*.

Four types of protective covenants are quite common: restrictions on (1) the issuance of additional debt, (2) dividend payments, (3) mergers, and (4) disposition of assets. Clearly, the stockholders benefit at the expense of the bondholders if the firm sells additional debt with a higher priority than existing debt, if the firm pays large cash dividends or repurchases large amounts of its stock in the market, if the firm merges and bondholders receive a riskier post-merger claim, or if the working assets of the firm are not properly maintained. Protective covenants try to prevent the stockholders from reducing the value of bonds.

One covenant to protect the bondholders against possible bondholder losses from mergers is a due-on-sale clause or *poison put,* requiring existing bonds to be repaid before a merger can occur. Corporate bonds without such protective covenants may have a premium added to the yield to compensate the bondholders for the possibility of merger.

The term *default* means a violation of any part of the bond indenture, including nonpayment of interest and/or violation of a protective covenant. For example, if a protective covenant in the indenture requires the firm's current ratio (i.e., current assets divided by current liabilities) to be above 2.0, the firm is in default if the ratio falls below 2.0. A default requires the trustee to act on behalf of the bondholders. After default, one possibility is a renegotiation of the contract; this is likely to occur if the default is a minor violation of the indenture. A second possibility is to file for bankruptcy. The possible scenarios following a default are shown in Figure 10.4.

FIGURE 10.4 Possible Results of Default.

Bankruptcy Courts

A bankruptcy is a legal proceeding administered by special bankruptcy courts. The firm itself or the creditors can file to begin a bankruptcy proceeding. During this proceeding, the court protects the firm's assets and appoints someone to run the firm's operations to avoid poor management practices and/or disappearance of the firm's assets.

Bankruptcy courts perform a special and important function for the legal system. To see the value of the bankruptcy courts, consider a situation of default without any bankruptcy courts. Imagine a firm that has defaulted on its financial obligations to its ten creditors. Without bankruptcy courts, the ten creditors of the firm would seek legal redress by suing the defaulting firm individually. All of these creditors will be competing with each other and may be filing court proceedings in different courts, creating extreme conflicts of interest between the different creditors. This type of competitive system forces the individual creditors to act in their own interest at the expense of the other creditors. The problem with this system is that the total amount of money available to pay creditors may be reduced by their acting in their self-interest. This has been called the *common pool problem*, described below.

The common pool problem is illustrated by the following example and is shown in Figure 10.5. Imagine a lake that has a fish population worth $100,000 if caught and sold immediately to consumers. If 25% of the fish are caught each year, reproduction is sufficient to maintain the fish population at a constant level, and a constant fish harvest of $25,000 can occur year after year. If there is only one fisherman, that fisherman is faced with the following choice: harvest $100,000 of fish in the current year or harvest $25,000 of fish indefinitely. If the discount rate for finding the present value of the perpetual harvest is less than 25%, then the present value of the perpetual harvest exceeds $100,000, the amount available from the single big harvest. For example, if the discount rate is 10%, the present value of the harvest is $250,000, and the single fisherman chooses to have a small annual harvest.

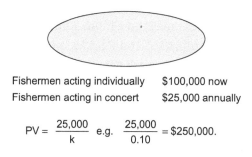

Fishermen acting individually $100,000 now
Fishermen acting in concert $25,000 annually

$$PV = \frac{25,000}{k} \quad \text{e.g.} \quad \frac{25,000}{0.10} = \$250,000.$$

FIGURE 10.5 The Common Pool Problem.

If there are many fishermen in this one lake, individual fishermen can maximize the present value of their own income by fishing as much as possible as quickly as possible. The fishermen have incentives to catch all the fish immediately. The total amount received by all the fishermen is $100,000. If the fishermen could design a system to harvest fish in concert, they would increase the present value of their catch.

The purpose of bankruptcy courts is to solve the common pool problem. Without bankruptcy courts, individual creditors have incentives to sue a defaulting firm and try to rapidly seize as many assets for themselves as possible. The actions of these competing creditors can easily destroy a sizable part of the value of a firm. Bankruptcy courts are a system for settling creditors' claims jointly so that the creditors can act in concert for their mutual benefit. Instead of individual creditors acting in ways to harm each other, the bankruptcy courts allow the settlement of their claims jointly.

Liquidation versus Reorganization

There are two possible resolutions of bankruptcy. First, a firm may be liquidated by the court. In liquidation, the individual assets of the firm are sold and distributed to the claimants according to the *rule of absolute priority*. Under the rule of absolute priority, the first claimant on the proceeds of the liquidation is the court, then tax obligations, followed by employees (up to some limit), secured creditors, unsecured creditors, preferred stockholders, and equity stockholders. In a typical liquidation, the stockholders can expect to receive nothing. Unsecured creditors can expect to get a small percentage of the face value of their obligations. Secured creditors have specific assets pledged as collateral. The proceeds from the liquidation of the pledged assets will depend upon market values.

Second, the firm may be reorganized by the court, a common result for large corporations. In reorganization, the claimants against the firm agree to surrender their old claims in exchange for a new set of scaled-down claims. The reorganized firm continues to operate during and after the bankruptcy. Firms are reorganized because a functioning business may have more value than the liquidating value of individual assets. A reorganization and liquidation do not have to be mutually exclusive, since reorganization can involve liquidation of some assets. The typical procedure in bankruptcy reorganization is for the stockholders to have a period of time to propose a reorganization plan. Next, the creditors have the right to propose reorganization plans. If no agreement can be reached on a reorganization plan, the bankruptcy court can impose a reorganization plan.

From a theoretical financial viewpoint, bankruptcy should occur when the value of equity is zero, or, equivalently, when the firm's fixed obligations exceed the value of the firm. This implies that stockholders should receive nothing from the resolution of bankruptcy. In practice, stockholders can receive positive payoffs from bankruptcy. In some cases, the management of a firm may initiate bankruptcy and ask the court to relieve the firm of some contractual obligations. Firms with very high contractually binding labor costs may be able to have labor contracts canceled as a result of the bankruptcy proceeding.

Costs of Bankruptcy

A bankruptcy proceeding involves costs. The most obvious costs are payments to the courts and to attorneys. These costs are a small percentage of assets for large bankrupt firms. The largest costs of bankruptcy are probably lost profit opportunities. Because opportunity costs are hard to measure, the size of total bankruptcy costs is difficult to estimate. Firms in bankruptcy may be unable to undertake profitable investment opportunities for two reasons. First, the court (which has the responsibility for running the firm) has protection of creditors' interest as its primary goal. Second, raising funds by issuing stocks and bonds is constrained during bankruptcy. In addition, sales from existing product lines may falter because customers may hesitate to buy from a bankrupt firm. Imagine the thinking of an individual considering the purchase of a car from a firm in bankruptcy. This potential buyer needs to consider the impact of the bankruptcy on the manufacturer's warranty, the availability of replacement parts, and the future trade-in value.

When a bankruptcy is imminent or publicly announced, trading of the firm's securities is typically stopped. After the suspension of trading, the securities of firms in bankruptcy continue to trade in the market at depressed prices. Investing in the bonds of a bankrupt firm is a high-risk, potentially high-return strategy. The majority of the bonds of bankrupt firms are not very good performers, but some of them will turn out to be very lucrative investments if the fortunes of the firm turn around sharply. Investing in bonds of firms in bankruptcy is a specialized field. It requires a detailed knowledge of bankruptcy law as well as knowledge about individual firms. A number of bond mutual funds and private investment funds have been established to focus on the securities of bankrupt firms.

FEATURES OF CORPORATE DEBT

Mortgage bonds are backed by specific assets. If there is default on mortgage bonds, the mortgage bondholders have the first claim on the pledged asset. *Equipment trust certificates* are another variety of secured debt in which specific equipment is pledged as collateral. Examples of firms financing equipment with equipment trust certificates include airlines pledging airplanes as collateral for these certificates and railroads pledging railroad cars.

Corporate debentures are unsecured debt. Unsecured debt has a general claim on the assets of the firm rather than a claim on specific assets. A firm may sell several different issues of debentures. These may be ordered in terms of priority of claims. Senior (or unsubordinated) debt has prior claim compared to junior (or subordinated) debt.

Income bonds arise out of a bankruptcy proceeding. They pay interest only if sufficient income is earned. The exact conditions when interest must be paid are specified in the bond indenture. Any interest not paid is owed for future payment. Income bonds give a firm that has gone through bankruptcy more "breathing room" compared to a straight bond. In contrast, nonpayment of interest on straight bonds constitutes default and most likely will precipitate bankruptcy. An income bond is similar to a preferred stock, except that interest is a tax-deductible business expense and preferred dividends are not.

CREDIT DEFAULT SWAPS

Beginning in the 1990s, over-the-counter contracts for insurance against fixed income defaults began to be traded. These contracts are called *credit default swaps*. Credit default swaps are now traded on corporate bonds, government bonds, and mortgage-backed securities.

Credit default swaps (CDS) constitute a guarantee by one party to pay the face value of a debt instrument (usually called the *notional amount*) to another party if an event such as default occurs. Most credit default swaps are *single-name* swaps, meaning that the debt instrument guarantees the debt of one issuer—perhaps one firm or one country. While the typical credit default swap is a contract for the debt of a specific company, market participants also trade contracts on baskets of companies.

The standard credit default swap arrangement is for a period of five years as illustrated in Figure 10.6. The buyer of protection pays the seller of the protection a quarterly fee for the life of the contract or until the date when the default event occurs. The fee is quoted on an annual basis. Thus a fee of 4% implies a quarterly payment of 1% every quarter. The 4% annual fee is called the *credit default swap premium*. The amount of the fee for a newly initiated contract changes as credit conditions change in the market, increasing as default becomes more likely and decreasing as default becomes less likely.

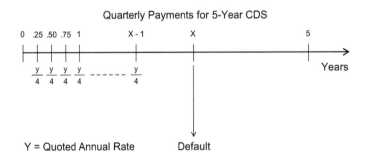

FIGURE 10.6 Example of Five-Year Credit Default Swap.

Figure 10.7 shows an example where investor *K* buys protection from a credit default swaps dealer. The swaps dealer also buys protection from investor *J*. Thus the dealer has a "balanced book." The dealer tries to make a profit by selling the default protection at a higher price to investor *K* than the purchase price from investor *J*.

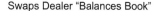

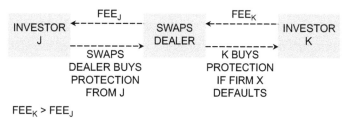

FIGURE 10.7 Example of a Dealer Position.

The International Swaps and Derivatives Association (ISDA) is a trade organization for participants in the market for credit default swaps. One of its primary roles is to create standard legal arrangements for credit default swaps. The ISDA has a variety of alternative specifications of the features for contracts between the protection seller and the protection buyer. In individual cases, the parties have to agree to precise terms from among a set of standard alternatives.

The ISDA has committees having the authority to determine when a "credit event" constitutes a trigger requiring the seller of the credit default swap to make payment to the protection buyer under the contract. Without the ISDA as decision-maker, many disputes would arise deciding when a credit event occurs. While bankruptcy is one triggering event, other triggering events are also possible. Other possible triggers include a fall in the debt rating or nonpayment of an obligation on a debt instrument.

In the event of a default, there are essentially two ways of settling the contract. Suppose that the notional amount is $100. If there is a default, one means of settling the contract is for the protection seller to pay $100 and receive the defaulted bond in exchange. If this defaulted bond is only worth $40, the protection seller will lose $60. A second method for settling contracts is for the protection seller to pay the difference between the notional amount and the market value of the debt instrument, in this example $60. This method is the most common method of settling defaulted contracts. To determine the market value of the defaulted instrument, an auction is conducted. The ISDA has set up procedures to try to ensure that the auction price is fair and has not been unduly influenced by some parties.

In working out the terms of the original agreement and setting the swap premium, the protection seller should require a swap premium sufficient to compensate for the risk of a triggering event and the resulting loss. This swap premium should depend upon the likelihood of default and the probable value of the debt instrument if default occurs.

Risk Transfer and Credit Default Swaps

Credit default swaps are over-the-counter contracts between two parties. These contracts are custom-made to meet the specific needs of the buyer of protection and the requirements of the seller of protection. Because they are traded over-the-counter, there is no public record of every transaction in contrast to organized stock exchanges such as the New York Stock Exchange. Electronic quotation services such as Bloomberg provide typical quotations, but not actual trading prices.

Credit default swaps allow the default risk of a particular debt instrument to be separated out and traded in the market. The seller of the protection may be better able to bear the risk of a default than a bond purchaser. The wide availability of credit default swaps allows default risk to be diversified and held by protection sellers willing to bear the default risk.

Credit Default Swaps versus Standard Insurance Contracts

A credit default swap is a type of insurance protection. With standard insurance contracts, one party buys protection to guard against a potential loss if an adverse event occurs. For example, a homeowner whose house is damaged by a hail storm is compensated by an insurance company for the losses from the hail. With credit default swaps, the buyer of protection may be the holder of the insured debt instrument, but other parties can buy protection without holding the particular debt instrument that is being guaranteed. Thus, third parties are able to buy credit default swaps, betting that a triggering event will occur. This feature allows anyone to place a bet that a particular debt instrument will default and benefit if a default is triggered.

There is major difference between insurance and credit default swaps. Insurance contracts are regulated in order to require companies writing insurance protection to have sufficient assets to live up to the insurance contract if an adverse event occurs. In contrast, credit default swaps are over-the-counter contracts between two parties. The contracting parties may have an agreement for the seller of protection to post collateral and perhaps even increase the posted collateral as the probability of an adverse event occurs. Since there is no regulator specifying mandatory collateral requirements, the probability of default on a credit default swap is higher than the risk of default by a regulated insurance company.

The lack of a mandatory requirement of posted capital for the seller of the swaps creates a moral hazard problem. That is, sellers of CDS may not worry about the consequences of defaulting on their agreement to buy defaulted debt instruments. A striking example of this moral hazard problem was American International Group (AIG), a very large insurance company located in New York State and technically regulated by New York State insurance regulators. Sometime after the year 2000, an office of AIG in London began to sell protection for large numbers of credit default swaps without posting any collateral to guarantee performance in the event of default. For writing these credit default swaps, the company received very large annual fees, making this London office appear to be extremely profitable for several years. Unfortunately, during the financial crisis of 2007–2008, many debt instruments that AIG guaranteed against default did actually default. The total liability from these credit default swaps exceeded the capital of the entire company. As a result, the US government did a bailout of AIG by injecting $180 billion into the company. This bailout money allowed AIG to pay its obligations for its credit default swaps.

OVER-THE-COUNTER TRADING VERSUS CLEARINGHOUSES

Trading of Credit Default Swaps is carried out over-the-counter through a network of dealers. In over-the-counter trading, there are pairwise contracts between dealers and buyers of protection and between dealers and sellers of protection. The dealers in turn usually have pairwise contracts with other dealers or investors. The result is a network of pairwise contracts as illustrated in Figure 10.8 for the case of six dealers. There are a total of fifteen pairs of contracts between these six dealers. With more dealers and investors, the number of possible contracts becomes extremely large.

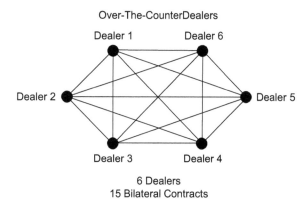

FIGURE 10.8 Contracts Between Multiple Dealers.

Suppose that dealer 2 suffers large losses because of defaults on underlying fixed income securities and failure by protection writers to honor their contracts. If dealer 2 is forced into bankruptcy, this dealer's contracts with other dealers can be forced into default. Because of the default of dealer 2 and this dealer's bilateral contracts with other dealers, other dealers may be forced to default. The consequence is an avalanche effect, sometimes called *systemic risk,* as illustrated in Figure 10.9.

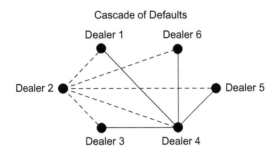

Cascade of Defaults

Dealer 2 fails and defaults.
Default by Dealer 2 causes Dealer 4 to fail and
default on other contracts.

FIGURE 10.9 Systemic Risk.

This problem of systemic risk can be resolved by having a central clearinghouse in which all buyers and sellers of credit default swaps have contracts with the central clearinghouse. The central clearinghouse requires the participants to post sufficient collateral to guarantee performance. Organized markets for futures contracts operate with central clearinghouses. We will discuss the operations of these clearinghouses in the chapter on futures contracts.

SUMMARY

Because there are very large numbers of bonds outstanding with many different features, bond rating agencies have developed. The three largest rating agencies are Moody's, Standard & Poor's, and Fitch. These agencies provide ratings as indicators of the relative probability of default. Corporate bonds with the highest rating of AAA have very low probabilities of default. Consequently, the yields on these bonds are relatively low. As the ratings decline, the probability of default increases and the bond yields increase.

A bond represents a contractual agreement between an issuer, bondholders, and a trustee. The obligations of the parties are spelled out in the bond indenture, which contains protective covenants. Violation of this contractual agreement constitutes default.

Bankruptcy is a legal proceeding, administered by special bankruptcy courts. There are two possible outcomes from bankruptcy. Either the assets of the firm are liquidated or the firm is reorganized. Bankruptcy is costly. Besides legal costs, there are lost sales and investment opportunities. Ratings of bonds provide valuable information about default probabilities. For corporations, ratings are a function of debt levels, firm profitability, the riskiness of the firm's assets, and firm size.

Credit default swaps are over-the-counter contracts. In a credit default swap, one party sells insurance against default on a fixed income security. Some other party buys this insurance. Credit default swaps allow the transfer of default risk.

QUESTIONS AND PROBLEMS

1. Describe the functions of a corporate bond indenture. What role does the bond trustee play?
2. Why do bond indentures include protective covenants? Give some examples of protective covenants and the reasons why they might be included.
3. Why do special bankruptcy courts exist?
4. Define financial distress. What alternatives are available to firms in financial distress instead of defaulting? Describe the pros and cons of each alternative.
5. Describe the costs associated with bankruptcy.
6. What does the term *secured debt* mean?
7. Describe the financial characteristics that determine bond ratings.
8. Are high-yield bonds good investments? Why or why not?
9. Would you expect the ratings of Fitch to be higher or lower than the ratings of Moody's and Standard and Poor's? If they are higher, would it be likely that these higher ratings are inflated because the ratings are solicited by the bond issuer?
10. What is a credit default swap? Why might credit default swaps create systemic risk?

CHAPTER 11

Mortgages

This chapter explains mortgage computations, the differences between fixed-rate mortgages and floating-rate mortgages, and the prepayment option. Then the discussion will shift to the securitization of mortgages, i.e., the packaging of many individual mortgages into pools that are then sold to individual investors.

A mortgage is a loan with real estate pledged as collateral. If the borrower defaults on the loan, the lender has first claim upon the real estate. The pledged real estate can be residential property or commercial property.

Interest rates on mortgages can be fixed over the life of the mortgage (fixed-rate), or the interest rate may be tied to some interest rate index and vary over time (called variable-rate, floating-rate, or adjustable rate). With fixed-rate mortgages, the lender bears the risk of changing interest rates, although the interest rate includes a premium for this risk. The fixed-rate borrower pays a higher interest cost to lock in the interest cost. With floating-rate mortgages, the interest rate is tied to a short-term interest rate and fluctuates as short-term interest rates change. The borrower bears the risk of changing interest rates. Since short-term interest rates are typically lower than long-term interest rates, the average interest cost is lower for floating-rate loans.

FIXED-RATE MORTGAGE COMPUTATIONS

Suppose a borrower takes out a fixed-interest-rate mortgage loan for a principal amount, P, and repays it in equal installments of M. The interest rate is fixed at R. To simplify the discussion, we assume n annual installment payments. The present value of the installment payments must equal the mortgage principal, P, that is

$$P = \frac{M}{1+R} + \frac{M}{(1+R)^2} + \ldots + \frac{M}{(1+R)^n} \qquad \textbf{11.1}$$

This may be expressed as

$$P = [M][PVA_n] = [M][\text{Present Value of an } n \text{ period Annuity}] \qquad \textbf{11.2}$$

PVA_n denotes the present value of an annuity of $1 per period for n periods at the interest rate R. Given the maturity, n, the interest rate, R, and the amount of the principal, P, the preceding equation can be solved for the installment payment, M:

$$M = \frac{P}{PVA_n} \qquad \textbf{11.3}$$

Consider a numerical example with a principal of $100, an interest rate of 10%, and a 20-year repayment period. Then the annual installment payment is

$$M = \frac{\$100}{8.5136} = \$11.75 \qquad \textbf{11.4}$$

Since there are 20 annual mortgage payments of $11.75, the total amount paid over the entire life of the mortgage is $235. $100 of this total is repayment of the original loan. The remaining $135 is interest. Even though the total amount of interest is quite large, these payments represent a fair price for an interest rate of 10%. The borrower is paying for receiving the $100 principal of the loan immediately.

The mortgage payment in the preceding problem can be found quite easily on a financial calculator by inserting a present value of –100, an interest rate of 10%, and 20 periods as the life of the mortgage.

As the interest rate on the mortgage decreases, the periodic mortgage payment is reduced. For example, if the interest rate is cut in half to 5%, the new mortgage payment will be substantially less. A 5% 20-year annuity of $1 has a present value of $12.4622. The annual mortgage payment is $100 / 12.4622 = $8.02, substantially less than the periodic payment of $11.75 with an interest rate of 10%. With a 5% interest rate the total payments over the life of the mortgage are $160.40 compared to total payments of $235 with interest rate of 10%.

Each mortgage payment, M, includes a payment for interest and repayment of part of the principal, often called amortization of principal. As the principal is reduced, the total interest on the principal is reduced, and more of the mortgage payment is repayment of principal.

The interest and principal repayment may be computed recursively. The interest payment is the previous period's principal times the interest rate. The repayment of principal is the mortgage payment minus the interest. The computations are illustrated in Table 11.1. Notice that the principal decreases over time, the amount of interest also decreases over time, and the repayment of principal (amortization) increases in later periods.

Table 11.1. Computation of Interest and Principal Repayment

Principal = $100; Interest Rate = 10%;
Maturity = 20 years; Mortgage Payment = $11.75

Point in Time	Principal	Interest = Principal at Previous Point in Time Times the Interest Rate	Repayment of Principal = Mortgage Payment Minus Interest
0	$100.00		
1	$98.25 = 100 − 1.75	$10.00 = .1(100)	$1.75 = 11.75 − 10.00
2	$96.34 = 98.26 − 1.92	$9.83 = .1(98.25)	$1.92 = 11.75 − 9.83
3		$9.63 = .1(96.34)	

Suppose that a mortgage starts out with n periods until the final mortgage payment. After j periods have elapsed, the remaining principal balance is simply the present value of an annuity of the mortgage payments for $n-j$ time periods. That is, the remaining principal at point in time j is

$$P_j = [M][PVA_{n-j}] \qquad \text{11.5}$$

As a numerical example, assume the previous 20-year mortgage with annual mortgage payment of $11.75. Five years into the mortgage, there will be 15 years left. The remaining principal after the mortgage payment made at the end of year five is simply the present value of a 15-year annuity of $11.75 at an interest rate of 10%. The remaining principal is $89.37. This amount can be found with a financial calculator by inserting a payment of $11.75, the number of periods as 15, and the interest rate as 10%.

The amortization or repayment of principal at a particular point in time j can be computed by computing the principal at the end of the previous time interval, $j-1$, and subtracting the principal at the current point in time. That is, $P_{j-1}-P_j$. Some algebraic manipulation shows that the principal repayment at point in time j can also be expressed as

$$\frac{\text{Principal}}{\text{repayment}} = M\left[\frac{1}{(1+R)^{n-j+1}}\right] \qquad \text{11.6}$$

To illustrate, the amortization of principal at the end of year five of the 20-year mortgage with the 10% interest rate is $11.75 times the present value of one dollar received six periods from now. ($11.75)(0.56447) = $6.63.

Monthly Payments

Most mortgage payments are paid on a monthly basis. To adjust the preceding discussion for monthly payments, use the number of months as the number of periods and divide the annual interest rate by 12 to get the monthly interest rate. For example, with an annual interest rate of 10% for 20 years, the monthly interest rate is (10 / 12) % = 0.8333% and the number of periods is 240 months. The monthly mortgage payment is the principal divided by the present value of a $1 annuity for 240 months, that is, 103.6246. The monthly mortgage payment is $100 / 103.6246 = $0.9650. On a financial calculator, this can be found by inserting the number of periods as 240, the interest rate as 0.8333%, and the present value as –100.

The Effective Interest Rate

Interest rates are often quoted in different ways. Mortgage interest rates are quoted as an annual rate, but the interest rate applied is a monthly rate equal to the annual rate divided by 12. The effective rate of interest is defined as the annualized monthly compounded rate. Suppose the quoted rate of interest is R. Then the annualized monthly compounded interest rate is $(1 + R / 12)^{12} - 1$. In the preceding example, the annualized monthly compounded interest rate is $(1.008333)^{12} - 1 = 10.47\%$.

The United States has a law called the Truth in Lending Act. Its goal is to provide sufficient information for consumers about loans. One of the requirements of the Truth in Lending Act is that consumer interest rates be stated as the effective annual rate or the annual percentage rate (APR). In general, if R is the stated annual rate and there are q compounding periods in a year, the APR is

$$APR = \left(1 + \frac{R}{q}\right)^q - 1 \qquad 11.7$$

VARIABLE-RATE MORTGAGES

With fluctuating interest rates, lenders with a short horizon have incentives to pass on interest rate risk in the form of variable-rate (floating-rate, adjustable-rate) loans with the interest rate tied to a widely available quoted interest rate index such as the one-year Treasury rate plus a premium. With variable-rate loans, the borrower bears the risks and the possible benefits of fluctuating short-term interest rates.

Most of the time short-term interest rates are lower than long-term interest rates. The interest rate on variable-rate mortgage loans is closely linked to the short-term interest rate, while the rates on long-term, fixed-rate mortgage loans are linked with the long-term interest rate. As a result, the interest rate on variable rate loans is lower than the interest rate on long-term, fixed-rate mortgages. Consequently, the potential benefit of a variable-rate loan to the borrower is the lower average short-term interest rates. The risk to the borrower is the possibility that interest rates might go up and the rate and periodic payment on the mortgage will increase.

Adjustable-rate mortgage loans typically have an initial rate of interest that is set below the market interest rate, the so-called teaser rate. The teaser rate might be fixed for two years, although the time can vary for individual mortgages. And then the rate is adjusted to the index level plus a premium. For example, a loan might have an initial teaser rate of 2% for two years. Then the rate is adjusted to the rate index plus a premium of 2.5%. If the new interest rate is higher, the periodic payment on the mortgage increases.[1]

Naïve variable-rate borrowers may not realize the possibility of substantially higher mortgage payments in the future. Consequently, they may be unable to afford the new higher payments and be forced to default if short-term interest rates increase. During the mortgage crisis of 2007–2009, many defaults occurred for floating-rate mortgages.

THE PREPAYMENT OPTION

Mortgages in the United States normally contain an option allowing the borrower to repay the remaining principal. Figure 11.1 shows the pattern of prepayments. This figure shows the percentages of mortgages that are prepaid on the vertical axis versus the change in interest rates on the horizontal axis. Since mortgages have a due-on-sale clause, there will typically be some prepayments for moving and other reasons. In addition, when interest rates decline, many mortgages will be replaced with lower interest rate mortgages. The larger the decline in interest rates, the greater the number of prepayments.

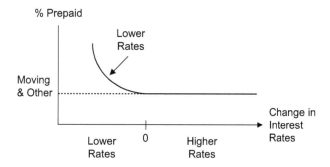

FIGURE 11.1 Refinancing Rate and the Change in the Interest Rate.

---

[1] The new payment depends upon the remaining principal. Since part of the principal will be reduced by amortization, the new payment depends upon the total amount of amortization.

Sometimes homeowners decide to make a larger payment than the required mortgage payment in individual months or every month. These payments reduce the remaining principal and shorten the life of the mortgage. A financial calculator allows the calculation of the impact of increasing the amount paid beyond the required mortgage payment. In the example that we have been using with a 20-year mortgage with interest rate of 10% and annual payments of $11.75, suppose that the borrower decides to increase the payments every year to $13 even though the contract calls for payment of $11.75. The remaining life of the mortgage becomes 15.38 years. $13 is paid for 15 periods. In the 16th time period, the rest of the mortgage is paid off. The remaining life of the mortgage can be found on a financial calculator by simply putting in $13 as the periodic payment, $100 as the present value, 10% as the interest rate, and have the calculator compute the remaining life. The result is 15.38. Since mortgage payments are made at discrete points in time, the mortgage will be fully repaid at year 16.

The Benefit of Refinancing after a Decline in Interest Rates

If interest rates decline after a mortgage is undertaken, repayment of the original mortgage and refinancing with a new, lower interest rate mortgage may be advantageous. We will first present a general framework for determining the benefit to the borrower of refinancing and then work through a detailed example. Note that a benefit to the borrower is a loss to the lender.

Suppose at time 0 a mortgage is taken out with a principal of P_0, maturity of n periods, an interest rate of R_{OLD}, and a periodic payment of M_{OLD}. After j periods have elapsed, the interest rate has dropped to R_{NEW}. The old mortgage has a remaining principal of P_j and is replaced by a new mortgage with $n-j$ periods until maturity. The new mortgage has periodic payments of M_{NEW}. The interest rate on the new loan is R_{NEW}. There are refinancing costs of REF. The refinancing costs include any prepayment penalties, legal costs, administrative costs, and loan initiation fees or points. The refinancing benefit is computed as follows

$$\text{Refinancing benefit} = [\; M_{OLD} - M_{NEW} \;] \; PVA_{n-j,\,R_{NEW}} - REF$$

$$= \begin{bmatrix} \text{Periodic} \\ \text{savings} \end{bmatrix} \begin{bmatrix} \text{Present value} \\ \text{of annuity} \end{bmatrix} - \begin{bmatrix} \text{Refinancing} \\ \text{costs} \end{bmatrix} \quad \textbf{11.8}$$

Finding the new mortgage payment requires first finding the remaining principal. Namely, $P_j = M_{OLD}[PVA_{n-j,R_{OLD}}]$. Then the new mortgage payments are simply the remaining principal divided by the present value of an annuity for the remaining number of years at the new interest rate.

$$M_{NEW} = \frac{P_j}{PVA_{n-j, R_{NEW}}} \qquad \textbf{11.9}$$

To illustrate, suppose that ten years ago a homeowner took out a 20-year mortgage that now has 10 years remaining. The old interest rate was 10%. Refinancing costs are assumed to be 3% of the remaining principal. For simplicity assume a principal of $100. From earlier calculations, the mortgage payment is $11.75, and the remaining principal is $72.20.

Assume interest rates have now dropped to 5% and the mortgage payment on the new loan is

$$M_{NEW} = \frac{P_j}{PVA_{n-j, R_{NEW}}} = \frac{\$72.20}{PVA_{10,.05}}$$

$$= \frac{\$72.20}{7.7217} = \$9.35 \qquad \textbf{11.10}$$

The savings from refinancing are computed as follows:

$$\begin{array}{c}\text{Refinancing}\\ \text{benefit}\end{array} = [\ M_{OLD} - M_{NEW}\ ]\ PVA_{n-j, R_{NEW}} - REF$$

$$= [\ \$11.75 - \$9.35\ ][\ 7.7217\ ] - [\ .03\ ][\ \$72.20\ ] = \$16.37 \qquad \textbf{11.11}$$

In this case, refinancing results in savings after deducting refinancing costs. The amount of the benefit of immediate refinancing depends upon the remaining life of the mortgage $(n-j)$. The new mortgage can be replaced with a longer maturity mortgage than $n-j$. For example, the new replacement mortgage might be a 30-year mortgage. This possibility makes the benefit of refinancing difficult to measure precisely.

Although a current refinancing may be advantageous, waiting to refinance in the future may be better. If future interest rates are lower, the benefit of refinancing can be larger. However, the borrower must continue to pay the old, higher interest rate until the refinancing takes place, at least partially offsetting the increased benefit from lower interest rates. In addition, if future interest rates are higher, the opportunity to gain from refinancing may be lost. The possibility of changing interest rates in the future makes the refinancing decision quite difficult.

CHANGES IN THE MORTGAGE MARKET OVER TIME

Since World War II, the mortgage market in the United States has changed significantly. To get a historical perspective, the mortgage market can be divided into several phases.

Phase I

For the time interval between World War II and approximately the mid-1970s, savings institutions and commercial banks were the primary sources of home mortgages. The typical mortgage was a long-term fixed-rate mortgage. The banks would typically finance these mortgages with bank deposits. Thus, the banks would borrow at relatively low short-term interest rates and lend at higher long-term rates, making a profit of the difference in rates minus operating costs.

Typically these financial institutions held the mortgages until they were paid off. As a result, the banks would incur any losses from default by the borrowers. This practice gave the lending institutions a large incentive to lend to high-quality (or prime) borrowers who were unlikely to default. A prime borrower would have a sizable down payment, verified income and/or assets sufficient to meet the mortgage payments, and a high credit rating. Because of the requirements of prime borrowers, default rates on mortgages were quite low.

Mortgages are amortized. Part of the monthly mortgage payment is interest on the remaining principal. The rest is repayment of principal, often called amortization. For simplicity, we shall call this Phase I as illustrated in Figure 11.2.

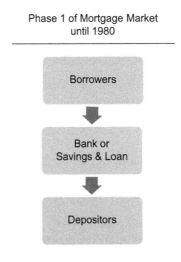

FIGURE 11.2 Mortgage Channel During Phase I.

Phase II

Phase II lasted from the mid-1970s until approximately the mid-1990s. During Phase II, the financing of mortgages followed two different channels shown in Figure 11.3. Many mortgages continued to follow the Phase I channel in which commercial banks and thrifts institutions would originate and hold mortgages financed by deposits.

In addition, a new channel developed in which mortgage loans made by banks were put into mortgage pools (*mortgage-backed securities*) and claims on the mortgage pools would then be sold to investors. These investors might be individuals, financial institutions, or even governmental units. This process of selling claims on mortgages (or other assets) to investors has become known as *securitization*.

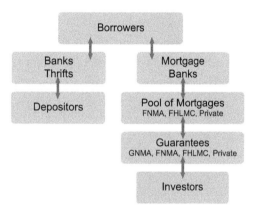

FIGURE 11.3 Mortgage Channels in Phase II.

During Phase II mortgages that were put into mortgage pools received default guarantees. One type of guarantee was from one of the following government agencies: The Federal Housing Administration (FHA), the Veterans Administration (VA), and the Government National Mortgage Association (GNMA). Since these agencies are part of the government of the United States, they are guaranteed by the government. Some mortgages were insured by private insurers. In addition, mortgages frequently received a second line of guarantee from one of two private but "government-sponsored entities" (GSEs): the Federal National Mortgage Association (FNMA or Fannie Mae), or the Federal Home Loan Mortgage Corporation (FHLMC or Freddie Mac).

Fannie Mae and Freddie Mac were established as private companies with a US government backup guarantee. They have performed several roles in the mortgage financing market. First, buying mortgages and holding them in their portfolio. Second, securitizing mortgages. That is, they have taken some mortgages and formed pools of mortgages that are then sold to investors as mortgage-backed securities.

In addition, these government-sponsored entities also have provided a guarantee of timely payment to investors. The guarantees of timely payment helped to keep mortgage interest rates lower.

During Phase II *mortgage brokers* began to appear. A mortgage broker is a firm that links home buyers seeking mortgages with mortgage pool organizers. Mortgage brokers do not lend money but merely connect a borrower with a lender. Mortgage brokers receive a fee from the borrower and the pool organizer. In contrast, *mortgage bankers* make an initial loan to the home buyer and then sell this loan to a pool organizer to be eventually sold to investors. The term *mortgage banker* includes both commercial banks and thrifts institutions originating loans. The term *originator* is used to describe both mortgage brokers and mortgage bankers.

The original pools of mortgages were called pass-throughs. Each investor in one of these pass-throughs would have a proportional share in the pool of mortgages. Investors would receive interest and scheduled repayments of principal (or amortization), as well as any principal repayments that were made early. See Figure 11.4.

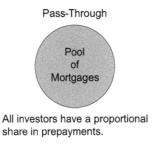

Pass-Through

All investors have a proportional
share in prepayments.

FIGURE 11.4 Mortgage Pass-Throughs.

Gradually many of these pools of mortgages were divided into *tranches*, or slices. Figure 11.5 illustrates a pass-through divided into tranches. There are many ways of dividing up the mortgage pools. One possible method might be to have all of the amortization (both scheduled and prepayments) paid to tranche 1. After tranche 1 was completely paid off, amortization would go to tranche 2, etc.

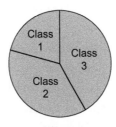

FIGURE 11.5 Pass-Through Divided into Tranches.

Figure 11.6 presents a more detailed picture of the securitization process in which mortgage borrowers approach several different originators of mortgages. The mortgages are then organized into a pool of mortgages. The mortgage pool is put into a trust called a special purpose vehicle. Then shares of the mortgage pool are sold to investors. Although investors technically have a claim against the originators and the pool organizers, the practical purpose of the trust is to insulate the pool organizer and the originators from investor claims. The mortgage pool is typically divided into tranches with different ratings and different interest rates.

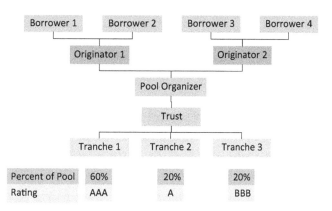

FIGURE 11.6 Illustration of the Securitization and Tranching of Mortgages.

The advantage of tranching is that particular investors might prefer the cash flow patterns of individual tranches and might be willing to pay a slightly higher price for the sum of all the tranches compared to the pass-through. Some investors may prefer a tranche that receives the prepayments sooner, and other investors may prefer a tranche that has the prepayments received at more distant dates. As a consequence, the sum of the value of the tranches may be worth more than the pool sold as a pass-through. The firm that divides the pool into tranches is able to sell all of the tranches for a higher price than simply selling the pool as a pass-through.

Tranching has disadvantages. First, dividing a pass through into tranches reduces the size of each part and consequently reduces the liquidity of the individual tranches. Second, because prepayments are not known with certainty, valuing tranches becomes more difficult especially for the tranches with lowest priorities.

Phase III

Phase III of the mortgage market began in the mid-1990s. Some mortgages continued to be held by banks and thrifts, but a very large proportion of mortgages were securitized and sold to investors.

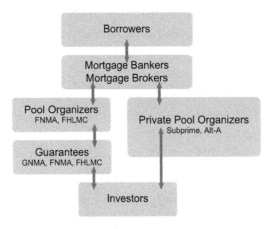

FIGURE 11.7 Mortgage Securitization During Phase III.

Phase III differs from Phase II in several ways and is illustrated in Figure 11.7. During Phase III, the number of mortgage brokers increased dramatically. A mortgage broker links a borrower and a pool organizer. The growth of the Internet greatly increased the ease of contacting mortgage brokers and contributed significantly to the growth of mortgage lending. In Phase I, a borrower had to physically visit an originator in order to initiate the lending process. With the growth of the Internet in Phase III, originations could be handled through the Internet and telephone. Documents could be sent by fax or as email attachments.

Subprime mortgages became increasingly common during Phase III until the housing bubble burst in 2006. A subprime mortgage is a mortgage that does not meet the standard criteria for prime mortgages, namely (1) a sizable down payment, (2) verifiable income sufficient to make mortgage payments, and (3) a good credit rating. Subprime mortgages met none of these three requirements for prime mortgages. The subprime loans were essentially loans to relatively poor individuals who were very likely to default. A similar type of loan was an Alt-A loan. This type of loan was missing one or two of the standard requirements for being a prime mortgage.

Lax lending standards helped to create a very large run-up in housing prices between 1997 and 2006. In fact, this was the largest housing boom in recorded US history. In some markets, housing prices tripled or quadrupled during this time interval. Prices behaved according to the *bigger fool theory,* namely that an asset is worth whatever the next fool is willing to pay.

During Phase III, the amount of variable interest rate mortgages with an initial teaser rate of interest increased significantly. Many borrowers choosing vari-able-rate mortgages were not sufficiently sophisticated enough to understand the risks involved. Some borrowers took out floating-rate loans in anticipation of being able to sell a property at a profit and repay the initial loan when the interest rate adjustment occurred. Other borrowers planned to refinance one floating-rate loan with a low teaser rate by another floating-rate loan with a low teaser rate when the first loan was scheduled to reset the interest rate. As long as housing prices increased, these strategies worked. But when housing prices peaked in 2006, the strategy of using variable-rate mortgages with low teaser rates of interest often resulted in catastrophe.

Second mortgages expanded dramatically during this period. Home equity lines of credit (HELOC) are one type of second mortgage. These are variable-rate loans from commercial banks. Anecdotal evidence indicates that some users of HELOCs regarded these as "money available from an ATM" that was frequently used for consumption expenditures. In a market of constantly rising market values of houses, borrowers might be able to refinance their existing first and second (HELOC) mortgages with a new first mortgage because the appraised value of the property went up.

Since loan originators and pool organizers earn profits each time they process mortgages, they have incentives to process as many mortgages as possible. The incentives were especially true for the individuals working as loan originators or pool organizers. The salaries and bonuses of the individuals working for these firms were directly related to the profits earned by the business, whose profits would depend primarily upon the volume of business. To increase their salaries and bonuses, individuals working for mortgage originators and pool organizers were strongly motivated to process as many mortgages as possible.

This compensation scheme was a ripe environment for fraud to occur if individual employees expected to not be held responsible for this fraud. For example, suppose a mortgage originator is approached by a borrower who clearly should not be granted a mortgage loan to buy a house. A mortgage originator might be tempted to grant this individual a mortgage since this mortgage becomes part of a pool of mortgages which may insulate the mortgage originator from liability if there is a future default. The CNBC video entitled *House of Cards* has interviews with mortgage originators and pool organizers who unabashedly state their goal of processing as many mortgages as possible regardless of the quality of the underlying mortgages.

Mortgage-backed securities receive default ratings from the rating agencies, Moody's, Standard & Poor's, or Fitch. The rating agencies provide ratings for the individual tranches of a mortgage-backed security. When a rating agency provides a rating for a publicly issued bond, the rating is considered an opinion. Therefore, a rating agency is not liable for incorrect forecasts of default. In contrast, underwriters of bond issues have a fiduciary responsibility to accurately provide information to investors in bond issues.

Because issuers of fixed income securities pay rating agencies to provide ratings, there may have been competition among rating agencies to provide higher ratings in order to get more fees from rating more mortgage-backed securities. The result of this competition for ratings business appears to have resulted in unrealistically high ratings for many mortgage-backed securities and the failure of many mortgage-backed securities with the highest ratings. Eventually in 2015, Standard & Poor's was fined $1.5 billion for its inappropriate behavior in rating mortgage-backed securities during the housing boom and was banned from providing ratings for mortgage-backed securities for one year.

Phase IV: Financial Crisis of 2007–2009

Housing prices reached a peak in 2006 and began to decline in the US. As a result, default rates on mortgages increased. The consequence was defaults on mortgage-backed securities and credit default swaps written on these mortgage-backed securities. These events caused great problems and eventual failure for three financial firms: Bear Stearns, Lehman Brothers, and AIG. The failure of these firms set off a panic in the financial markets with a dramatic drop in stock prices. The result was an unwillingness to make loans. A sharp downturn in business activity followed, along with a large increase in unemployment. This downturn in business has been called *The Great Recession*.

For many years, the US government had created entities to promote the flow of funds into the housing market. These included three government agencies, namely the Federal Housing Administration (FHA), the Government National Mortgage Association (GNMA), and the Veterans Administration (VA). In addition, the US government created two private firms, the Government National Mortgage Association (Ginnie Mae) and the Federal Home Loan Mortgage Corporation (Freddie Mac). Both of these were private firms with traded stock, but with a government guarantee. The purpose was to increase the flow of funds into the housing market and reduce the cost of housing. These goals were achieved by investing in mortgages and in creating mortgage-backed securities.

Both Fannie Mae and Freddie Mac became insolvent during the financial crisis. As a result, the US government took over the running of these firms by putting them into government run conservatorship.

Phase V: Recovery

By 2010, the economy began to recover, although housing prices declined on average in the US through 2012. After 2012, the steady recovery became stronger, and the economy has expanded through 2019. Since 2012, housing prices have risen considerably. The average housing price in the United States went up 50% between 2012 and 2018.

SUMMARY

Mortgages are used to finance real estate properties, both homes and commercial properties. Fixed-rate mortgages have a constant interest rate over the life of the mortgage. Floating-rate mortgages have an interest rate that moves up and down as market interest rates change. Borrowers have the option to prepay a mortgage loan before maturity.

The mortgage market has undergone dramatic changes since the mid-1970s. The amount of money flowing into mortgages has increased as a percentage of gross domestic product. Mortgage-backed securities were developed, allowing originators of mortgage loans to sell the mortgages into mortgage pools that are then sold to investors. These mortgage pools were often divided and subdivided into many different varieties. There was a housing boom from approximately the mid-1990s through 2006, with home prices rising dramatically. Subsequently, home prices fell dramatically and many borrowers have defaulted on their mortgage loans.

The bursting of the housing bubble significantly contributed to the Great Recession. Since then, both the economy and the housing market have recovered.

QUESTIONS AND PROBLEMS

1. For a standard fixed-rate mortgage, compute the annual mortgage payment for a 15-year annual mortgage loan with principal of $100 and interest rate of 5%.
2. In problem 1, break each mortgage payment into interest on remaining principal and amortization for the first three years.
    (a)   Also, compute the remaining balance on the mortgage at each point in time.
    (b)   What is the total amount of interest paid over the mortgage's life?
3. Assume that you take out a 15-year mortgage at a 5% interest rate and $100 principal.
    (a)   Compute the mortgage principal in the years 12 and 13.
    (b)   Compute the amortization in year 13.
    (c)   How many years does it take for half of the original principal to be repaid?
4. Suppose Susan has a 15-year mortgage with $100 principal. In year 8, the amortization of the principal is $5.93. Compute the interest rate on the mortgage.

5. Assume that you take out a 15-year mortgage at a 5% interest rate and $100 principal. After one year, the interest rate on new loans is 4%. If you refinance, there are refinancing costs of 3%.

    (a) Compute the immediate gain from refinancing.

    (b) Also, compute the refinancing benefit if the refinancing occurs five years after the mortgage is taken out.

6. Explain what it means to originate a mortgage loan. Who are the originators?

7. A bank has a choice of making a 2-year loan at 5% or a variable-rate loan at the 1-year Treasury bill rate plus 2%. Currently, the Treasury bill rate is 1%. Under what circumstances is the 2-year loan better than the variable-rate loan and vice versa?

8. Assume a standard fixed–rate mortgage.

    (a) Compute the annual mortgage payment for a 15-year annual mortgage loan with principal of $100 and interest rate of 6%.

    (b) Also compute the monthly and annual payments if the mortgage is paid monthly and the monthly interest rate is (6%) / 12. Why is there a difference between the total annual payments with annual versus monthly payments?

9. Assume that you take out a 15-year mortgage at a 6% interest rate and $100 principal.

    (a) Compute the amortization in year 10.

    (b) Repeat the calculation assuming monthly payments with interest rate of (6%) / 12.

10. Suppose that you take out a 15-year mortgage loan with principal of $100. The annual mortgage payment is $8.99. What is the interest rate?

CHAPTER 12

Futures Contracts

Futures contracts on physical commodities have been traded for many years. In recent years, active markets have developed for financial futures contracts. This chapter describes futures contracts for physical commodities and the use of futures contracts in risk reduction and hedging. The next chapter examines bond futures contracts and their uses.

A futures contract involves a contractual agreement to purchase or sell something at a future point in time, called the *delivery date*.[1] The buyer is called the *long* and the seller is called the *short*. Futures contracts are *zero-sum games;* that is, the short and the long are playing against each other. The long's gains equal the short's losses and vice versa.

The actual purchase of the commodity is not scheduled to take place until the delivery date, as shown in Figure 12.1. For example, suppose a contract is signed for the short to deliver one ounce of silver in one year for a price of $18. Figure 12.2 shows the futures obligations.

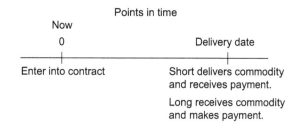

FIGURE 12.1 Futures Contracts Cash Flows.

---

[1] For some futures contracts, the delivery date is actually a month. The seller has the option to pick the exact day during the month to make delivery of the contract and be paid.

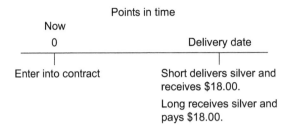

Points in time

Now
0
Delivery date

Enter into contract

Short delivers silver and receives $18.00.

Long receives silver and pays $18.00.

FIGURE 12.2 Silver Futures.

In fact, most futures contracts are closed out by an offsetting position before delivery occurs. A long offsets by going short; a short offsets by going long. Imagine an investor who has taken a short position in silver futures at $18.00 per ounce on March 15 as shown in Figure 12.3. The scheduled delivery date is September 15. Any time before that delivery date, the short can offset the short position by going long. For example, suppose that on March 16 the short decides to close the position by *offsetting*—that is, going long at $18.05 per ounce. Going long one contract offsets the original short position for a loss of $0.05 per ounce. There is a loss because the investor has sold (shorted) at $18.00 and bought (gone long) at $18.05. Had the position been closed at a price below $18.00, the short would have gained.

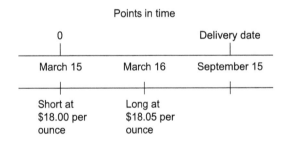

Points in time

0
Delivery date

March 15   March 16   September 15

Short at $18.00 per ounce

Long at $18.05 per ounce

FIGURE 12.3 Offsetting a Futures Position.

Offsetting does not involve any incremental brokerage fees because the fee to establish the initial short position includes the commission to take the offsetting long position—a so-called *round-trip commission*. If actual delivery is made on the contract on September 15, silver has to be purchased and delivered to the location specified in the futures contract. Sizable transactions costs may be incurred. Therefore, most futures contracts are offset, not delivered. Even with financial futures contracts, the transactions costs involved in purchasing the securities in the spot market generally exceed the cost of an offsetting futures position.

Historically, futures contracts have been traded in a designated "pit" at the exchange. A pit is a series of steps above the trading floor. The traders stand on the steps and engage in open outcry and hand signal trading. Because of the rapid ups and downs in futures prices, the pressures of being a trader are quite intense. In recent years, some of the trading in the futures markets has been shifted to automated systems with electronically executed orders.

OPEN INTEREST

Futures markets have clearinghouses which keep track of the total number of outstanding contracts, the open interest. The shorts and longs deal with the clearinghouse, not with each other. For every outstanding contract, one person is short and one is long. For the open interest to change, the number of shorts and longs must change. Consider the example in Figure 12.4. On March 15, the open interest is five contracts. In total, investors are long five contracts and short five contracts. For every contract long, there must be a contract short.

Longs		Shorts	
Bill	4	Sherman	3
Will	1	Herman	2

Total Longs = Total Shorts.

FIGURE 12.4 Open Interest—Day 1.

On March 16, Bill decides to offset one long contract by going short, reducing Bill's net position to three contracts long. When Bill goes short one contract, someone else must be going long. The identity of this long determines the change in the open interest.

The first possibility occurs if there is another long investor, Phil. Then the open interest remains the same. See Figure 12.5.

Open Interest--Day 2			
Longs		Shorts	
Bill	3	Sherman	3
Will	1	Herman	2
Phil	1		
	5		5

Open Interest is unchanged.

FIGURE 12.5 A New Long Enters the Market.

If an investor with an existing short position goes long, the open interest is reduced. For example, suppose Sherman decides to offset one contract. Then the new open interest is shown in Figure 12.6.

Open Interest--Day 2			
Longs		Shorts	
Bill	3	Sherman	2
Will	1	Herman	2
	4		4

FIGURE 12.6 Bill Offsets 1 and Sherman Offsets 1.

To summarize, if a particular transaction involves a new long *and* a new short, the open interest increases by one contract. If a transaction involves offsetting by an existing long *and* offsetting by an existing short, the open interest declines by one contract. If a transaction entails offsetting by an existing short or long, and if the other side of the transaction is a new investor, the open interest remains unchanged. The clearinghouse cancels the offsetting positions.

The amount of trading is different from the open interest. For example, if fifty longs decided to offset by going short and the other sides of the transactions were taken by fifty new long investors, there would be fifty trades and an unchanged open interest. But there can also be fifty trades if fifty long positions offset and fifty short positions offset.

MARGIN AND MARKING-TO-MARKET

Every long and short position is required to post a performance bond called *margin* with the clearinghouse. The margin allows the clearinghouse to guarantee the financial integrity of contracts. If one side defaults, the clearinghouse should have sufficient margin funds to ensure that the other side of the contract does not suffer financially.

Because an investor in futures markets must put down margin equal to only a small proportion of the market value of the underlying commodity, the investor's position is highly levered and quite risky. A small percentage change in the price of the futures contract brings about a much larger percentage change in the value of the margin. If the investor puts down $m\%$ of the futures price, the margin will change $1 / (m\%)$ for every 1% change in the futures price. For example, if an investor puts down 10% of the futures price, the margin will change $1 / 0.10$, or 10 times as fast as the futures price.

Each day the exchange computes a *settlement price*. The settlement price is used to figure the amount of cash transfer between shorts and longs after trading closes. The settlement price is not the closing price, the price from the very last trade of the day. Instead, the settlement price is an average of the prices near the end of trading. If the closing price were used, some traders might be able to manipulate prices at the close to their advantage since the settlement price is used for daily marking-to-market.

If the settlement price increases (decreases) from one day to the next, the long has a gain (loss) and the short has a loss (gain). Consider an example for silver futures. Suppose the settlement price on March 15 is $18.00 per ounce and at the end of trading on the next day, March 16, the settlement price becomes $18.20. Then the long gains $0.20 per ounce and the short loses $0.20 per ounce. The clearinghouse transfers funds between the accounts of the short and the long in a process called *marking-to-market*. In the futures markets, every contract is marked-to-market every day. Every day, the longs and the shorts must "settle up." The funds used to settle the accounts of the shorts and the longs come from the collateral deposited by investors with the clearinghouse. When prices increase, the collateral of the longs is increased and the shorts' collateral is reduced by the same amount. If an individual investor's collateral becomes too small as a result of market price changes, the investor is required to put up more margin or the position is closed. Thus, marking-to-market helps to guarantee performance on the contract.

Futures exchanges set price limits on some individual futures contracts except during delivery months. Price limits restrict the change in price on a particular day to some maximum amount up or down. For example, suppose a futures contract settles on Monday at $8. If a price limit of $1 is applicable, on Tuesday the contract is not allowed to trade at less than $7 or more than $9. The motivation for price limits is to restrict the price volatility of futures contracts. If a contract is up or down the limit, trading may stop until the following day, allowing the traders some time to cool down. The price limits also allow the clearinghouse time to collect more collateral from traders who have taken losses. Thus, price limits help to maintain the financial integrity of traders' positions. Instead of having price limits, the clearinghouse could require greater amounts of collateral.

In addition, limits may be set on the total number of contracts in which a position can be taken. Position limits are motivated by the desire to keep markets competitive. There is fear that price manipulation might occur if one trader, or a syndicate of traders, controls too many contracts. These position limits, combined with price limits and margin requirements, guarantee the financial integrity of contract positions. Thus, one side of a contract can expect to suffer no financial harm if the other side defaults.

FORWARD VERSUS FUTURES CONTRACTS

In some markets, forward contracts are traded. Forward contracts have a number of similarities and differences with futures contracts, as summarized in Table 12.1.

There are several differences between forward markets and futures markets. First, futures markets are organized public markets where information about prices, the volume of trading, and positions outstanding are publicly available. This information disclosure increases the transparency and the liquidity of futures markets. Forward markets are over-the-counter markets. Over-the-counter markets typically have no public record of trading prices, volumes, or positions.

Second, futures markets have clearinghouses. The shorts and longs deal with the clearinghouse, rather than each other. The clearinghouse requires collateral as a guarantee of performance on contracts. Futures markets have marking-to-market on a daily basis. The combination of collateral and daily marking to market makes defaults on futures contracts rare. In the theoretical forward contracts discussed in this book, default is assumed to be impossible. In practice, the chance for default on a forward contract can be considerable. The markets for forward foreign exchange attempt to solve the problem of default by having a small and private market in which the parties are unlikely to default because of their close ties.

Third, futures markets trade a standardized commodity while forward markets trade customized contracts. Standardized futures markets are typically much more liquid than customized contracts in forward markets.

Table 12.1. Forward versus Futures Contracts

	Forward	Futures
Collateral	None	Yes
Marking-to-Market	None	Daily
Compensating Balances	Usually	None
Resale	Limited	Active trading on organized exchanges
Contract Terms	Custom made	Standardized
Delivery	Usually delivered	Usually offset
Market Size	Small, private. Participants know each other.	Large, public, impersonal

If all interest rates are certain, futures and forward prices are identical, even though futures contracts have marking-to-market. Since interest rates are uncertain in practice, a difference between futures and forward prices may exist. Empirically, any difference between futures and forwards appears to be a second-order effect—perhaps a fraction of a percent. The subsequent discussion of futures markets overlooks the possible differences between futures and forward contracts created by collateral requirements and marking-to-market.

DETERMINANTS OF FUTURES PRICES

On the delivery date, a futures contract and a spot market contract are identical. If not, arbitrage opportunities are available from buying in the lower-priced market and simultaneously selling in the higher-priced market. If the futures price is higher than the spot price, an arbitrager can make a profit by shorting futures, buying the commodity, and delivering it into the futures contract for an immediate risk-free profit. If the futures price is below the spot price, an arbitrager can go long futures and short sell the commodity; when delivery occurs on the futures contract, the delivered commodity can be used to close the short position.

Before the delivery date, there are two cases to consider. First, for a nonstorable commodity, the futures price is determined by the market's expectation of the future spot price on the delivery date. As an example, consider a hypothetical futures market for fresh tomatoes with a delivery date one year into the future. Since fresh tomatoes are storable only for short periods, the futures price for delivery one year hence is set by the market's expectations of demand and supply for fresh tomatoes on the delivery date. These expectations depend on population trends, weather conditions, availability of substitutes, etc. In recent years, an increasing number of contracts have been created for nonstorable items, such as electricity.

Second, the commodity may be storable. In practice, most existing futures contracts are for storable commodities. Let the current (time 0) futures price for delivery at time d in the future be $F_{0,d}$ and the current (time 0) spot price be P_0. Then, for storable commodities such as grains and metals, the cost of carry model implies the following relationship between futures prices and spot prices:

$$F_{0,d} = P_0 + \text{Interest} + \text{Storage until Delivery} \qquad \textbf{12.1}$$

In other words, purchasing a futures contract is the equivalent of borrowing the purchase price of a commodity, buying the commodity, and storing it until the delivery date (see Table 12.2). At the delivery date, the loan principal, interest charges, and storage costs must be paid. The total of these three costs should equal the futures price.

Table 12.2. Creating a Forward Position from a Spot Position

Actions	Points in Time	
	0	Delivery Date
		Cash Flows
Borrow	$+P_0$	Repay $-[P_0 + \text{Interest} + \text{Storage}]$
Buy Commodity	$-P_0$	
Net Cash Flows	0	$-[P_0 + \text{Interest} + \text{Storage}]$

Futures Price above Equilibrium Level

In the case of zero storage costs and unrestricted, cost-free short selling, arbitrage forces the futures price to equal the spot price plus interest. To prove this, the cases where the futures price is above (below) its equilibrium value are shown shortly to provide arbitrage opportunities. Arbitrage forces the prices back to their equilibrium values.

Table 12.3 shows the arbitrage if the futures price rises above its equilibrium price. The arbitrager can short futures, borrow money, purchase the commodity in the spot market, and store until the delivery date. On the delivery date, the arbitrager delivers the commodity, gets paid by the long, and repays the loan plus interest. There is a sure profit. To simplify the discussion, the storage cost is assumed to be zero. R is defined as the total interest from time zero until delivery expressed as a percentage.

Table 12.3. Arbitrage If Futures Price Is above Equilibrium Level

Actions	Points in Time	
	0	Delivery Date
		Cash Flows
Short Futures		$+F_{o,d}$
Borrow	$+P_0$	
Buy Commodity	$-P_0$	
Repay Loan + Interest		$-P_0(1+R)$
Deliver Commodity in Futures Market		
Net Cash Flows	0	$F - P_0(1+R)$

If $F_{o,d} - P_0(1+R)$ is positive, there is a sure arbitrage profit. The actions of arbitragers shorting futures and buying in the spot market drive the futures price F down and the spot market price P up until $F_{o,d} - P_0(1+R)$ equals zero.

Consider the following numerical example of arbitrage. If the spot price of gold is $1400 and the one-year spot interest rate is 10%, the futures price for delivery in one year should be $1540 [i.e., 1400 (1.10)]. If the futures price is actually $1600, arbitrage profits are available from shorting futures, borrowing $1400, buying gold, and storing it until the delivery date. The actions and cash flows are shown in Table 12.4.

Table 12.4. Arbitrage Example If Futures Price Is above Equilibrium Level

	Points in Time	
	0	Delivery Date
Actions		Cash Flows
Short Futures		+ 1600
Borrow	+1400	
Buy Commodity	−1400	
Repay Loan + Interest		−1400(1.10)
Deliver Commodity in Futures Market		
Net Cash Flows	0	1600 − 1400(1.10) = 60

Futures Price below Equilibrium Level

Table 12.5 shows the arbitrage. The arbitrager goes long futures, short sells the commodity, and invests the proceeds from the short sale. On the delivery date, the arbitrager purchases the commodity through the futures contract, uses this to close the short position, and receives the amount lent plus interest for a sure profit.

Table 12.5. Arbitrage If Futures Price Is below Equilibrium Level

	Points in Time	
	0	Delivery Date
Actions		Cash Flows
Long futures		$-F_{o,d}$
Short commodity	$+P_o$	
Invest proceeds	$-P_o$	$+P_o(1+R)$
Take delivery on futures and close short position		
Net cash flows	0	$-[F_{o,d} - P_o(1+R)]$

If the futures price F is less than the spot price plus interest, $P_o(1 + R)$, the net cash flow from this arbitrage is positive with complete certainty. The actions of arbitragers repeatedly profiting from this arbitrage force the futures price up and the spot price down until the arbitrage profits are eliminated—that is, until the futures price equals the spot price plus interest.

Consider the arbitrage opportunities for the following numerical example. The spot price of gold is $1400 and the one-year interest rate is 10%, again implying a futures price of $1540. If the futures price is actually $1400, the arbitrage opportunity is as shown in Table 12.6.

Table 12.6. Example of Arbitrage If Futures Price Is below Equilibrium Level

	Points in Time	
	0	Delivery Date
Actions		Cash Flows
Long Futures		−1400
Short Commodity	+1400	
Invest Proceeds	−1400	+1400(1.10)
Take Delivery on Futures and Close Short Position		
Net Cash Flows	0	$-[1400 - 1400(1.10)] = 140$

The Length of Time until Delivery

Futures contracts for more distant delivery dates typically have higher price quotations because of higher interest and storage costs for carrying the commodity for a longer time period. With zero storage costs, the futures price for delivery in d periods is the spot price times 1 plus the spot interest rate for d periods (R_d) to the power d [i.e., $(1 + R_d)^d$]. Figure 12.7 shows the theoretical futures prices for several delivery dates. The theoretical futures price for immediate delivery is the same as the spot price. As the delivery date becomes more distant, the theoretical futures price in the cost of carry model increases by the total interest between the current point in time and the delivery date (as well as the storage costs, which we have omitted for simplicity).

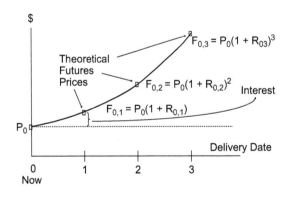

FIGURE 12.7 Futures Price for Several Delivery Dates.

Convenience Yield

For most futures contracts, the futures price increases as the delivery date becomes more distant because the total interest and storage costs increase as the delivery date becomes more distant. For some commodities, possession of the commodity may have a convenience value to a firm. This convenience yield may reduce the futures price below the spot price plus interest and storage. Figure 12.8 illustrates the impact of convenience yield. In a perfect market, there would be an arbitrage from going long in the futures, shorting the commodity in the spot market, lending the proceeds, and closing all positions at the futures delivery date. For commodities with convenience yield, short selling the commodity in the spot market is impossible in practice. For such commodities, the actual futures price lies below the theoretical futures price.

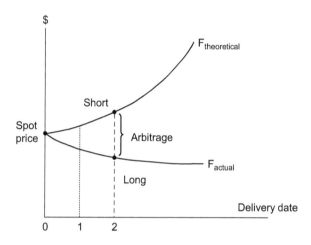

FIGURE 12.8 The Impact of Convenience Yield.

The case of oil futures prices during the war with Iraq in the fall of 1990 is a striking example of convenience yield, although many other similar examples can be found. Table 12.7 presents the futures price per barrel for light sweet crude oil observed on September 28, 1990, for various delivery dates. At the time, the spot price of oil was approximately $41 per barrel.

Table 12.7. Futures Price of Light Sweet Crude Oil Observed on September 28, 1990

Delivery Month	Futures Price ($ per Barrel)
November 1990	39.51
December 1990	38.31
January 1991	36.72
February 1991	35.40
March 1991	34.15
April 1991	33.00
May 1991	31.95
June 1991	31.00
July 1991	30.20
August 1991	29.55
September 1991	29.05
October 1991	28.62
November 1991	28.27
December 1991	27.98
January 1992	27.71
February 1992	27.45
March 1992	27.20
April 1992	26.96

If arbitrage is possible, the futures price for distant delivery dates should exceed the spot price by the amount of interest and storage until the delivery date. With the spot price of oil at $41 in September 1990, the sum of the spot price plus interest and storage until April 1992 is considerably higher than $41. Yet, the futures price for April 1992 delivery was only $26.96. Consequently, the convenience yield exceeded $14.04 ($41 − 26.96).

The earlier discussion indicated an arbitrage opportunity if the futures price is less than the cost of carrying. The arbitrage is to (short) sell the commodity, invest the proceeds, go long futures, and use the oil purchased from the futures contract to cover the short sale. To short sell, a lender of the commodity has to be found. Given fears about oil shortages resulting from the war, no lenders of oil were available. The potential lenders of oil were unwilling to lend because the convenience yield of oil was very high. A second possibility is for holders of oil to switch their position by selling their own oil, lending the proceeds, and buying back oil in the futures market. Again, the war uncertainties made holders of oil unwilling to give up the convenience yield of their inventories, making arbitrage impossible. In short, the war and the resulting high convenience yield created a divergence between the theoretical futures and the actual futures.

SPECULATIVE FUTURES POSITIONS

Going short or long in futures without any offsetting position is often described as taking a *speculative position*. As an example, suppose you anticipate a sharp rise in the price of silver and go long in silver futures for 1,000 ounces at $15.00 per ounce. Happily, you are correct. The futures price goes to $16.00 and you make a profit of $1.00 per ounce, or $1,000.

To set up your original futures position, margin is required in the form of marketable securities or cash. The broker will inform you of the exact amount of margin. For simplicity, assume that the initial margin is $1500 (10% of the original value of the contract). If, in fact, the actual gain on your short position is $1,000, the percentage gain is 1000 / 1500 = 66.67%, ten times the 6.667% gain on an outright purchase for $15,000. The percentage gains and losses on futures can be very large. All of your margin can be lost in a few days. For this reason, speculative positions (i.e., either short or long with no offsetting position) in futures contracts are very risky.

The percentage changes in collateral (or equity) are related to the percentage changes in the underlying futures price in the following way (overlooking interest and dividends):

$$\% \text{ change equity} = \frac{\% \text{ change futures price}}{\% \text{ put down}} \qquad \textbf{12.2}$$

For example, if the margin percentage is 5%, then

$$\% \text{ change equity} = \frac{\% \text{ change futures price}}{0.05}$$
$$= 20[\% \text{ change futures price}] \qquad \textbf{12.3}$$

Since 1 / 0.05 = 20, your collateral changes 20 times as fast percentage-wise as the futures price.

HEDGING WITH FUTURES CONTRACTS

In a futures *hedge,* an investor offsets a position in the spot market with a nearly opposite position in the futures market with the objective of reducing the overall risk of the position. Hedges allow those unwilling or unable to bear the risk to transfer the risk to another party willing and able to take on the risks and possible rewards.

In a *long hedge,* the investor takes a long position in futures. In a *short hedge,* the investor takes a short position in futures. A very important type of short hedge occurs when an investor with a long position in the spot market simultaneously shorts futures contracts. This variety of a short hedge is illustrated by the following example.

Suppose a farmer plants a wheat crop in the spring, expecting to harvest and sell the wheat in the fall. Effectively, the farmer's planted wheat is a long position in wheat. Because the price of wheat at the harvest time is uncertain, the farmer bears considerable risk about the eventual profits earned on the wheat. To protect against this risk, the farmer shorts wheat futures (a short hedge) and locks-in the selling price of the wheat. If the futures price is $6 per bushel and production costs are $4 per bushel, the farmer's short position in wheat futures allows the wheat to be sold at $6 per bushel, locking-in a profit of $2 per bushel.

The short futures position is a two-edged sword. While the farmer can avoid losses if the wheat price at harvest is low, the farmer also gives up large profits if the wheat price is quite high at the harvest date. The farmer is willing to give up the chance of large profits in order to avoid possible catastrophic losses on the downside. The futures contract allows the farmer to transfer the risks to someone else better able to bear these risks.

As an example of a *long hedge*, consider a bread manufacturer in need of wheat to make the bread. To lock in the purchase price of wheat on the harvest date, the bread manufacturer goes long wheat futures (a long hedge). The bread manufacturer forgoes windfall gains if the wheat price is low on the harvest date. In exchange, potentially large losses are avoided if wheat prices are high on the harvest date. The futures contract permits the bread manufacturer to pass on the price risks of wheat.

The outcome from a hedge depends on the length of time that the hedge is held. There are two cases to consider for a short hedge. One possibility is for the short hedger to hold the position until delivery and then deliver the commodity at time 2. In this way, the short hedger locks in the selling price. See Table 12.8.

Table 12.8. Short Hedge Held until Delivery.

Points in Time	0	1	Delivery Date 2
Action	Long Spot & Short Futures		Deliver Spot
Cash Flows	$-P_0$		$+F_{0,2}$

Second, the hedger may close the position before delivery. See Table 12.9.

Table 12.9. Close Short Hedge before Delivery.

Points in Time	0	1	Delivery Date 2
Action	Long Spot & Short Futures	Sell Spot & Long Futures	
Cash Flows	$-P_0 + F_{0,2}$	$P_1 - F_{1,2}$	

The net cash flows are $-P_0 + P_1 + F_{0,2} - F_{1,2}$, overlooking any time differences or interest. Notice that $-P_0 + P_1$ is the change in the spot price and $F_{0,2} - F_{1,2}$ is the change in the futures price. If the net cash flows are exactly zero, the hedge is perfect as shown in Figure 12.9.

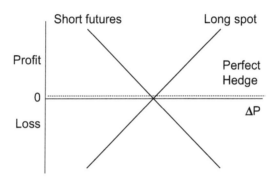

FIGURE 12.9 Profit Profile for Short Hedge.

In short hedging, the hedger may be able to find a futures contract for a virtually identical item as the hedger's spot position. Then the gains (losses) in the spot market are offset by the losses (gains) in the futures market as shown in Figure 12.9. As the spot price increases (decreases), the investor gains (loses) dollar for dollar. Gains (losses) in the spot position are offset dollar for dollar by the short futures position. The profit profile for the net position is a horizontal line, indicating no change in the value of the net position.

CROSS HEDGING

Many times, futures contracts that are identical to spot commodities do not exist. The hedger must utilize a short position in a similar, but different, item. This is called a cross hedge. Then the hedge is not perfect and $-P_0 + P_1 + F_{0,2} - F_{1,2}$ does not equal 0.

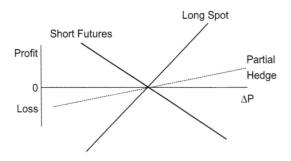

FIGURE 12.10 Profit Profile for Cross Hedge.

Suppose a farmer is long in the spot market in wheat, but futures trade for a different commodity. The prices of the two commodities are related, but different. Suppose the farmer engages in a one-for-one hedge. For every bushel of wheat in the farmer's long spot position, the farmer shorts one bushel of futures. Figure 12.10 shows the profit profiles for long spot wheat, short futures, and the net position. The futures prices are assumed to move half as fast as spot wheat prices. The slope of the profit profile for long spot is 1.0; the slope of the profit profile for short futures is –0.50. The net position has a slope of +0.50. Thus, the gains and losses on the spot position in wheat are cut in half by the short hedge.

FINE-TUNING THE HEDGE

In a simple hedge, the short hedger shorts one unit of futures for every one unit of a spot position. If the price changes in the futures and spot markets do not follow a one-for-one relationship, the hedge will not be perfect, although the risk of the net position will be lower than the risk of a simple spot position. The effectiveness of the hedge may be improved by changing the number of futures contracts per unit of spot contracts.

Suppose a $1 change in the spot price results in a change in the futures price of $b as shown as the slope in Figure 12.11. The hedge can be improved by short selling $1 / b$ units of futures for every unit of spot.

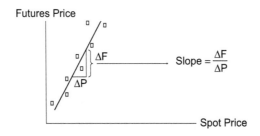

FIGURE 12.11 Spot and Futures Prices.

Suppose that the futures price changes by $1.25 for every $1 change in spot prices as shown in Figure 12.12.

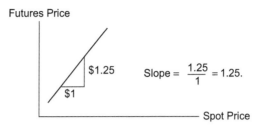

FIGURE 12.12 Example of the Optimal Hedge Ratio.

Then, the optimal hedge ratio is 1 / 1.25 = 0.80. For every unit of spot, .80 units of futures are shorted. The change in the net position is zero. That is,

$$\Delta\text{Net} = (\Delta\text{Spot})(\# \text{ Units}) - (\Delta F)(\# \text{ Units}) \qquad \textbf{12.4}$$

$$\Delta\text{Net} = (\$1)(1) - (1.25)(0.80) \qquad \textbf{12.5}$$

$$\Delta\text{Net} = 0 \qquad \textbf{12.6}$$

In practice, the relationship between a spot position and a futures contract in a cross hedge is typically not a perfect straight line, but rather the dots shown in Figure 12.13. Using regression analysis, the hedger can estimate the slope of the best-fitting relationship, b. The optimal hedge is not a perfect hedge since the link between the spot and futures is not perfect. The optimal hedge is the best hedge in the sense that the expected change in the hedged position is zero.

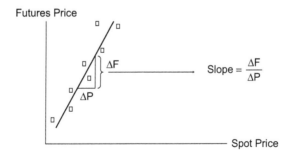

FIGURE 12.13 Actual Spot and Futures Prices.

INTERACTION BETWEEN SPOT AND FUTURES PRICES

The earlier discussion focused on the effect of spot prices of commodities on futures prices. The discussion focused on the causation running from spot prices to futures prices. In reality, prices in the futures market have an influence on spot prices. The causation runs in both directions. The futures and the spot prices are jointly determined.

The joint determination of spot and futures markets has practical implications. At the beginning of 2007, the price of crude oil in the United States was approximately $50 per barrel. By the middle of 2008, the price had risen to $140. During this interval of time, there were relatively small changes in the supply and the demand for oil. In the same time interval, the open interest in oil futures approximately doubled.

Historically, positions in the futures markets were dominated by long and short hedgers, firms that used futures markets to reduce the risk of their operations. A small proportion of futures positions were taken by speculators, who are gambling on their ability to predict changes in futures prices.

A large increase in the open interest beginning in 2007 was driven by a large increase in long positions in oil futures by commodity index funds. These commodity index funds went long in futures to diversify their holdings of stocks and bonds into commodities, an asset class with low correlations of returns with stocks and bonds. Consequently, the open interest in oil futures doubled, resulting in the oil futures price jumping to approximately $140 per barrel. In the second half of 2008, commodity index funds exited the futures market, resulting in a decline in the open interest and a decline in the oil futures price back down to approximately $50 per barrel. Commodity funds also took large long positions in the other commodities in the Goldman Sachs 20 commodity index and these commodities had a cycle similar to that of oil. This example clearly shows how activity in the futures market can have an impact upon the price in the spot market.

The influence of commodity index funds has been hotly debated. Some have argued that commodity index fund long positions must necessarily be matched by some other party going short. Therefore, any price changes that occur are not the result of increases in the open interest. This argument overlooks the simple fact that increases in prices of commodities in the futures market create the opportunity for producers of commodities to lock in sale prices and make enormous profits. As the oil price went from $50 a barrel to $140 a barrel, many oil producers with production costs below the futures price were quite willing to take short positions in oil futures and lock in enormous profits. Producers of the other commodities in the Goldman Sachs 20 Commodity Index were also quite pleased to enter into highly profitable short positions in the futures markets as these commodities went way up in price in the futures market.

SUMMARY

Futures contracts are obligations to buy and sell commodities at future delivery dates. These contracts allow businesses and individuals to transfer price risks to those who choose to bear the risks. The short is obligated to sell the commodity at a fixed price. The long is required to buy the commodity at the contractually agreed price.

The futures price of storable commodities equals the spot price plus interest and storage until the delivery date. Arbitrage guarantees this result in the absence of convenience yield.

In a hedge, a position in the spot market is offset with a futures position to reduce the overall risk. A short hedge involves a short futures position. A long hedge includes a long futures position.

QUESTIONS AND PROBLEMS

1. The open interest includes:

Longs		Shorts	
Bob	15 contracts	Bill	10 contracts
Lois	5 contracts	Will	10 contracts

   Determine the new open interest under the following assumptions:
   (a) Bill goes long one contract and Gene shorts one contract.
   (b) Bill goes long one contract and Bob shorts one contract.
2. Explain the differences between forward and futures contracts.
3. What are price and position limits on futures contracts? What are the purposes of price and position limits?
4. Suppose you go long in gold futures at $1300 per ounce. Your broker requires you to put up 5% of this price as collateral. The net day gold futures settle at $1320. Compute the gain as a percentage of your equity in the position. What is the general relationship between the percentage change in the investor's equity and the percentage change in the futures price?
5. Assume no marking-to-market or storage costs. The spot price of gold is $1300 and the futures price for delivery in one year is $1360. The annual interest rate is 10%. Is the preceding information mutually consistent? If not, how can investors exploit the situation for their own profit?
6. Suppose that oil in the spot market is selling for $100 per barrel. Oil futures for delivery in two years are quoted at $80 per barrel. The two-year spot interest rate is 5%. Explain the perfect market arbitrage to profit from this situation. In practice, what would prevent this arbitrage from occurring?

7. Investors can reduce their risk by using a futures market hedge to offset a spot market position. What happens to this risk? What are the consequences for the hedger?

8. A farmer plants enough wheat to harvest 1000 bushels. The cost of planting the wheat is $2.50 per bushel. On the harvest date, the wheat price will be one of three prices with equal probability: $2.00, $4.00, or $6.00. Compute the farmer's profit for each of these possibilities. The futures price for wheat is $3.80. Compute the farmer's profit for this price. When is hedging with futures the best choice for the farmer?

9. You buy gold in the spot market at $1280 per ounce. You decide to hedge the gold position with a cross hedge in platinum futures. Suppose platinum futures are quoted at $1400 per ounce. For every dollar that gold advances (or declines), platinum futures are likely to change by $1.25. Draw a profit profile for a one-to-one hedge—one ounce of short platinum futures for each ounce long spot gold. Then, derive the hedge ratio for a perfect hedge and draw the profit profile.

10. Gold is selling for $1280 in the spot market. Gold futures for delivery in one year are quoted at $1315 per ounce. You observe that one-year Treasury strips are selling at $99 per $100 of par and two-year strips are selling at $97 per $100 of par value. Are there are any arbitrage opportunities?

CHAPTER 13

Bond Futures

Bond futures contracts allow market participants to agree to buy or sell bonds at delivery dates in the future. Investors who are long in bond futures are able to lock in future lending interest rates. Investors taking short positions in bond futures are able to lock in future borrowing interest rates. Bond futures contracts can also be used for hedging, i.e., transferring risks to other parties.

TREASURY BOND FUTURES

In 1977, the Chicago Board of Trade (CBT) introduced a US Treasury bond futures contract. Since then several different bond and note futures contracts have been introduced. To simplify the discussion, we will focus on one Treasury bond futures contract requiring the delivery of $100,000 par value of United States Treasury bonds. Currently, the contract allows the short to deliver any US Treasury bond with between 15 and 25 years to maturity as of the delivery date. Figure 13.1 illustrates the contract.

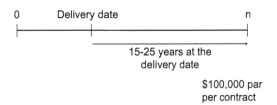

FIGURE 13.1 Treasury Bond Futures.

Besides the Treasury bond futures contract, the CME Group also offers trading in Treasury notes with maturities of 2, 3, 5, and 10 years. Recall that Treasury notes are securities issued with original maturities of 10 years or less, while Treasury bonds have original maturities greater than 10 years. In addition, the CME Group offers an Ultra Treasury Bond Futures Contract in which the deliverable bond has at least 25 years to maturity at the beginning of the delivery month of the contract. Interested readers should check the CME Group website for the full details of each contract.

Multiple Deliverable Bonds

One of the important features of the Treasury bond futures contract is the ability of the short position to deliver Treasury bonds with maturities between 15 and 25 years at the delivery date. Having a number of deliverable securities means that a set of rules must be established for the relative value of delivering individual securities. A later section of this chapter will discuss the impact of multiple deliverable bonds on the pricing of Treasury bond futures.

Having multiple deliverable bonds increases the supply of deliverable items enormously. The reason for multiple deliverable bonds is the prevention of *corners*. In the past, various individuals or groups of individuals have tried to manipulate prices in the futures market for personal gain. Since futures contracts are obligations to do something at the delivery date, the shorts or the longs may be contractually bound to close their positions at very unfavorable terms, i.e., to be *cornered*.

One of the more well-known corners involved the three Hunt brothers in the 1970s. The Hunt family had made a large amount of money in the oil business. In conjunction with several foreign individuals, the group devised a strategy of buying enormous amounts of silver in the silver spot market and going long in large amounts of silver futures. The intent was to accumulate large spot and futures positions at relatively low prices and then drive the price of silver in the spot and futures markets to very high levels. At the delivery date of silver futures contracts, the shorts were contractually obligated to either offset their positions at very high prices or buy silver in the spot market at very high prices and deliver into the futures contract. Either option would result in very large profits for the Hunt brothers and large losses for investors who had established short positions at relatively low prices.

Before the delivery date, the futures exchange, which is controlled by the futures brokers, became concerned that many of the shorts would default, leaving the brokers contingently liable for losses. Widespread defaults would jeopardize the future existence of this contract. To remedy the situation, the exchange tripled the margin requirements. The Hunt brothers and associates were forced to close out their long positions, driving the price markedly lower and preventing widespread contract defaults.

Subsequently, the Hunt brothers were prosecuted by the US government for manipulation of security prices under various federal government statutes. The brothers were found guilty and were heavily fined for their actions.

Other Contract Features

US Treasury bond futures are quoted per $100 of par value in 32nds of a dollar. The quote is a percentage of the par value of $100,000 per contract. As an example, if the quotation is 91–10, the dollar amount is $91,000 plus 10 / 32 times $1000, which is $312.50. Thus, a quote for Treasury bond futures of 91–10 translates into $91,312.50.

As in many futures contracts, the Treasury bond futures contract has a delivery month. The short is able to deliver into the contract on a number of dates during this delivery month. In addition, on a possible delivery date, the short has the option to deliver for several hours after trading closes on the futures exchange. If the price of the cheapest-to-deliver bond drops after the futures market closes, the short may be able to buy in the spot market and deliver into the futures market for a gain. Since traders who are long in Treasury bond futures during the delivery month are aware of these options, the futures price should reflect the potential impact of these options.

FUTURES PRICE ON THE DELIVERY DATE

On the delivery date, the futures price must equal the spot price of the deliverable commodity because arbitrage forces the futures price to equal the spot market price.[1] If the futures price is too high, the arbitrager shorts futures, buys the deliverable bond, and delivers the bond into the futures contract. If the futures price is too low, the arbitrager goes long futures and shorts the bond in the spot market; the bond acquired from the long futures position is used to cover the short position. If there are multiple deliverable bonds, the arbitrage applies for the cheapest bond to deliver.

FUTURES PRICE BEFORE THE DELIVERY DATE

The Treasury bond futures contract is different from metals futures contracts because the underlying bond pays coupons. A long futures position is not entitled to any cash flows from the underlying securities before the delivery date. For contracts on commodities such as gold with no cash payments made to gold investors, the futures price equals the current spot price plus interest and storage until delivery date. For Treasury bond futures, the futures price is shown below to equal the spot price plus interest until the delivery date minus the delivery date value of the coupons not received between now and the delivery date. Before covering the general case, let us consider several cases below.

---

[1] Strictly speaking, this statement is valid only if there is one delivery date. With multiple delivery dates during the month and with the wildcard option described below, market prices may deviate slightly from the spot price.

Delivery in One Year and Deliverable Bond Matures in Two Years

For this case, the futures cash flows are as shown in Table 13.1.

Table 13.1. Delivery in One Year and Two-Period Bond

		Points in Time	
	0	1 (Delivery Date)	2 (Bond Maturity)
Action	Contract signed	Futures price paid	Coupon + par value received
Cash Flows	0	$-F_{0,1}$	$+c+$ par

The futures price, $F_{0,1}$, is the price observed at time 0 for delivery at time 1. $F_{0,1}$ is the time 1 value of the coupon and par values discounted at the forward interest rate $f_{0,2}$ for period 2. That is,

$$F_{0,1} = \frac{c + \text{Par}}{1 + f_{0,2}} \qquad \textbf{13.1}$$

A little algebra indicates that

$$F_{0,1} = P_{0,2}\left(1 + R_{0,1}\right) - c \qquad \textbf{13.2}$$

where $P_{0,2}$ is the spot price of a 2-period bond and $R_{0,1}$ is the 1-period spot interest rate. The futures price is mathematically equivalent to the time 1 value of the current bond price, $P_{0,2}$, minus the coupon paid at time 1. The time 1 coupon is subtracted since the buyer of futures is not entitled to this coupon. The buyer of the futures contract is entitled only to the time 2 coupon and the par value. Thus, the futures price for delivery at time 1 is the spot price times 1+ the interest rate until the delivery date minus the coupon that is not received (because the futures purchase is made after the coupon payment).

As an example, assume the following term structure: $R_{0,1} = 2\%$, $R_{0,2} = 5\%$, implying that $f_{0,2} = 8.09\%$. Suppose a deliverable bond has a $5 coupon and $100 par value. The current or spot price of the bond is $100.14. Then,

$$F_{0,1} = \frac{105}{1.0809} = 97.14 = 100.14(1.02) - 5 \qquad \textbf{13.3}$$

Delivery in One Year and Deliverable Bond Matures in Three Years

The futures cash flows are shown in Table 13.2.

Table 13.2. Delivery in One Year and Three-Period Bond

		Points in Time		
	0	1 Delivery Date	2	3 Bond Maturity
Action	Contract Signed	Futures Price Paid		Coupon + Par Value Received
Cash Flows	0	$-F_{0,1}$	$+c$	$+c+\text{par}$

The futures price for delivery at time 1 should be the cash flows at time 2 and 3 discounted at the appropriate forward rates. That is,

$$F_{0,1} = \frac{c}{1+f_{0,2}} + \frac{c+\text{Par}}{(1+f_{0,2})(1+f_{0,3})} \qquad \textbf{13.4}$$

A little algebra indicates that:

$$F_{0,1} = P_{0,3}(1+R_{0,1}) - c \qquad \textbf{13.5}$$

As a numerical example, suppose the following term structure: $R_{0,1} = 5\%$, $f_{0,2} = f_{0,3} = 5\%$. Assume a \$5 coupon and par value of \$100. Then:

$$\begin{aligned} F_{0,1} &= \frac{5}{1.05} + \frac{105}{(1.05)(1.05)} \\ &= 100(1.05) - 5 = 100 \qquad \textbf{13.6} \end{aligned}$$

Delivery in One Year and Deliverable Bond Matures in n Years

The futures cash flows in this case are as shown in Table 13.3.

Table 13.3. Delivery in 1 Year and n-Period Bond

		Points in Time			
		Delivery Date			Bond Maturity
	0	1	2	...	n
Action	Contract signed	Futures price paid	Coupon received	Coupon received	Coupon + par value received
Cash Flows	0	$-F_{BOND}$	$+c$	$+c$	$+c+\text{par}$

The buyer of the futures contract receives the coupons from time 2 until time n and the par value at time n. The futures price is the time 1 value of these cash flows.

$$F_{0,1} = \frac{c}{1 + f_{0,2}} + \frac{c}{(1 + f_{0,2})(1 + f_{0,3})} + \ldots + \frac{c + \text{Par}}{(1 + f_{0,2})(1 + f_{0,3})\ldots(1 + f_{0,n})} \quad \textbf{13.7}$$

The long futures position for delivery at time 1 is entitled to receive the bond cash flows from time 2 through time n. To arrive at the time 1 value, each of these cash flows must be discounted by the appropriate forward interest rates. A little algebra indicates that the futures price may be expressed in terms of the current spot price of the bond as follows:

$$F_{0,1} = P_{0,n}(1 + R_{0,1}) - c \quad \textbf{13.8}$$

The futures price is mathematically equivalent to $P_{0,n}(1 + R_{0,1}) - c$. The intuition is that the buyer of futures pays the time 1 value of the bond less the value of the time 1 coupon, which is not received. This result holds true as long as the delivery date for the futures contract is time 1.

Delivery in d Years and Deliverable Bond Matures in n Years

The futures cash flows in this case are as shown in Table 13.4.

Table 13.4. Delivery in d Years and n-Period Bond

				Points in Time			
	0	1	...	d (delivery date)	$d+1$	...	n (bond maturity)
Action	Contract signed			Futures price paid	Coupon received	Coupon received	Coupon + par value received
Cash Flows	0	0	0	$-F_{0,d}$	$+c$	$+c$	$+c+\text{par}$

The buyer of the futures contract receives the coupons from time $d+1$ until time n and par value at time n. The futures price is the time d value of these cash flows. The forward price can be derived by looking at the time d value of each individual cash flow. The coupon c received at time $d+1$ must be discounted one period to time d at the forward rate $f_{0,d+1}$ for a time d value of $c/(1 + f_{0,d+1})$. The coupon received at time $d+2$ has a value at time d of $c/(1 + f_{0,d+1})(1 + f_{0,d+2})$. In general

$$F_{0,d} = \frac{c}{1 + f_{0,d+1}} + \frac{c}{(1 + f_{0,d+1})(1 + f_{0,d+2})} + \ldots$$

$$\ldots + \frac{c + \text{PAR}}{(1 + f_{0,d+1})(1 + f_{0,d+2})\ldots(1 + f_{0,n})} \qquad \textbf{13.9}$$

This equation is mathematically equivalent to the following:

$$F_{0,d} = (P_{0,n} - c\,A_{0,d})\,(1 + R_{0,d})^d \qquad \textbf{13.10}$$

$P_{0,n}$ is the spot price of an n-period bond, $A_{0,d}$ is the present value of an annuity of $1 per period for d periods, and $R_{0,d}$ is the spot interest rate for d periods. The forward price is equal to the current spot price $P_{0,n}$ of a bond with coupon c and maturity n minus the annuity of $c of coupons from time 1 to time d (i.e., $cA_{0,d}$) times $[1 + R_{0,d}]^d$ to adjust for the fact that the cash flows are received at time d.

To illustrate, suppose the futures delivery date is in two years. The deliverable bond has a maturity of 4 years and a coupon rate of 5%. Assuming $R_{0,1}$ is 4%, $R_{0,2}$ is 5%, $R_{0,3}$ is 6%, and $R_{0,4}$ is 7%, the current price of the bond is $93.64. The futures price is:

$$F_{0,2} = \left[P_{0,4} - c \left(\frac{1}{1 + R_{0,1}} + \frac{1}{(1 + R_{0,2})^2} \right) \right] (1 + R_{0,2})^2$$

$$= \left[93.64 - 5(.9615 + .9070) \right] (1.05)^2 = 92.94 \qquad \textbf{13.11}$$

COMPARISON WITH OTHER FUTURES CONTRACTS

There are many other types of futures contracts besides those for bonds. Comparison of the pricing of these other contracts with the pricing of bond futures is informative. Suppose we consider the case of a delivery date in one period. Then for bond futures we have

$$F_{0,1}^B = P_{0,1}^B (1 + R_{0,1}) - c \qquad \textbf{13.12}$$

Futures contracts for metals, grains, and other physical commodities are priced in very much the same way as Treasury bond futures with the exception that these physical commodities do not have coupons. Thus, the futures price for a metal such as gold for delivery at point in time one is

$$F_{0,1}^G = P_{0,1}^G (1 + R_{0,1}) \qquad \textbf{13.13}$$

Several stock index futures contracts are traded. These are also priced in a similar way as Treasury bond futures. The one difference is that stocks pay dividends as opposed to coupons paid on bonds. For bond futures contracts, the delivery date value of coupons received through the delivery date is subtracted. For stock futures contracts, the delivery date value of dividends received through the delivery date is subtracted. With stock futures, the dividends are not contractually set and consequently finding the delivery date value of the dividends involves dealing with the uncertainty of these dividends. Thus, for stock index futures the futures price for delivery at time one is:

$$F_{0,1}^{ST} = P_{0,1}^{ST}(1+R_{0,1}) - \left[\begin{array}{c} \text{Delivery date value of} \\ \text{dividends not received} \end{array} \right] \qquad \text{13.14}$$

HEDGING WITH FINANCIAL FUTURES

In a futures hedge, a spot position is (partially) offset with hedging in a futures position. The net position has reduced risk. The futures market allows many types of investors to transfer risks to other investors more willing to bear these risks.

There are many types of hedges. The ensuing discussion concentrates on short hedges, in which a long position in the spot market is offset by a short position in futures. These may be used by any investor who has a long position in the spot market. Apart from small investors, many financial institutions might hedge, including bond dealers, banks, insurance companies, and pension funds.

Short Hedge with Treasury Bond Futures

Suppose a bond dealer in the course of its business has net holdings at the end of Friday trading of $100,000 of Treasury bonds. Over the course of the weekend, the value of this inventory may go down. In order to protect against this risk, suppose the dealer shorts one contract of T-bond futures with $100,000 par value at 96–24.

Suppose on Monday morning, interest rates have risen. Consequently, the bond dealer is forced to sell the bonds at $99,000 for a $1000 loss. During the same period, the futures contract declines in value to 96–00, resulting in a gain of $750 on the short futures position. The net loss on the hedge position is $250. The bond dealer has moderated the downside risk by having a partially offsetting position in futures.

Table 13.5 shows the gains and losses from a short hedge. $-P_{0,n}$ is the value of the spot position purchased at time 0. $P_{1,n-1}$ is the value of the spot position sold at time 1. $+F_0$ is the value of the futures position shorted at time 0. $-F_1$ is the value of the long futures position at time 1.

Table 13.5. Gains and Losses from a Short Hedge

	Points in Time					
	0	1	$d = 2$ (delivery date)	$d + 1$	...	n (bond maturity)
Action	Long spot & Short futures	Sell spot & long futures				
Cash Flows	$-P_{0,n}$ $+F_{0,2}$	$+P_{1,n-1}$ & $-F_{1,2}$				

The net gain or loss on the hedge is:

$$\text{Net Gain (Loss)} = -P_{0,n} + P_{1,n-1} + F_0 - F_1 \qquad \textbf{13.15}$$

In the numerical example,

$$\text{Net Gain (Loss)} = -100{,}000 + 99{,}000$$
$$+ 96{,}750 - 96{,}000 = -250 \qquad \textbf{13.16}$$

Hedging is a two-edged sword. Losses are reduced by hedging and so are gains. If interest rates drop, the bond dealer makes a profit on the bonds but suffers a loss on the short futures position. The net gain is smaller, or negligible. Hedgers are willing to forgo both losses and gains because the hedger is risk-averse. For a hedger, the penalties from losses are greater than the advantages of gains. Large losses from a sharp increase in interest rates might bankrupt a bond dealer. To avoid this adverse possibility, the bond dealer is willing to forgo large gains. On average, the bond dealer will still profit by the bid-ask spread. Taking a futures position allows the bond dealer to protect the firm's position from the risk of sudden large increases in interest rates.

Hedges can be fine-tuned by changing the number of futures contracts in the hedge. In the bond dealer hedge, if the bond price changes $1.25 for every $1.00 change in the futures price, the expected payoff from the hedge can be improved by shorting 1.25 futures contracts for every bond ($100,000 par) purchased.

The difference between the futures price and the spot price (i.e., $F - P$) has been called the basis (B). Note that the net gain (loss) on a hedge equals the change in the basis. That is,

$$\text{Net Gain (Loss)} = +F_0 - P_{0,n} - \left[+F_1 - P_{1,n-1} \right]$$
$$= +B_0 - B_1 = \text{basis change} \qquad \textbf{13.17}$$

where B_0 is the basis at time 0 and B_1 is the basis at time 1. Hedges are effective if the change in the basis is relatively small. The hedge is perfect if the change in the basis is zero. Then the change in the futures and spot prices exactly offset.

CHEAPEST DELIVERABLE BOND

The investor who is short Treasury bond futures contracts is allowed to deliver many possible US Treasury bonds with $100,000 par value. A delivered bond must also have at least 15–25 years to the smaller of maturity or first call date. As discussed earlier, the purpose of having many bonds deliverable is to reduce the likelihood of a corner by increasing the total supply of deliverable securities.

Invoice Price

If delivery is made on a futures contract, the long pays the short the invoice price for delivering a particular bond. The *invoice price i*s equal to the settlement futures price times an *adjustment factor*. In trying to figure the best bond to deliver, the short has to do the following calculation for every bond:[2]

$$\text{Proceeds} = (F)(\text{adj}) - P$$

$$= \begin{bmatrix} \text{futures} \\ \text{price} \end{bmatrix} \begin{bmatrix} \text{adjustment} \\ \text{factor} \end{bmatrix} - \begin{bmatrix} \text{spot} \\ \text{price} \end{bmatrix} \qquad \textbf{13.18}$$

where F is the settlement futures price, adj is the adjustment factor, and P is the market price of the bond. The best, or *cheapest-bond-to-deliver*, from the short's viewpoint is the bond for which the proceeds in the preceding expression are the largest. In general, the proceeds are negative for all bonds. If the proceeds are positive, there are arbitrage profits from shorting futures and delivering the bond with positive proceeds. In equilibrium, all arbitrage opportunities should be eliminated, resulting in the net proceeds being zero or negative. The short tries to find the bond for which the proceeds are closest to zero; this minimizes the cost to deliver. On the delivery date, the cheapest bond to deliver is the bond for which the proceeds are zero in frictionless markets. Typically, there are several bonds that are relatively cheap to deliver. This makes corners very difficult.

---

[2] This overlooks accrued interest. The long must pay the short the invoice price plus accrued interest. The short delivers a bond which entitles him to the accrued interest. Technically, the accrued interest should be added to the invoice price and added to the bond price. But these two terms cancel.

The Adjustment Factor

To establish a relative value in delivery, the futures exchange uses an adjustment factor (adj) for each security. The adjustment factor for Treasury bond futures is computed from the following formula for a bond with n years to maturity, coupon of c:

$$adj = \frac{c/2par}{(1.03)} = \frac{c/2par}{(1.03)^2} + \ldots + \frac{c/2par + 1.0}{(1.03)^{2n}} \qquad \textbf{13.19}$$

$$adj = \left(\frac{c/2}{par}\right)\left(\begin{array}{c}\text{Present value of}\\ \text{an annuity at 3\%}\\ \text{for } 2n \text{ periods}\end{array}\right) + \frac{1}{(1.03)^{2n}} \qquad \textbf{13.20}$$

To compute the adjustment factor, the coupon rate divided by 2 (i.e., dollars of coupon divided by 2 par) and an assumed par value of 1.0 are discounted at a 3% discount rate for $2n$ half-year periods. The value of the adjustment factor (adj), depends upon the coupon rate. If the annual coupon rate is 6% of par, adj equals 1.0. If the annual coupon rate is greater (less) than 6%, adj is greater (less) than 1.0.

Table 13.6 illustrates the computation of the adjustment factor for 20-year bonds with annual coupon rates of 4% and 6% and par values of $100. If there are 20 years, there are 40 half-year periods. Note that the present value of a 40 annuity at 3% is 23.1148 and $1/(1.03)^{40}$ equals 0.3066.

Table 13.6. The Adjustment Factor

Coupon	Price	Computation of Adjustment Factor				
4%	$80.41	(.02)(23.1148)	+	.3066	=	.7689
6%	$100.00	(.03)(23.1148)	+	.3066	=	1.00

The short has the choice of bond to deliver. The adjustment factor attempts to adjust the invoice price for the relative worth of the bonds. Recall that the invoice price is the futures price times the adjustment factor. The invoice prices for the two bonds are computed in Table 13.6, assuming that the settlement futures price is $100.

Table 13.7. Invoice Price versus Market Price

Coupon	Invoice Price = (Futures Price)(Adjustment Factor)			Market Price
4%	(100)(.7689)	=	76.89	$80.41
6%	(100)(1.0)	=	100.00	$100.00

Table 13.7 shows the objective of the adjustment procedure to adjust the invoice price for the relative value of the bond delivered. The shorts search for the best bond to deliver, the so-called cheapest-to-deliver. The cheapest bond to deliver has an invoice price very close to the market price of the bond. Frequently, the difference between the invoice price and the market is close to zero for many bonds. Then the deliverable supply of bonds is large, and corners are hard to achieve.

Table 13.8 shows the invoice price, market price, and the proceeds from delivering each bond. The 4% coupon bond has negative net proceeds, while the 6% coupon bond has zero net proceeds and is cheaper to deliver. This bond will set the equilibrium futures price.

Table 13.8. Proceeds

Bond Coupon	Invoice Price	Market Price	Proceeds from Delivery
4%	$76.89	$80.41	− $3.52
6%	$100.00	$100.00	$0.00

Other Aspects of the Delivery Process

The delivery process for CBT Treasury bond futures has some other interesting complications. As with many futures contracts, there is a delivery month. The short position has the option to deliver at any point during the month.

In the beginning of the month, the settlement price for that day is used for deliveries initiated on that day. On the seventh business day before the end of a delivery month, the settlement futures price is determined. This price is used for computing the invoice price for deliveries made in the rest of this delivery month. The fixing of the futures price gives the short an option to choose the day for delivery. This delivery option may turn out to be quite valuable. If the futures price is fixed at $90 seven days before the end of the month and if spot prices subsequently decline, the short may be able to buy a deliverable bond for much less than its invoice price and deliver it for a profit. If bond prices subsequently rise during the last seven business days, the short would have to buy a bond at a high price and suffer a loss at delivery.

During most of the delivery month, the settlement futures price is set every day at 3 p.m. central time. The short has the option to deliver until 8 p.m. If the short chooses not to deliver, the same position is simply maintained until the next day, when the same choice is made. The option to initiate delivery between 3 p.m. and 8 p.m. has value to the short, since the trading of bonds continues after the futures markets close.[3] This option is called the *wildcard option*. If bond prices go down after 3 p.m., the short's option has positive value, and delivery may be desirable. It

---

[3] The actual delivery process covers three business days. On day 1, the short position gives notice that delivery is being initiated. Actually, delivery of the commodity and payment of the invoice price occurs on day 3.

has been suggested that this wildcard option tends to push the 3 p.m. futures price below the price that would prevail without the wildcard option.

SUMMARY

Treasury bond futures contracts are widely traded. The futures price for delivery on a particular delivery date equals the coupon payments plus par value discounted back to the delivery date at the appropriate forward interest rates. Treasury bond futures are widely used to hedge spot positions by investment banking firms, bond dealers, banks, and hedge funds. Treasury bond futures allow the short to deliver one of several bonds. The short will choose the cheapest bond to deliver. This cheapest-to-deliver bond sets the futures price.

QUESTIONS AND PROBLEMS

1. A bond futures contract with one deliverable bond has a maturity date in 2 years from now have par value of $100 and annual coupon of $5. If the futures delivery date is in 1 year, determine the futures price if
   (a) $R_{0,1} = R_{0,2} = 5\%$.
   (b) $R_{0,1} = 2\%, R_{0,2} = 6\%$.

2. Consider a bond futures contract with one deliverable bond having a maturity date in 3 years from now, par value of $100, and annual coupon of $5. If the futures delivery date is in one year, determine the futures price if
   (a) $R_{0,1} = R_{0,2} = R_{0,3} = 5\%$.
   (b) $R_{0,1} = 2\%, R_{0,2} = 6\%, R_{0,3} = 9\%$.

3. A bond futures contract has one deliverable bond with a maturity date in 3 years from now, par value of $100, and annual coupon of $5. If the futures delivery date is in 2 years, determine the futures price if
   (a) $R_{0,1} = R_{0,2} = R_{0,3} = 5\%$.
   (b) $R_{0,1} = 2\%, R_{0,2} = 6\%, R_{0,3} = 9\%$.

4. Suppose a bond futures contract has one deliverable bond with a maturity date in 25 years from now, par value of $100, price of $99, and annual coupon of $5. If the futures delivery date is in 1 year, determine the futures price if $R_{0,1} = 4\%$.

5. Assume that the price quotation of the CBT Treasury bond futures contract changes from 98–14 to 100–09. What are the gains and losses to the short and long as a result of marking-to-market for one contract with $100,000 par value?

6. An individual owns a 21-year maturity bond with an annual coupon of 5%, a face value of $100,000, and a price of $98,000. To protect against rising interest rates, this individual shorts one CBT Treasury bond futures contract with a delivery date 2 years hence and a futures price of 98–16. In the course of the next year, interest rates change. The bond price drops to $95,000 and the futures price drops to 96–16.

   (a) Overlooking bond coupon and marking-to-market, compute the gains or losses on the bond position, the futures position, and the net position.

   (b) Suppose we knew the relationship between the futures and spot prices. For every dollar change in the futures, the spot price changed $1.10. Determine the optimal hedge ratio.

7. A bond dealer owns a 21-year maturity bond with an annual coupon of 5%, a face value of $100,000, and a price of $95,000. To hedge against rising interest rates, the dealer shorts one CBT Treasury bond futures contract with a delivery date 2 years hence and a futures price of 92–16. In the course of the next year, interest rates drop. The futures price goes to 97–16. At what interest rate on the bond would the hedge just break even?

8. A bond futures contract has one deliverable bond that has a maturity date in 2 years from now, par value of $100, and annual coupon of $4.50. If the futures delivery date is in one year, determine the spot price of two-period strips per $100 of par if the futures price is $101.98 and if one-period strips have a price of $91.50 per $100 of par value.

9. A bond futures contract has one deliverable bond that has a maturity date in 3 years from now, par value of $100, and annual coupon of $6.75. If the futures delivery date is in one year, determine the futures price if the prices of 1-, 2-, and 3-period strips per $100 par are $99, $96, and $92.

10. Suppose there is a Treasury bond futures contract traded with three deliverable bonds. One bond has a maturity of 15 years, price of $110, and coupon rate of 7%. The second deliverable bond has a maturity of 18 years, price of $105.50, and a coupon rate of 6.5%. The third deliverable bond has a maturity of 20 years, price of $94.75, and a coupon rate of 5.5%. On the delivery date of the futures contract the futures price is $100. Which is the cheapest to deliver?

CHAPTER 14

Callable Bonds

FEATURES OF CALLABLE BONDS

Call features are widely used for corporate and municipal government bonds. The call feature on a bond gives the bond's issuer the right to force the bondholders to turn in their bonds for the *call price*. In the years immediately after bond issuance, the call price starts out at par plus one year's interest. As the bond ages, the call price declines toward par (see Figure 14.1). The exact terms and dates are stated in the bond indenture.

Frequently, callable corporate bonds have a period of call protection after the bond is originally issued as shown in Figure 14.1. During the call-protected period, the bond cannot be called by the issuing firm and replaced by another bond. However, most bonds can be called for reasons other than replacement with another lower-cost bond. Thus, bonds can be *redeemed* and replaced by stock during the period of call protection.

Over time the proportion of corporate bonds containing call options has varied. At times, the large majority of bonds have had call features. At other times, the majority of bonds have been noncallable. The proportion of callable bonds has been relatively high when interest rates have been high by historical standards. The proportion of callable bonds has been relatively low when interest rates have been low relative to historical standards.

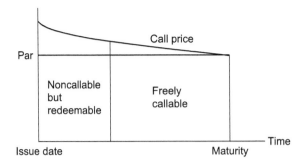

FIGURE 14.1 Callable Bonds.

Reasons for Calling a Bond

A firm might exercise a bond's call option for several reasons. First, calling a bond allows a firm to retire a debt issue to remove an undesirable protective covenant in the bond indenture. Second, if a firm has improved its credit rating, a higher-coupon bond can be called and replaced with a lower-coupon bond. This higher-coupon bond would have been issued in the past when the firm had a poorer credit rating.

The third reason for calling a bond is a decline in market interest rates. Then, a bond with a high coupon is called and replaced by a lower-coupon bond. The firm gains the present value of the coupons saved minus any costs of refunding. Refunding costs include paying the premium above par, flotation costs for the replacement bond issue, and loss of the opportunity to call the bond in the future if interest rates were to drop even further.

Refunding is a zero-sum game. That is, the gains to the firm from a refunding are losses to the bondholders. If a high coupon bond is called after a decline in interest rates, the bondholders are able to reinvest the call price but at a lower interest rate. The bondholders' loss of interest is the firm's gain.

When a callable bond is issued, the bondholders are aware of the *possibility* of a future call. To compensate for the risk of possible future calls, the bondholders require a higher coupon for a callable bond, a call premium above par, and, typically, a period of call protection during which the original coupon is locked in. See Figure 14.1.

In an efficient market, the bondholders have the same information about prospects for future exercise of the call option as the firm. Therefore, the compensation for call risks (i.e., the higher coupon, call premium, and period of call protection) should be fair at the issue date. This conclusion has the following interesting implication. In a perfectly efficient market, there is no net advantage for a firm to issue callable versus noncallable bonds. That is, the higher cost of the callable bond should exactly offset the anticipated gains from future refunding.

Embedded Call Option

Much corporate debt, municipal debt instruments, and all mortgages contain a call option that allows the borrower to repay the principal of the loan. Since borrowing corresponds to short selling a noncallable bond, borrowing with an embedded call option is equivalent to short selling a debt instrument and buying a call option with exercise price equal to the remaining principal. The price of the call option is included in the higher coupon payment for the callable debt.

To illustrate, assume a perpetual noncallable bond par value of $100 and annual coupon of $6. Also assume a perpetual debt callable at par of $100 with coupon of $7. The borrower pays $1 more per year for the call option. Thus, a callable bond has a higher coupon and yield to maturity than an otherwise identical noncallable bond. If the callable debt suddenly lost its call feature, its value would become $116.67, that is, $7 discounted at 6%, 7 / .06. Therefore, the value of the call option is $16.67. In general, the value of a noncallable debt equals the value of a callable debt plus the value of the call option.

$$\frac{\text{Noncallable}}{\text{Bond}} = \frac{\text{Callable}}{\text{Bond}} + \frac{\text{Call}}{\text{Option}}$$

$$116.67 = 100 + 16.67 \qquad 14.1$$

Yield to Call

Since bonds are callable at the option of the issuer, the yield to maturity for callable bonds may be misleading since the bond is assumed to be held until the final maturity. In order to account for the possibility that the option might be exercised before the bond matures, market participants also compute the yield until the first call date. The computation of yield until first call is similar to the computation for yield to maturity with the exceptions that the end of the bond's life is the first call date and the call price is used instead of par value. The yield to first call date (R) is computed from the following equation:

$$\text{Price} = P = \frac{c}{1+R} + \frac{c}{(1+R)^2} + \ldots + \frac{c+\text{callprice}}{(1+R)^n} \qquad 14.2$$

where n is the number of periods until the first call date.

By convention, the market reports the lower of the yield to maturity or the yield to first call date.

BOND REFUNDING

The value of the embedded call option increases when interest rates drop. If rates decline sufficiently, the borrower will want to exercise the call option and refinance the debt at a lower interest rate. For example, consider a perpetual bond with 10% interest rate callable at par. Now suppose that all interest rates drop and that the interest rate on new par debt (callable at par) is 7%. Then the old debt can be replaced with a new debt with the same call price, but a coupon $3 lower for each future period. The savings are shown in Tables 14.1 and 14.2. The present value of the savings is $3/0.07 = $42.86. The costs of refinancing must be subtracted to arrive at the net benefit of refinancing. In general, the net refinancing benefit equals the interest savings discounted at the interest rate on new callable debt minus the refinancing costs as shown in equation 14.3. The refinancing costs include any call premium.

$$\frac{\text{Refinancing}}{\text{Benefit}} = \begin{bmatrix} C_{OLD} - C_{NEW} \end{bmatrix} \begin{bmatrix} \text{Present Value} \\ \text{of an Annuity} \\ \text{for remaining life} \end{bmatrix} - \begin{bmatrix} \text{Refinancing} \\ \text{Costs} \end{bmatrix} \qquad \text{14.3}$$

If we assume a perpetual bond and if the costs of refinancing are 1.25% of par, then:

$$\frac{\text{Refinancing}}{\text{Benefit}} = \begin{bmatrix} 10 - 7 \end{bmatrix} \begin{bmatrix} \dfrac{1}{.07} \end{bmatrix} - \begin{bmatrix} (100)\,(.0125) \end{bmatrix}$$

$$= 42.86 - 1.25 = \$41.61 \qquad \text{14.4}$$

Table 14.1. Coupon Savings in General

	Points in Time			
	0	1	2	...
Old coupon		C_{OLD}	C_{OLD}	C_{OLD}
New coupon		C_{NEW}	C_{NEW}	C_{NEW}
Savings		$C_{OLD} - C_{NEW}$	$C_{OLD} - C_{NEW}$	$C_{OLD} - C_{NEW}$

Table 14.2. Coupon Savings Example

	Points in Time			
	0	1	2	...
Old coupon		10	10	10
New coupon		7	7	7
Savings		3	3	3

Refinancing costs include the call premium, underwriter fees, loan initiation fees, points, appraisal fees, survey fees, taxes, and search time. For mortgages, refinancing costs can vary, with 2–3% being quite common. For marketable bonds, refinancing costs generally include a call premium plus underwriter fees ranging from 0.50% to 5%.

If interest rates have fallen substantially, a firm may find extending the maturity of its existing debt to be desirable. The alternative may be to keep the existing debt until it matures and then refinance at some future, currently unknown, interest rate. Waiting to refinance runs the risk of higher interest rates in the future. The next section discusses timing in more detail.

The Timing of Refunding

In addition to cash flows resulting from an immediate refunding, firms must consider the possibility of waiting to refund on potentially better terms. To clarify this point, consider the courses of action to the firm at time t as shown in Figure 14.2. At time t, the firm can either refund and realize a net refunding benefit of B_t or wait. If the firm refunds at time t, it cannot refund this same bond again. If the choice at time t is to wait, then, at time $t + 1$, the choices are to wait or to refund for a benefit of B_{t+1}, which may be greater than, equal to, or less than B_t. However, by waiting the firm continues to pay the old coupon of c, a cost of waiting. Thus, waiting may result in an additional benefit, no change, or a reduced benefit. The same scenario applies for waiting and refunding at later points in time. Because waiting and refunding in the future may result in a greater refunding benefit, the call option may have some value beyond the current intrinsic value of refunding immediately.

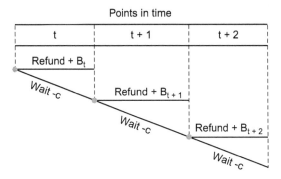

FIGURE 14.2 Timing of Refunding.

Advance Refunding

Typically, callable bonds are issued with a period of call protection. If interest rates drop considerably before the period of call protection ends, the firm might consider an advance refunding. In advance refunding, the firm offers to purchase call-protected debt at a price above the call price. Bondholders are *not* required to sell their bonds back to the firm. However, the offer can be made attractive enough for most bondholders to sell their bonds and for the firm to reap a refunding benefit as well.

To illustrate, assume that a bond has 2 years of call protection remaining, a call price of $112 per $100 of par value, and an annual coupon of $12. If current interest rates are 6%, the firm has an incentive to refund. Instead of waiting 2 years and refunding at possibly higher or lower rates, the firm can offer to retire the issue right now and refund.

The first step is to estimate a price sufficient to induce the bondholders to sell but not eliminate too much of the firm's refunding benefit. If current interest rates are low enough, refunding when the bond becomes freely callable in 2 years seems almost inevitable. From the bondholders' viewpoint, the bond's value is the present value of the $12 coupon for the next 2 years plus the present value of the call price 2 years from now. If d is the appropriate discount rate, then:

$$\text{Value} = \frac{12}{1+d} + \frac{12+112}{(1+d)^2} \qquad 14.5$$

If d is 6%, the value is $121.68. By offering slightly more, the firm may be able to induce the bondholders to sell their bonds. An advance refunding allows a firm to realize some refunding benefits immediately. This must be weighed against the added cost of open market purchase.

REASONS FOR ISSUING CALLABLE BONDS

In a perfectly efficient market, the added coupon on a callable bond, the call premium, and the period of call protection should reflect the fair value of the prospect of exercise of the call option. There should be no net advantage to issue debt with call features. Several possible explanations have been suggested.

A possible explanation of call features centers on corporate management's superior knowledge of a firm's individual prospects: asymmetric information. According to this scenario, the management of a firm issuing callable bonds has a more favorable view of the firm's prospects than the bondholders' perceptions. By issuing callable debt now, the corporate management expects to refinance at a future date on more favorable terms when the firm's performance has improved.

An alternative to issuing long maturity callable bonds is issuing short maturity debt. The short maturity debt would have to be rolled over repeatedly. These rollovers involve flotation costs. Additionally, there is uncertainty about the future course of interest rates. For some firms, paying the added coupon on a callable bond is worth avoiding the uncertainty of future rollovers.

SINKING FUNDS

Many corporate bonds contain a sinking fund provision, which requires the issuing firm to retire part of the bond issue at intervals stated in the bond indenture. Suppose a firm issues 25-year bonds with annual sinking fund payments of 2% of principal beginning in the tenth year. This means 15 annual sinking fund payments of 2%, leaving 70% of par value to be repaid at final maturity.

Every sinking fund bond issue has a special call provision allowing the firm to call bonds at random on the required sinking fund dates. The firm has the option to purchase the required number of bonds in the open market. At each sinking fund date, the firm chooses the cheaper option.

A sinking fund provision may signal lower default risk. A sinking fund may show the availability of sufficient internal funds from current operations or the availability of external funding to meet sinking fund payments. Thus, sinking funds indicate the favorable future prospects of the firm, implying lower default risk and reduced yields on the bonds.

SUMMARY

Corporate and municipal bonds often have a call feature, allowing the issuer to call the bonds at a stated call price. This call feature permits the issuer to replace the issue at a later date with another bond issue or other source of financing.

In an informationally efficient market in which the bondholders and the firm have the same information, the market sets the features (i.e., coupon, call price, and period of call protection) on a callable bond to make the marginal bondholder and issuing firm indifferent between callable and noncallable bonds. In imperfect markets, firms may have incentives to issue callable bonds.

QUESTIONS/PROBLEMS

1. Explain the impact of call deferment and call premiums on the coupon of a callable bond.

2. Instead of refunding a callable bond issue immediately, a firm has the choice of waiting to refund until some future date. Explain the possible advantages and disadvantages of waiting to refund.

3. A firm has a perpetual callable bond outstanding with a par value of $100 and an annual coupon of $8. The firm can refund this with a new noncallable perpetual bond having a 4% coupon. The call price on the old bond is $108. Flotation costs for a new issue are 1% of par. What is the myopic benefit of refunding?

CPSIA information can be obtained
at www.ICGtesting.com
Printed in the USA
LVHW060029270522
719862LV00003B/31

9 781516 592784